GOING INFINITE

MICHAEL LEWIS

GOING INFINITE

THE RISE AND FALL OF A NEW TYCOON

W. W. NORTON & COMPANY

Celebrating a Century of Independent Publishing

For information about permission to reproduce selections from this book,
write to Permissions, W. W. Norton & Company, Inc., 500 Fifth Avenue, New York, NY 10110

For information about special discounts for bulk purchases, please contact
W. W. Norton Special Sales at specialsales@wwnorton.com or 800-233-4830

Manufacturing by Lakeside Book Company
Book design by Chris Welch
Production manager: Julia Druskin
Prepress production director: Joe Lops

ISBN 978-1-324-07433-5

W. W. Norton & Company, Inc., 500 Fifth Avenue, New York, N.Y. 10110
www.wwnorton.com

W. W. Norton & Company Ltd., 15 Carlisle Street, London W1D 3BS

1 2 3 4 5 6 7 8 9 0

IN MEMORY OF DIXIE LEE LEWIS

YOU REMAIN INSIDE OF ME

The infinite is nowhere to be found in reality, no matter what experiences, observations, and knowledge are appealed to. Can thought about things be so much different from things? Can thinking processes be so unlike the actual processes of things? In short, can thought be so far removed from reality?

—*David Hilbert, German mathematician (1862–1943)*

CONTENTS

PREFACE

first heard about Sam Bankman-Fried at the end of 2021 from a
friend who, oddly enough, wanted me to help him figure out who
he was. My friend was about to close a deal with Sam that would
bind their fates, through an exchange of shares in each other's companies worth hundreds of millions of dollars. He remained uneasy.
He thought he understood FTX, the crypto exchange that Sam had
built, but he didn't have as good a feel for Sam himself. He'd asked
around about Sam and discovered that, as little as he felt he really
knew him, other people, even people who had invested millions of
dollars in Sam's company, knew even less. My friend thought that the
general ignorance might be explained by Sam's circumstances. FTX
had been around only two and a half years. Sam was only twenty-nine
years old, a bit odd, and had spent most of the previous three years
outside the United States. All that could explain why no one seemed
to really know him. My friend asked me if I could meet with Sam and
report back whatever I made of him.

A few weeks later, Sam was on my front porch in Berkeley, California. He'd emerged from an Uber in cargo shorts, a T-shirt, limp
white socks and ratty New Balance sneakers—which I soon learned
were basically the only clothes he owned. We went for a walk—the
only time in the next two years I would ever see this person who was
always dressed for a hike actually go for one. During our walk I prod-

ded him with questions, but after a while I was mostly just listening. The stuff he was telling me—all of which, I should say here, turned out to be true—was incredible. The sums of money in his life, for a start. Not just the tens of billions of dollars he'd accumulated in the previous two years but the hundreds of millions being thrown at him by leading Silicon Valley venture capitalists who (as one later told me) thought Sam had a real shot at being the world's first trillionaire. FTX's revenues were growing at an astonishing rate: from $20 million in 2019, to $100 million in 2020, to $1 billion in 2021. On our walk I asked him how much it would take for him to sell FTX and go do something other than make money. He thought the question over. "One hundred and fifty billion dollars," he finally said—though he added that he had use for "infinity dollars."

Everything about him was peculiar, starting with motives—or at least what he believed his motives to be. He didn't come right out with all of it on our walk, maybe because he realized how implausible it'd sound to a total stranger. He needed infinity dollars because he planned to address the biggest existential risks to life on earth: nuclear war, pandemics far more deadly than Covid, artificial intelligence that turned on mankind and wiped us out, and so on. To the list of problems Sam hoped to tackle he'd recently added the assault on American democracy, which, if successful, would make all of the other big problems far less likely to be solved. One hundred fifty billion was about what was needed to make a dent in at least one of the big problems.

There were also a bunch of smaller problems that money might solve that had Sam thinking about whether to throw it at them, too. The Bahamas, for instance. A few months before I met him, apparently in response to the crackdown on cryptocurrencies by the Chinese government, Sam had moved his entire company from Hong Kong to the Bahamas. The good thing about the Bahamas, from Sam's point of view, was that it had created regulations, which the United States had not, to legitimize a crypto futures exchange. The bad thing was that Covid had gutted its economy. The country lacked the infrastructure to support the global financial empire Sam hoped to build, and it was now too broke to create one. He was just then trying to persuade forty or so employees, many of whom had grown up in or around China, to move nine thousand miles to an island without a school to which they'd be willing to send their kids. Sam explained that he was trying to decide whether to simply pay off the $9 billion Bahamas national debt himself, so the country could fix their roads and build schools and so on. He'd recently met with the new prime minister to discuss this idea and some others. I learned later from one of the prime minister's aides that after the Bahamian general election in September 2021, Sam was the first person the prime minister had wanted to meet.

All of this would have sounded even more preposterous if Sam hadn't already done what he'd done—or if he hadn't been so unusual. He hadn't been warped by money in the ways people often are. He wasn't braggy. He had opinions, but he didn't seem to expect his listener to share them, and he pretended to listen to mine even when what I was saying clearly didn't interest him. He didn't even seem all that taken with his own fantastic story. His mom and dad were law professors at Stanford who had basically zero interest in money and were bewildered by what had become of their son—that's pretty much all I got out of him that day, and the next few months. On the other hand, on subjects other than himself he was refreshingly unguarded: he seemed willing to answer any question I could think to ask about the crypto industry or his business. His ambition was grandiose, but he wasn't.

By the end of this walk I was totally sold. I called my friend and said something like: *Go for it! Swap shares with Sam Bankman-Fried! Do whatever he wants to do! What could possibly go wrong?* It was only later that I realized I hadn't even begun to answer his original question: Who was this guy?

ACT I

1

YUP

Most of the people who went to work for Sam Bankman-Fried ended up in jobs for which they were not obviously qualified, and Natalie Tien was no exception. She'd been raised in Taiwan by middle-class parents whose only real hope for her was that she'd find a rich husband. She was small and agreeable and ill-designed for rebellion. She still reflexively covered her mouth with her hand when she laughed. And yet she'd been determined to prove to her parents that they'd underestimated her. After college she'd gone hunting not for a husband but for work. She'd been so anxious about her own ambition that, before each interview, she'd write out and memorize exactly what she wanted to say about herself. She'd landed the first real job she'd applied for, at an English-language training company, and it had bored her to tears. But then, in 2018, at the age of twenty-eight, she'd discovered crypto.

The previous year, the price of bitcoin had risen almost twenty-fold, from $1,000 to $19,000, and the daily trading volumes had boomed by some massive amount that was hard to precisely quantify. (The closest thing to an accurate accounting of what occurred was from the Coinbase crypto exchange, where trading volume in

2017 was thirty times greater than in 2016.) Across Asia, new crypto-currency exchanges were popping up every month to service the growing gambling public. They all had deep pockets and an insatiable demand for young women. "Requirements are: pretty, big boobs, have done live streaming before, born in 2000 or later, good at chit-chatting," read the job ad for a salesperson at the fastest-growing new exchange. By 2018 a lot of young Asian women were trying to meet those requirements. Natalie took a different approach. She spent a month reading everything she could find about cryptocurrencies and blockchains. "Everyone called it a scam," she said, and she worried about that. Once on the inside, she was struck by how few of the people who worked in crypto could explain what a bitcoin was. The businesses themselves didn't always know what they were doing, or why. They were hiring lots of people because they could afford to, and big headcounts signaled their importance. What kept Natalie going, and ignoring the feeling that whatever talent she might possess was being wasted, was her feeling that crypto might be the next big thing. "I thought of it as a gamble with nothing to lose," she said.

By June of 2020 she was working for her second Asian crypto exchange when she heard about the opening at FTX. Like the other exchanges, FTX hired her quickly, after a single interview, and she became the company's forty-ninth employee. FTX was different from the other exchanges, mainly because the guy who ran it, Sam Bankman-Fried, was different. Every man Natalie Tien had ever met in crypto had been chiefly interested in money and women, and Sam was chiefly interested in neither—though it took her a while to figure out what it was he was chiefly interested in. *Everything here is five times*, she thought. Five times more work, five times more growth, five times more money, five times more responsibility. No one came out and said that you had to work all the time, or that there was no room for a life outside work, but anyone at FTX who tried to live a normal life simply didn't stick. Natalie stuck, and within months of moving to FTX's Hong Kong offices found herself named head of the company's public relations. What was peculiar about this—apart from the fact that she had no real experience in public relations—was that FTX had no public relations. "When I joined, Sam didn't believe in PR," said Natalie. "He thought it was all bullshit."

At the start, Natalie found herself trying to persuade Sam that he should talk to journalists, while at the same time trying to persuade journalists that they should talk to Sam. "In July 2020 no journalist was interested in Sam," she said. "Zip." The mania for crypto recalled Rotterdam circa 1637, when a single tulip bulb traded for roughly triple the price of a Rembrandt. And every day more of it was being traded on FTX. And Natalie kept pushing on journalists, and on Sam.

On the morning of May 11, 2021, Sam Bankman-Fried made his first television appearance. He sat at his trading desk and talked into his computer screen to two female reporters on Bloomberg TV. Thick black curls exploded off his head in every direction. People who tried to describe Sam's hair would give up and call it an "afro," but it wasn't an Afro. It was just a mess, and like everything about Sam's appearance felt less like a decision than a decision not to make a decision. He wore what he always wore: a wrinkled T-shirt and cargo shorts. His bare knee jackhammered up and down at roughly four beats per second, while his eyes darted left and right and collided with his interviewers' gaze only by chance. His general demeanor was that of a kid pretending to be interested when his parents hauled him into the living room to meet their friends. He'd done nothing to prepare, but the questions were so easy that it didn't matter. *Crypto Wunderkind*, read the Bloomberg chyron, while the numbers on the left of the screen showed that, in just the past year, bitcoin's price had risen by more than 500 percent.

That first TV show Natalie watched from her own desk, but later, during future interviews, she'd walk around behind Sam to confirm that, yes, his eyes moved around so much because he was playing a video game. On live TV! Often, on live TV, Sam would not only play a video game but respond to messages, edit documents, and tweet. The TV interviewer would ask him a question and Sam would say, "Ahhhh, interesting question"—even though he never found any of the questions interesting. And Natalie knew he was just buying time to exit whatever game he was playing and reenter the conversation. Natalie didn't know how a person was supposed to behave on live television, but she suspected it wasn't like this. Yet even as she watched Sam's first television performance she sensed it might play well. Sam was odd on TV, but he was also odd in real life. In real life people who encountered him often thought he was the most interesting person they'd ever met. She decided against media training—or anything that might make Sam seem less like Sam.

Not long after that first Bloomberg interview, *Forbes* magazine showed up. Back in 2017, when *Forbes* had begun to track crypto fortunes, Sam's name hadn't even made the list of people whose fortunes they should track; but back in 2017, Sam could not have told you what a bitcoin was, and in any case he had been worth approximately zero dollars. "He kind of came out of nowhere," said Steve Ehrlich, the reporter *Forbes* assigned to figure out the net worth of this twenty-nine-year-old nobody. "It shocked me. It wasn't that he had bought bitcoin and it had gone from zero to twenty thousand." Inside of three years, it appeared, Sam Bankman-Fried had created a business so valuable that his share of it implied that he was now the richest person in the world under the age of thirty. "When I first looked at the numbers, I was like, Can this really be true—can this guy really be worth twenty billion dollars?" said Chase Peterson-Withorn, who led the *Forbes* team of investigators. "It was pretty much unprecedented. No one else had gotten richer faster except for Mark Zuckerberg, and it was very close."

From that question they soon jumped to another: *Exactly how much more than twenty billion dollars might this guy be worth?* In addition to the crypto exchange, FTX, Sam also owned and controlled a crypto quant trading firm called Alameda Research. The year before, 2020, with just a handful of employees, Alameda had generated a billion dollars in trading profits, and was accumulating stakes in other companies, and crypto tokens, at a bewildering rate. The closer you got to Alameda Research, the less it seemed like a hedge fund and the more it resembled a dragon's lair, stuffed with random treasures. The *Forbes* wealth analysts had always tried to keep things simple: your assets were worth only what other people were willing to pay for them. That approach had worked during the dot-com bubble, when everyone could agree that even though Pets.com was ridiculous it was still worth $400 million, because investors were willing to buy it at that valuation. But with these new crypto fortunes, the *Forbes* approach to wealth only got you so far. What to do, for instance, with the Solana tokens Sam owned inside of Alameda Research? Hardly anyone knew what Solana was—a new cryptocurrency minted to rival Bitcoin— much less how to value it. On the one hand, the current market price implied that Sam's Solana stash was worth maybe $12 billion; on the other hand, Sam owned roughly 10 percent of all the Solana in the world. It was hard to know what anyone would pay for it if Sam tried to sell it all. *Forbes* pretty much just ignored Sam's Solana holdings, along with most of the rest of the contents of his dragon's lair.

As Sam went back and forth with the *Forbes* reporters, he—and Natalie—worried mainly that they'd publish a number that would require him to explain more than he wanted to explain. He'd walked the *Forbes* people through what they knew, or thought they knew. "There were two reasons I talked to them," he said. "First, it was going to be in there anyway. And second, it makes them trust us more." Still, he was worried that if he told *Forbes* everything, they might tell everyone that he was as rich as he thought himself to be. "I didn't just send them the number: here's what I'm worth," he said. "It would set the wrong tone. The number was too big. If it comes out in *Forbes* that I'm worth one hundred billion dollars, it's going to be weird and it's going to fuck things up." He hadn't sent them the list of the one hundred or so businesses he'd acquired over the previous two years, for example. His story might be fantastic, but he needed it to be believable.

It turned out that Sam had nothing to worry about. In November 2021, *Forbes* listed his net worth at $22.5 billion, a notch below Rupert Murdoch and a notch above Laurene Powell Jobs. Twenty-

two and a half billion dollars was roughly what you got if you simply agreed with the world's leading venture capital firms that FTX's
crypto exchange business by itself was worth $40 billion. Sam owned
60 percent of FTX: 60 percent of $40 billion was $24 billion. Still, in
the forty years since *Forbes* began tracking rich people's money, he
was an outlier. "He was the richest self-made newcomer to the *Forbes*
list, ever," said Peterson-Withorn. "And we could easily have justified
a much bigger number. We tried to be conservative." Sam's number
was so believable that *Forbes*'s executives were soon asking if he might
like to buy their company, too.

When Sam saw the response to the *Forbes* billionaires list, and the
Forbes cover that followed, any doubts he had about the value of public relations evaporated. Natalie's job became both simpler and more
complicated. Simpler, because basically everyone now wanted to talk
to Sam, and Sam was game to talk to anyone—so long as he could
play a video game while doing it. Sam went from being totally private
to being a media whore. He was as happy to yak for an hour in a completely unguarded way with the reporter from the *Westwego Crypto
Daily* as he was to speak with the *New York Times*. Natalie compiled
lists for Sam, with notes on the hundred or so journalists likely to
walk into his field of vision, and advice on how to handle them. For
example: "This person is just, like, an asshole so be very careful with
him." Or: "You can't avoid the Financial Times guy but be very cau-
tious around anyone from the Financial Times because the Financial
Times is very anti-crypto."

Being the head of public relations for a booming multinational
corporation wasn't all that difficult. "You just do and learn at the
same time," Natalie said brightly. The hard part of her job was Sam.
The demand for his time soon reached the point that Natalie took
on a second role, as Sam's personal scheduler. It always had been
Natalie the *Financial Times* reporter was meant to call if he wanted
to set a time with Sam; now it was Natalie Sam's father also needed
to call if he hoped to get fifteen minutes with his son. By the end of
2021 Natalie, and Natalie alone, knew where Sam was at any given

moment, and where he might next go, and how to get him to do what he needed to do. She didn't actually have all that much in common with her boss, but to do her job she had to be inside his head. "You need to learn how to get along with him," she said. "And it's kind of mysterious how to get along with him."

A year into her job, Natalie had become as good as anyone at predicting what Sam might do, and why. And yet even to Natalie, Sam remained a puzzle. She could never be sure where he was, for a start. "Don't expect that he'll tell you where he's going to be at when," said Natalie. "He'll never tell you. You need to be smart and fast to find out by yourself." And Sam might be anywhere, at any hour. She'd book him a room for two nights at the Four Seasons in Washington, DC, and Sam might even check in, but never enter the room. He had more trouble with sleep than anyone she'd ever known. At two in the morning, she might find him at his desk talking to some journalist halfway around the world, or wandering around some deserted street tweeting up a storm, or really anyplace but in his bed. But then at two in the afternoon, when he was meant to be on live television, he might be asleep on the beanbag chair beside his desk. "There is not such a thing as on times and off times with him," said Natalie. There had been nights Natalie had gone to bed at 3:00 a.m., set an alarm for 7:00, woken up to see what public relations shitstorm Sam might have caused in the interim, set a second alarm for 8:00, checked again, then set another alarm and fallen back to sleep until 9:30.

Sam's approach to his commitments was an even bigger issue. Natalie mapped out every minute of Sam's days—not just the TV appearances but the meetings with other CEOs, and curious celebrities, and rulers of small countries. She put nothing on Sam's schedule that he had not agreed to. More often than not, it was Sam who had suggested some meeting or public appearance. And yet Sam treated everything on his schedule as optional. The schedule was less a plan than a theory. When people asked Sam for his time, they assumed they'd posed a yes or no question, and the noises Sam made always sounded more like "yes" than like "no." They didn't know that inside

Sam's mind was a dial, with zero on one end and one hundred on the other. All he had done, when he said yes, was to assign some non-zero probability to the proposed use of his time. The dial would swing wildly as he calculated and recalculated the expected value of each commitment, right up until the moment he honored it or didn't. "He'll never tell you what he's going to do," explained Natalie. "You have to always be prepared it's going to change every second." Every decision Sam made involved an expected value calculation. The numbers in Sam's mind were always shifting. One midnight, for instance, he had sent Natalie a message that read: "There's a 60 percent chance I'll go to Texas tomorrow." "What does that mean, a sixty percent chance?" asked Natalie. "I can't book sixty percent of an airplane and sixty percent of a car, or sixty percent of a hotel room in Texas."

Of course, she didn't say that to Sam directly. Instead, she tried to anticipate the shifting odds before Sam made his calculations. She learned to humor the professor at Harvard, for example, by saying, "Yes, Sam told me he agreed to come and speak to a room full of important Harvard people at two next Friday. It's on his schedule." Yet even as she uttered those words, she'd already invented the excuse she'd make to that same Harvard person, likely next Thursday night, to explain why Sam would be nowhere near Massachusetts. *Sam has Covid. The prime minister needed to see Sam. Sam is stuck in Kazakhstan.*

The funny thing about these situations was that Sam never really meant to cause them, which in a way made them feel even more insulting. He didn't mean to be rude. He didn't mean to create chaos in other people's lives. He was just moving through the world in the only way he knew how. The cost this implied for others simply never entered his calculations. With him it was never personal. If he stood you up, it was never on a whim, or the result of thoughtlessness. It was because he'd done some math in his head that proved that you weren't worth the time. "You're always going to be apologizing to different people, and you'll do that every day," said Natalie.

Natalie loved her job. Sam had never once been cruel or abusive or even flirty. Just the opposite: she felt protected by him from the abuse of others. He'd occasionally surprise her with some kindness—for example, after he'd met privately with President Clinton, and asked him what the United States might do if China invaded Taiwan. Whatever Clinton had told Sam had prompted him to seek her out afterward and suggest that she move her parents out of Taiwan. Sam seldom even disagreed with her. He'd invariably seem open to her ideas—and sometimes, as with Bloomberg TV, he'd actually do what she suggested. "Yup," he'd always say. "Yup" was Sam's go-to word, and the less he'd actually listened to whatever you'd just said, the longer he drew it out. *Yuuuuuuuup.* "He's not direct, most of the time," said Natalie. "He'll say 'yup' or 'that's interesting' and he doesn't really mean that. So you need to figure out when he is just avoiding conflict, and when he means it."

By early 2022 Sam's situation was totally out of hand. Every important person on the planet seemed to want to get to know him. He had said yes to them all. Anyone else in Sam's situation would have built out a huge network of schedulers and advisors and gatekeepers. Sam had only Natalie, who was no longer just Sam's public relations head and Sam's private scheduler but, on occasion, Sam's bodyguard. She was a circus juggler with a thousand balls in the air. No one ball was all that important, but Natalie sensed that any given ball, if dropped, might trigger a cascading crisis. And on the morning of February 14, one of those balls had her especially worried.

Three days earlier, Sam had boarded a private plane in the Bahamas bound for Los Angeles, with nothing but his laptop and a change of underwear. Since then, he'd had brunch with Shaquille O'Neal and dinner with the Kardashians, and had watched the Super Bowl with the owner of the Los Angeles Rams. He'd chatted with Hillary Clinton and Orlando Bloom. He'd attended four parties and had met with entrepreneurs who wanted him to buy their businesses, and also with the CEO of Goldman Sachs, who was eager to get to know Sam better. For the previous three nights Natalie hadn't been entirely sure where, or if, Sam had slept, but she knew he'd checked into the room she'd booked for him at the Beverly Hilton, because she'd watched him do it.

Now, on the fourteenth, the hotel room looked as if he'd never arrived. The sheets were still crisp, the pillows undented, the trash cans empty, the bathroom sparkling. The only sign of a human presence in the room was Sam himself. He sat at the desk in the same wrinkled T-shirt and baggy cargo shorts he'd worn on the plane ride in. As always, he was doing several things at once: checking his phone, applying ChapStick to his perpetually parched lips, opening and closing windows on his laptop—all while his knee jackhammered at four beats a second. His assigned task—the one Natalie had reminded him about the night before, and again this morning—was being on time for his Zoom meeting. He was already late. Yet another very important person who really wanted to meet him was waiting for him inside his laptop.

"Hey, this is Sam!" said Sam, to his laptop, as his Zoom box opened.

Onto his screen popped Anna Wintour, editor in chief of *Vogue* magazine. She wore a tight yellow dress and careful makeup and a bob cut so sharply that its fringes plunged and curved down around her face like the blades of two scythes. "I'm so happy to finally meet you!" she said.

"Hey, it's great to meet you too!" Sam replied.

Sam didn't really know who Anna Wintour was. Natalie and others had briefed him, but he hadn't paid attention. He knew Anna Wintour edited a magazine. He might or might not have been dimly aware that Meryl Streep had played her in *The Devil Wears Prada*, and that she'd ruled the treacherous world of women's fashion since— well, since before Sam was born. She looked like a million bucks, but her art, like all art, was wasted on Sam. When you asked Sam to describe a person's appearance—even a person he'd slept with— he'd say, "I don't really know how to answer that. I'm not good at judging how people look."

As Anna Wintour began to speak, he clicked a button and she vanished from his screen. In her place popped his favorite video game, *Storybook Brawl*. He had only a few seconds to choose his character.

He picked the Hoard Dragon. The Hoard Dragon was maybe Sam's favorite hero to play.

"Yup," said Sam, to whatever Anna Wintour was saying. He could still hear her through headphones. Unless she watched his eyes, she had no reason to think that he wasn't paying attention. Sam didn't want to seem rude. It was just that he needed to be playing this other game at the same time as whatever game he had going in real life. His new social role as the world's most interesting new child billionaire required him to do all kinds of dumb stuff. He needed something, other than what he was expected to be thinking about, to occupy his mind. And so, oddly, the more important he became in the eyes of the world, the more important these games became to him.

Storybook Brawl had everything Sam loved in a game. It pitted him against live opponents. It required him to make lots of decisions quickly. Games without clocks bored Sam. It energized him to have seconds ticking away as he assembled his platoon of fantasy characters—dwarves, witches, monsters, princesses, and so on. Each character came with two numbers attached to it: how much damage it could inflict on other characters and how much damage it could itself survive. Each also had more complex traits—for example, the ability to cast random spells, or to interact in peculiar ways with specific treasures it collected along the way, or to strengthen comrades in some quantifiable way. The game was too complicated to know with certainty its optimal moves. It required skill, but also luck. It required him to estimate probabilities, but also to guess. This was important; Sam didn't care for games, like chess, where the players controlled everything and the best move was in theory perfectly calculable. Chess he'd have liked better if robot voices wired into the board hollered rule changes at random intervals. *Knights are now rooks! All bishops must leave the board! Pawns can now fly!* Or almost anything—so long as the new rule forced all players to scrap whatever strategy they'd been pursuing and improvise another, better one. The games Sam loved allowed for only partial knowledge of any situation. Trading crypto was like that.

"Yuuuuuup," said Sam, to whatever Anna Wintour had just said. His dwarf platoon, to which he'd added a princess or two, was defending the Hoard Dragon. At the same time, it was attacking its new foe, his opponent's hero, a fat white penguin named Wonder Waddle. A dwarf named Crafty assaulted a sad-looking wimp called the Lonely Prince. Sleeping Princess wiped out the Labyrinth Minotaur. A sleeping maiden awakened to cast a spell that caused a dying character to turn into three arbitrarily generated living ones. So much was happening all at once! It would have been impossible for him to follow the action, even if that were all he was following.

"Yuuuuuuuuup," said Sam. The noises the woman was making were still entirely ceremonial. No real content here. But each of Sam's yups was warmer, more animated, than the last. And she was clearly warming to him. Everyone did these days. When you had $22.5 billion, people really, really wanted to be your friend. They'd forgive you anything. Their desire freed you up from having to pay attention to them, which was good, because Sam had only so much attention to give. Another battle was about to begin. As the seconds ticked down, he hastily selected a new army of killer trees and dwarves. At the same time, he pulled up a document: the notes Natalie had created for this very meeting. Sam now looked them over for the first time. Anna Wintour was definitely the editor of *Vogue* magazine.

"That's interesting," he said, as the battle commenced. Again, it was over in seconds. Already the Hoard Dragon was in trouble. Its health number was declining faster than the competition's. A lot of the heroes were front-loaded; the Hoard Dragon was one of the rare ones that acquired its special powers only later in its life. The way to play the Hoard Dragon was to buy treasures that paid off more for it than for any other hero—but the payoff came way down the road, like eight battles later. In the meantime, you were diverting resources from the battle at hand. Sam didn't need to win these early battles. He just needed to keep the Hoard Dragon alive long enough to enjoy the future gargantuan payoffs from the treasures he was accumulating. Anna Wintour was making that difficult. She wanted so much

attention! And she was arriving at the reason for the call: the Met
Gala. Organized by *Vogue* magazine. But rather than simply explain it
to him and leave him in peace, she asked Sam what he knew about it.

Sam shifted in his chair. From his wrinkled cargo shorts he pulled
his ChapStick. He twiddled it. Valuable seconds ticked away. Finally,
he hit a button. The Hoard Dragon vanished, and Anna Wintour reappeared.
Curiously, only when he was talking did he want to see her.

"I don't know as much about your industry as obviously you do,"
he said, cautiously. "I know some of the public information, but I
don't know much of the behind-the-scenes information." *Some* information.
Strictly speaking, that was true: Sam knew some information.
He knew that the Met Gala was a party. Attended by celebrities.
Beyond that, he didn't know much. For example, he could not have
told you if the "Met" was the Metropolitan Opera or the Metropolitan
Museum or, for that matter, the Metropolitan Police.

Anna Wintour was clearly used to this situation. To Sam's great
relief, she now began to explain the thing. The moment she opened
her mouth, Sam switched out her face for a page from Wikipedia:

> The **Met Gala**, formally called the **Costume Institute Gala** or the
> **Costume Institute Benefit** and also known as the **Met Ball**, is an
> annual fundraising gala for the benefit of the Metropolitan Museum
> of Art's Costume Institute in New York City. It marks the opening of
> the Costume Institute's annual fashion exhibit.[4] Each year's event
> celebrates the theme of that year's Costume Institute exhibition,
> and the exhibition sets the tone for the formal dress of the night,
> since guests are expected to choose their fashion to match the
> theme of the exhibit.

"Interesting!" said Sam. "That's super interesting." But even as he
expressed this interest, he pressed a button that caused the Wikipedia
page to vanish. In its place appeared an enormous golden tomahawk.
The Hoard Dragon was hanging by a thread. Another battle was
about to begin, against a character named Peter Pants. Peter Pants was

the opposite of the Hoard Dragon. Peter Pants was a make-or-break character whose powers dwindled over time. Peter Pants was all about killing you quickly. Peter Pants might finish off the Hoard Dragon in a single battle. Sam had only a few seconds to organize his fighting force. He needed to focus. Anna Wintour was making that impossible.

"Yuuuup," said Sam.

Anna Wintour now said she wanted to hear more about what FTX had done, giving-money-away-wise. Compelled to speak, Sam allowed her face to return to his computer screen. "We've done sponsorship deals with some places," he said. "But it's somewhat of an accident what we jumped into first. We really try to look hard at what partnerships would be most impactful. That's why we've partnered with Tom and Gisele." *Partnered.* Again, strictly true. It didn't capture the spirit of the relationship. Sam had agreed to pay Tom Brady $55 million, and his then-wife, Gisele Bündchen, another $19.8 million, for twenty hours of their time each, over the next three years. Sam was paying people more money per minute than anyone had ever paid them to do anything in their entire lives. He'd paid Larry David $10 million to create a sixty-second ad—over and above the $25 million the ad cost to produce and air during the Super Bowl—which Sam had watched just the day before. It was a great ad.

The Hoard Dragon was dying.

Sam might not have been entirely sure what the Met Gala was, or exactly what role he might play in it, but he could sense what Anna Wintour was after. She didn't want only his money; she wanted him. Present, on her Met Gala red carpet, beside her, creating buzz. Sam also understood what he might get in return for his sacrifice: women. Or, rather, access to the female crypto speculator. FTX had spent vast sums to capture the minds of men. Fashion, to Sam's way of thinking, occupied roughly the same place in the female imagination that sports did in the male imagination. He'd asked some marketing people for a list of things he might do in fashion to appeal to women. The Met Gala was on the list. And so here he was, on a Zoom call with Anna Wintour herself, who now seemed to be hinting that Sam might pay for the entire shindig.

"Yeah, absolutely," said Sam, but his mind was elsewhere. The Hoard Dragon was dead. Anna Wintour had killed it. What to do? He made a half-hearted bid to begin another game and pick another hero but then changed his mind and shut the game down. He could often occupy two worlds at once and win in both. In this case he clearly stood no chance of winning in one world unless he paid less attention in the other. And this woman somehow had acquired a spell that interfered with his abilities to multitask. For now she was asking him not only for his money and his time. She wanted to know all about his political activities.

"My mom is working full-time on the effectiveness of political campaign donations, and my brother is in DC with policymakers," Sam said, returning Anna Wintour's face to his laptop. "We're doing a decent amount to see just how hard we can make it to steal an election. It's sad that's the forum we have to fight in, but it is."

For a surprisingly long time, Sam's spending on American elections had flown under the radar. Back in 2020, he'd sent $5.2 million to Joe Biden's presidential campaign without anyone asking or even thanking him for it. He was Biden's second- or third-biggest donor, and yet the campaign had never even bothered to call him. Since then, Sam had tossed tens of millions more dollars at one hundred different candidates and political action committees (PACs), in ways that made his identity difficult to detect. It was yet another game— *How to Influence American Politics*—that he was learning by doing, and it was pretty fun, especially when you had the special power of invisibility. But then he "fucked up," as he put it. He let it slip in some interview that he was thinking of hurling a billion dollars into the next presidential election. That remark had awakened the beast. And now Anna Wintour was professing her love for Pete Buttigieg. She was asking where, exactly, Sam planned to be in the next few weeks. To talk more about Pete Buttigieg.

"I certainly would love an introduction," said Sam. "He's someone who I'd love to see as president." If he thought that would satisfy Anna Wintour, he was wrong. She wanted to nail down a place in the real world where Sam might be, and a time he might be there.

"I'm in the Bahamas sixty percent of the time," said Sam, neatly evading the question. "I'm in DC some. For better or worse, my job is now thirty percent telling the regulators about what regulation should look like for crypto in the United States." His bare left leg now curled under his bottom on the hotel desk chair; his right heel, encased in a white athletic sock, bounced up and down off the hotel carpet. He looked less like a crypto tycoon than a first grader who needed to pee. *But now Anna Wintour was talking again, thank God.* Liberated, he scrolled through his Twitter feed. Two nights earlier, Sam had been introduced to Katy Perry. Katy Perry had wanted to know all about crypto. Now she was posting on Instagram: "im quitting music and becoming an intern for @ftx_official ok 👋."

Anna Wintour's tone was changing. She had gotten what she came for and was now warmly ending the conversation. To be free of her, all Sam needed to do was make his usual sounds of total agreement with whatever she said.

Yup.

Awesome!

That makes a ton of sense.

Yeah, I would love to!

See ya!

With that, Sam hit a button and Anna Wintour was gone for good. With the understandable impression that Sam Bankman-Fried, the most openhanded billionaire ever to have walked the earth, had agreed to be her special guest at the Met Gala. That Sam might even pay for the entire thing. Sam, for his part, hadn't really thought about it. He'd not even begun to do his Met Gala math. "I would have to think hard if this is a thing I want to go to," he said, as he stowed his laptop in his backpack with his spare underwear and headed for the door of his Los Angeles hotel room, on his way back to the Bahamas.

"I would certainly be out of place there. It's going to be a difficult needle to thread."

In the ensuing weeks, Sam gave Anna Wintour's people no reason to think he was doing anything but threading needles. FTX's marketing people sounded out Louis Vuitton about creating a red-carpet-worthy version of Sam's T-shirt and cargo shorts look. Other FTX employees, perhaps hedging the company's bets, paid Tom Ford to design a more conventional outfit, complete with sixty-five-thousand-dollar cuff links. Behind the scenes, wheels spun and gears ground but Sam himself never really engaged with the process, or even said what was on his mind. He viewed the entire list of fashion plays dreamed up by the FTX marketing people with suspicion. "I have no idea which of these things matters and which doesn't," he said. "It's not clear that there is any way to know."

His whole life, as far back as he could remember, he'd been perplexed by the way people allowed physical appearance to shape their lives. "You start by making decisions on who you are going to be with based on how they look," he said. "Then, because of that, you make bad choices about religion and food and everything else. Then you are just rolling the dice on who you are going to be." Anna Wintour, now that he thought of it, represented much of what he disliked about human beings. "There are very few businesses that I have strong moral objections to, and hers is one of them," he said. "I actually have disdain for fashion. I have general disdain for the importance that physical attractiveness has, and this is one thing emanating out of that."

Very briefly, Sam set aside his disdain for the fashion industry and tried to do some math. *Four billion women on the planet. Let's say one in a thousand of them pays attention to the Met Gala. Let's say one in a hundred of those gets interested in FTX . . .* But it felt like trying to comb his hair when he had chewing gum stuck in it. His mind couldn't even really get past the need for him to change out of his cargo shorts. And yet he allowed the decision to just sit there, festering, for months. The Met Gala would not occur until May 2. In Sam's mind he had until roughly the night of May 1 before he had to tell Natalie what he planned to do.

Natalie Tien was prepared for Anna Wintour's people to be disappointed when she told them that Sam wouldn't be there. It was their outrage that surprised her. "They called and shouted and said Sam will never set foot in fashion again!" said Natalie. So much for pulling more women into crypto. Natalie didn't understand why the Met Gala was such a big deal. Sam's last-minute decision not to go would not create anything like the havoc caused by some of his other internal calculations. CEOs had flown to the Bahamas under the mistaken impression that Sam had agreed to buy their companies. The World Economic Forum had to scramble to fill a stage and cancel media interviews after Sam decided, the night before he was meant to deliver a big speech in Davos, not to. Sam had failed to fly to Dubai to give the keynote at *Time* magazine's party for the world's 100 Most Influential People, even after *Time* had named him to their list and flattered him in print. "In a crypto landscape ridden with scams, hedonism, and greed, Bankman-Fried offers a kinder and more impactful vision brought forth by the nascent technology," *Time* had written, the week before Sam stiffed them. Tyra Banks and will.i.am and all the rest of the world's other most influential people were treated to hastily prepared remarks delivered by a not entirely sober FTX employee named Adam Jacobs, who was bewildered to be standing in for Sam. "I'm like, What is the head of payments doing giving this speech?" said Jacobs. "Why am I drinking with will.i.am?"

But the people at *Time* magazine hadn't made a stink. No one except Anna Wintour's people did: the general rule of life as late as May 2, 2022, was that Sam got to be Sam. It didn't cross Natalie's mind to feel even a tiny bit irritated with Sam. She could never be upset with him for the mess he left for her to clean up, because she knew that he never intended to make a mess. She could even forgive people who called to scream at her about Sam. If she herself didn't fully understand Sam, how could anyone?

2

THE SANTA CLAUS PROBLEM

When I'd asked Sam for a list of people who could describe what he was like before the age of eighteen, he'd taken a deep breath and said, "That's slim pickings." He suggested his parents, Joe Bankman and Barbara Fried. He mentioned that he had a younger brother, Gabe. Apart from that, he said, he had no early relationships that would cast any light on him, and there were no experiences in his childhood that mattered much. "I'm a little confused about my childhood," he said. "I just can't figure out what I did with it. I look at the things I did, and I cannot successfully add up to twenty-four hours a day. I daydreamed some. I read some books. I played some video games, but that wasn't until high school. I had one or two friends I'd hang out with now and again." The names of those friends, with one exception, would not ever spring to mind. He was happy to supply me with his date of birth: March 5, 1992. Beyond that, he didn't have much to say, and didn't think his childhood had anything to say about him—which struck me as odd, as he had spent roughly two-thirds of his life in it.

He'd gone to school for thirteen years with other children. He'd been admitted to colleges, which would have required teachers to write him recommendations. His parents were well-known professors. Most Sundays, I'd learn, Joe and Barbara hosted a dinner that guests remember fondly to this day. "The conversation was intoxicating," recalls Tino Cuéllar, a Stanford law professor who would go on to become a judge on California's supreme court and then head of the Carnegie Endowment for International Peace. "Fifteen percent of it was what was going on in your life, fifteen percent was politics, and the rest was ideas. How we thought about what we thought about—aesthetics, music, whatever." Sam had been at those dinners but could not think of any one of their guests who'd be worth my talking to. Pressed, he suggested I call his brother, who was now employed by Sam to distribute Sam's money to political candidates. Gabe, three years younger, told me that I was wasting my time. "We weren't close growing up," he said, when I reached him. "I don't think Sam liked school that much, but I don't really know. He kept to himself. I would interact with him as another tenant in my house."

Sam's parents were only a bit more helpful. Sam had been their first child, and so it had taken them longer than it might have to figure out that there was no point in parenting him by any book. "Childhood was a funny thing for Sam," said Joe. "He was never comfortable with kids, or with being a kid." They'd briefly attempted to inflict upon him a normal childhood before realizing that there was no point. The trip to the amusement park was a good example. When Sam was a small child, his mother had located a Six Flags or Great America park. She'd hauled him dutifully from amusement to amusement until she realized Sam wasn't amused. Instead of throwing himself into the rides, he was watching *her.* "Are you having fun, Mom?" he asked finally, by which he meant, *Is this really your or anyone else's idea of fun?* "I realized I had been busted," said Barbara.

By the time Sam was eight she had given up on the idea that his wants and needs would be anything like other children's. She remembered the instant that happened. She had been at Stanford for over a decade, a frequent contributor of difficult papers to academic journals. "I was walking him to school, and he asked me what I was doing," recalled Barbara. "I told him I was giving some paper, and he asked, 'What's it on?' " I gave him a bullshit answer, and he pressed me on it, and by the end of the walk we were in the middle of a deep conversation about the argument. The points he was making were better than any of the reviewers'. At that moment my parenting style changed."

To their friends who came to dinner on Sunday nights, Joe was always light, Barbara more serious. Joe was funny, Barbara trenchant. Gabe was a bright and cheery little kid whom everyone loved. Sam was always a presence, but he was quieter and more watchful and less accessible than his little brother. To their dinner guests it seemed that Joe and especially Barbara were both a little afraid for, and of, their elder son. And that they were concerned about how he would ever fit into the world. "We worried that Gabe's light was going to shine, and Sam would hide his under a bushel," said Barbara.

Sam himself took a bit longer to recognize the gulf between himself and other children. He didn't really know why he didn't have friends the way other kids did. Between the ages of eight and ten, he was sideswiped by a pair of realizations that, taken together, amounted to an epiphany. The first came one December day during the third grade. Christmas was approaching, and a few of his classmates brought up the critical subject of Santa Claus.

The Bankman-Frieds weren't big on the usual holidays. They celebrated Hanukkah but with so little enthusiasm that one year they simply forgot it, and, realizing that none of them cared, stopped celebrating anything. "It was like, 'Alright, who was bothered by this fact? The fact that we forgot Hanukkah.' No one raised their hand," Sam said. They didn't do birthdays, either. Sam didn't feel the slightest bit deprived. "My parents were like, I dunno, 'Is there something you want? Alright, bring it up. And you can have it. Even in February. Doesn't have to be in December. If you want it, let's have an open and honest conversation about it instead of us trying to guess.' " Sam, like his parents, didn't see the point in anyone trying to imagine what someone else might want. The family's indifference to convention came naturally and unselfconsciously. It was never, *Look how interest-*

ing we are, we don't observe any of the rituals that define so many American lives. "It's not like they said, 'Gifts are dumb,'" recalled Sam. "They never tried to convince us about gifts. It didn't happen like that."

None of what the Bankman-Frieds did was for show; they weren't that kind of people. They just really thought about what they did before they did it. In his twenties Sam would learn that his parents had never married. In silent protest of the fact that their gay friends could not legally marry, they'd joined in a civil union. And they never said a word about it to their children, or to anyone else, as far as Sam could tell. Later, Sam understood that "they were clearly being driven by a different underlying belief system." As a small child he knew only that there were things other children took for granted that he did not. One was Santa Claus.

Of course Sam was aware of Santa. "I'd like heard of it," he said. "I hadn't thought that deeply about it." He thought of Santa roughly the same way he thought of cartoon characters. Bugs Bunny existed too, in some sense, but Bugs Bunny wasn't *real*. Now, at the age of eight, he realized that other children believed that Santa was real, in a way that Bugs Bunny was not. It blew his mind. He went home that afternoon, shut himself in his room, and thought it over. "Imagine you had never been introduced to the idea of Santa as a real thing," said Sam. "And then one day someone tells you that ninety-five percent of the people your age in the world believe in him. That this guy lives in the North Pole and has these elves. That he takes off with these flying reindeer. He flies into your chimney and brings you presents. Unless you've been naughty, in which case he brings coal. Though for some reason no one actually knows anyone who has gotten coal. And he does this just once a year. You're like, 'What the fuck? Where did that come from?'"

He found his way to a solution that offered temporary relief: only children suffered from this madness. Yes, kids believed in Santa. But grown-ups did not. There was a limit to the insanity. But then, a year or so later, a boy in his class said he believed in God.

Sam had heard of God too. "God was like a thing on TV," he said. "God came up. But I didn't think anyone actually believed in God." It told you something not just about Sam but about his upbringing that he could live for almost ten years inside the United States of America without realizing that other people believed in God. "I never asked myself, 'Why does God come up if no one believes in it?'" he said. "I had never gone through that process before. I hadn't drilled down into 'Do people believe in it?'" Now Henry was telling him not only that he believed in God but that his parents did too. So did lots of other grown-ups. "And I freaked out," recalled Sam. "Then he freaked out. We both freaked out. I remember thinking, *Wait a minute, do you think I'm going to hell?* Because that seems like a big deal. If hell exists, why do you, like, care about McDonald's? Why are we talking about any of this shit, if there is a hell. If it really exists. It's fucking terrifying, hell."

This was Santa all over again, only worse. God—or rather the fact that anyone believed in him—rocked Sam's world. Just sideswiped his view of other people and what was going on inside their minds. He tried to confront adults—mainly friends of his parents' who came to dinner—about God. He always found it easier to talk to grown-ups than to children and had always been better at it than other children—a fact he attributed to the idiotic childishness of other children. His parents' friends were at their dinner table every Sunday, and available for inspection. "I'd ask them, 'Do you believe in God?' They'd equivocate—like, say something about a Being that started the Clock of the Universe. And I'd think, Quit fucking around: it's a binary question. Just yes or no." He didn't understand the unwillingness of even really smart grown-ups to get the right answer to this question. "It was weird to me," he said. "I never understood why people bothered pretending about this shit."

From the widespread belief in God, and Santa, Sam drew a conclusion: it was possible for almost everyone to be self-evidently wrong about something. "Mass delusions are a property of the world, as it turns out," he said. He had to accept that there was nothing he could do about this. There was no point in arguing with other kids' belief in Santa Claus. Yet he didn't feel the slightest need to pretend to agree. He simply came to terms with the fact that the world could be completely wrong about something, and he could be completely right. There could be a kind of equilibrium in which everyone in the world could remain wrong and he could remain right, and neither side would even try to change the other's mind. "There are times when we're just going to stare at each other," said Sam.

One interpretation of Sam's childhood is that he was simply waiting for it to end. That's how he thought about it, more or less: that he was holding his breath until other people grew up so he could talk to them. "A lot of childhood just never made sense to me," he said. "If you don't find it magical to think about Santa Claus then it's just fucking dumb." Although he found it easier to talk with adults than with children, the connections he made with the adults were no stronger than those he made with other kids. In some deep way, he sensed, he remained cut off from other human beings. He could read them, but they couldn't read him. "There were some things I had to teach myself to do," he said. "One is facial expressions. Like making sure I smile when I'm supposed to smile. Smiling was the biggest thing that I most weirdly couldn't do." Other people would say or do things to which he was meant to respond with some emotional display. And instead of faking it, he questioned the premise. *What's the whole point of facial expressions in the first place? If you're going to say something to me, just say it. Why do I have to grin while you do it?*

Very early on, Sam realized that he'd need to acquire abilities most people just took for granted. But he also knew that he could take for granted abilities that other people sweated to learn. When the teacher said that Sally had thirteen apples in her basket, then picked twice as many apples as she already had and added them to that same basket, Sam knew faster than the other kids how many apples Sally had in her basket. In kindergarten a teacher had suggested to Barbara and Joe that they remove him from public school and enroll him in a school for gifted kids. "We thought she was bats," said Barbara. For the next seven years they were given no reason to think they'd made a mistake. Right through middle school Sam was a good but not great student, defined mainly by his disinterest in whatever his teacher was saying. "I was obedient in that I wouldn't do shit I wasn't supposed to do," said Sam. "But I wouldn't necessarily do shit I was supposed to do. I would just be sitting there in a stupor."

It was in middle school that he became conscious of the fact that he was not a happy person. Depression took many forms, and his was of the low-level, simmering kind. "I think in general when people are depressed they know they are depressed," he said. "My form of it was not out-of-control negative. My form of it was lack of positive." He had a fault line inside him, pressure was building on it, and one day, in the seventh grade, it slipped. His mother returned from work to find Sam alone, in despair. "I came home, and he was crying," recalled Barbara. "He said, 'I'm so bored I'm going to die.'" Barbara and Joe organized a small group of parents to beseech the school to offer an advanced math class. The school relented and brought in a special teacher. "The class met at seven," recalled Barbara. "And for the first time Sam just jumped out of bed at six thirty. Up till then there wasn't a real clear indicator that he was special." It was then that Barbara and Joe decided to spend the money to send him to a fancy private high school, Crystal Springs Uplands.

Crystal Springs made no difference. "I hated it there too," said Sam. "The whole way through. I didn't like classes. I didn't like my schoolmates. I was bored." The student body was a who's who of Silicon Valley children. (Steve Jobs's son, Reed, was in Sam's class.) By most standards it was a nerdy school. A jock was a person who ran track. To Sam it still felt unserious. "It was a lot of moderately unambitious really rich kids," he said. "The one thing they knew is they didn't have to worry. So there was not a lot of drive, and not a lot of pressure. Everyone went to Stanford." He wanted to think about things the other kids had no interest in—including thinking—and he had no interest in what they wanted to think about. He didn't even bother trying to fit in. Everyone else carried a backpack; he alone showed up with a rolling bag whose wheels thump-thump-thumped over the cobblestones as he moved from class to class. When weaker students conferred before a test, they sometimes tried to get him to join in, in the hope that he might save them. Sam wanted no part of it. "He was like, 'Sorry, you're on your own,'" recalled one classmate. "I think he felt above a lot of it. In class he had the attitude of being above a lot of things. He was not liked or disliked. He was just kind of there." Said another classmate, "He was the butt of jokes made by people who sort of pretended he was in on them, but he wasn't." During the school campout Sam hadn't even tried to go to sleep. Everyone just thought that was weird. "I was viewed as smart, as a nerd, not as a good guy or a bad guy," said Sam. "Not really viewed as a person. Smart and inoffensive and maybe not all that human." Worse, he didn't totally disagree with his classmates' assessment. "I didn't feel misunderstood. I felt like their half-assed guesses were in the right ballpark."

By high school Sam had decided that he just didn't like school, which was odd for a person who would finish at the top of his class. He'd also decided that at least some of the fault lay not with him but with school. English class, for instance. His doubts about English class dated back to the sixth grade. That was when the teachers had stopped worrying about simple literacy and turned their attention to deeper questions. "As soon as English class went from 'can you read a book' to writing an essay about a book, I completely lost interest," recalled Sam. He found literary criticism bizarre: Who cared what you felt or thought about a story? The story was the story, with no provably right or wrong way to read it. "If they said talk about what you like or don't like, okay, I would do that," he said. That's not what they were asking him to do, however. They were asking him to interpret the book, and then judging him on his interpretations.

In elementary school he'd read the Harry Potter books over and over. By the eighth grade he had stopped reading books altogether. "You start to associate it with a negative feeling, and you stop liking it," he said. "I started to associate books with a thing I didn't like." He kept his thoughts about the literary-industrial establishment to himself through middle school, but by high school they began to leak out of him. "I objected to the fundamental reality of the entire class," said Sam of English. "All of a sudden I was being told I was wrong—about a thing it was impossible to be wrong about. The thing that offended me is that it wasn't honest with itself. It was subjectivity framed as objectivity. All the grading was arbitrary. I don't even know how you grade it. I disagreed with the implicit factual claims behind the things that got good grades." He'd sat through middle school in a stupor, but by high school he was sure enough of his own mind that he was willing to challenge his English teachers' cherished beliefs on grounds unrecognizable to English teachers. Their belief, for instance, that Shakespeare was an especially good writer.

> The plot twist in Much Ado About Nothing—typical of Shakespeare—relies on, simultaneously, one-dimensional and unrealistic characters, illogical plots and obvious endings. I mean, come on—kill someone because he thinks, with good reason, that his fiancée is cheating on him? Beatrice is absurdly out of line in an unrealistic way; Benedick is absurd for listening to her, and this is all supposed to be taken in stride.

To Sam's way of thinking, the case against Shakespeare could be made with basic statistics:

> I could go on and on about the failings of Shakespeare . . . but really I shouldn't need to: the Bayesian priors are pretty damning. About half the people born since 1600 have been born in the past 100 years, but it gets much worse than that. When Shakespeare wrote almost all Europeans were busy farming, and very few people attended university; few people were even literate— probably as low as ten million people. By contrast there are now upwards of a billion literate people in the Western sphere. What are the odds that the greatest writer would have been born in 1564? The Bayesian priors aren't very favorable.[*]

---

[*] From a blog Sam wrote as a college sophomore, but he'd made this argument as a high school junior.

That he still received good grades from his English teachers didn't lessen his skepticism of their enterprise. Why were they giving him an A? Why were they giving any grade to anyone for what amounted to an opinion? "I convinced the teachers that I was a good student, and thus I got good grades," he said. "It was self-fulfilling to a decent extent." They gave him an A because they didn't want to explain why they *didn't* give him an A. All of humanities was like this for him: dopey stuff he wanted mainly to escape but that somehow always lurked just around every corner. In choosing a college to attend, Sam sought to ensure he'd never again be made to write an essay about Jane Austen.

But even MIT, where he eventually landed, had a humanities requirement. A single liberal arts class, which he satisfied by taking film history, but even that grated on him. "Whatever cease-fire existed earlier in my life was gone," he said. "I was starting to get a little bit of a whiff of 'I don't have to put up with it anymore.'" The very first question on the final exam set him off. *What's the difference between art and entertainment?* "It's a bullshit distinction dreamed up by academics trying to justify the existence of their jobs," wrote Sam, and handed the exam back.

He felt nothing in the presence of art. He found religion absurd. He thought both right-wing and left-wing political opinions kind of dumb, less a consequence of thought than of their holder's tribal identity. He and his family ignored the rituals that punctuated most people's existence. He didn't even celebrate his own birthday. What gave pleasure and solace and a sense of belonging to others left Sam cold. When the Bankman-Frieds traveled to Europe, Sam realized that he was just staring at a lot of old buildings for no particular reason. "We did a few trips," he said. "I basically hated it." To his unrelenting alienation there was one exception: games. In sixth grade Sam heard about a game called *Magic: The Gathering*. For the next four years it was the only activity that consumed him faster than he could consume it.

Magic had been created in the early 1990s by a young mathematician named Richard Garfield. It was the first of a new kind of game, designed, perhaps, for a new kind of person. Garfield had started with an odd question: Could a strategic game be designed that allowed the players to come to it with different equipment? He wasn't sure if it was even possible. You couldn't allow poker players to show up with their own privately curated decks, or chess players to come equipped with whichever pieces they wanted to. You didn't want players to be able to simply buy better material and thus victory.

In the game Garfield designed, players did indeed buy their own playing cards, and assembled their own decks for competition. Each of the cards had a picture of some mythical character—a witch, a demon, and so on—and each character had its own special traits and a quantified ability to inflict and withstand damage. (If *Magic* sounds similar to *Storybook Brawl*, it's because *Storybook Brawl* was one of many games modeled on *Magic*.) But you couldn't just buy the best cards— because you never knew which cards would be the best. The game itself was unstable. The cards constantly changed in ways that were impossible to anticipate: new cards were introduced, and old cards were banned. The interactions between the cards were too complicated to fully understand—at some point Garfield realized even he could not predict what might happen in his own game, which he liked. "The game is shallow if you know when you create it what the best play is," he said. "There should exist within the game a scenario where it is impossible to determine a winning strategy."

This was a radical notion: the game was ultimately unknowable. Merely playing a lot and memorizing the best moves only got you so far, as from one game to the next the best moves would change. "It makes it so players have to constantly adapt the strategy to things no one could have anticipated," said Garfield. The people who were good at *Magic* were those who found it easy to adapt their strategies. As the best strategy was not just hard to know but unknowable, the people who were good at *Magic* were also comfortable making decisions while being certain that they were uncertain.

Sam was good at *Magic*. Inside the game he interacted more easily with other people than he could outside it. Playing the game, he made his one meaningful childhood friend, a boy named Matt Nass.[*] Matt was as chill as a twelve-year-old boy could be. He had none of the neediness of other kids. "Given the backdrop of *I don't understand kids in the first place*, neediness was a problem," said Sam. Matt made zero social or emotional demands on him. He didn't need Sam to generate facial expressions, or to ask him questions about himself, or really to do anything but play *Magic*.

Matt's sheer lack of needs opened Sam up as much as Sam ever opened up. Sam and Matt bought their cards together, and got driven together by their parents to play local tournaments against grown men.[†] Eventually they went on the junior circuit together—reaching, at the end of tenth grade, the national championships in Chicago. Matt saw Sam as maybe no one else did. "I think it's easy to think of people who are extremely rational as robotic," he said, "but I really don't think that applies to Sam. He was a really rare combination of hyper-rational and extremely kind." They drifted apart in high school but attended colleges an hour's drive from each other. In the fall of Sam's junior year, he knocked on Matt's dorm room door. "I was playing video games and too distracted to check my phone, so I had no idea what had happened," recalled Matt. That afternoon, Matt's father, with whom he was very close, had died of a heart attack. "Sam told me the news in person and then drove me back to his nerd frat at MIT, where we played board games and video games all night to distract me before I flew back home the next day."

Every life is defined not just by what happens in it but by what doesn't. The beginning of Sam's life is as striking for what didn't happen in it as for what did. He could see he was different from most other kids. He made no effort to join their games, and they didn't

---

[*] Matt grew up to be an inventor of games. He created *Storybook Brawl*.
[†] These events were overwhelmingly male. Populated by a certain kind of guy. It tells you something about *Magic* culture that tournament rules eventually included standards of personal hygiene, after players began to weaponize their body odor.

understand his. He maintained what he later called a "romantically positive" view of himself. "I didn't think it was a happy thing that I was different," he said. "I thought it was a cool thing." His only weapon for defending himself against the derision of his schoolmates was a shallow contempt, and a weak sense of his own superiority. "But I never had a super principled reason for it. It was, *I better think that, or what do I have going for me?*" He was perfectly positioned, emotionally and intellectually, to make a religion of himself. What were the odds of a mathematically gifted kid in the middle of Silicon Valley in the early 2000s *not* picking up *The Fountainhead* and finding his inner life inside? But that never happened.

Sam saw some merits in a certain kind of libertarianism. But he listened to actual libertarians argue why, for instance, they shouldn't need to pay taxes. And he thought, *Yeah, of course no one likes to pay taxes, but that's not exactly a philosophy.* "They blurred the line between libertarianism as a philosophy and selfishness as a philosophy," he said. His internal wiring didn't carry this particular signal. "The notion that other people don't matter as much as I do felt like a stretch," he said. "I thought it would be bizarre even to think about." It was one thing to feel isolated; it was another to believe that one's place of isolation was the center of the universe. Or that you and what happened to you were the only things that mattered. "It felt unambitious to not care about what happened to the rest of the world," said Sam. "It was shooting too low to only think about what was going to impact me."

In their day jobs, his parents continually wrestled with the tension, in American law, between individual freedoms and the collective good. Both identified, broadly speaking, as utilitarians: any law should seek not to maximize some abstract notion of freedom but rather the greatest good for the greatest number. They never pushed their views on Sam, but Sam of course heard them. And his parents mostly made sense to him. Around the time he stopped reading books, he turned to utilitarian message boards on the internet. He might not have felt connections to individual people, but that only made it easier for him to consider the interests of humanity as a whole. "Not being super close to that many particular people made it more natural to care not about anyone in particular but about everyone," he said. "The default wiring I had was, 'Yeah, there's not anyone who doesn't matter. So I guess I should care the same amount about everyone.'" One day, at the age of twelve, he had popped out of his room and made an impassioned point in defense of utilitarianism. "I was just stunned when I realized that's what he was doing in his bedroom," said Barbara. As Sam would later explain:

> When I was about 12 years old I was first becoming politically aware and started to think through social issues. Gay marriage was a no brainer—you don't have to be a hardcore utilitarian to see that making people's lives miserable because they're completely harmlessly a little bit different than you is stupid. But abortion was nagging me a bit. I was pretty conflicted for a while: having unwanted kids is bad, but so was murder.

Then Sam framed abortion as a utilitarian might. Not by dwelling on the rights of the mother or the rights of the unborn child but by evaluating the utility of either course of action.

> There are lots of good reasons why murder is usually a really bad thing: you cause distress to the friends and family of the murdered, you cause society to lose a potentially valuable member in which it has already invested a lot of food and education and resources, and you take away the life of a person who had already invested a lot into it. But none of those apply to abortion. In fact, if you think about the actual consequences of an abortion, except for the distress caused to the parents (which they're in the best position to evaluate), there are few differences from if the fetus had never been conceived in the first place. In other words, to a utilitarian abortion looks a lot like birth control. In the end murder is just a word and what's

important isn't whether you try to apply the word to a situation but the facts of the situation that caused you to describe it as murder in the first place. And in the case of abortion few of the things that make murder so bad apply.[*]

This was how Sam figured out who he was: by thinking about things for himself, without a whole lot of concern for the thoughts of others. There were two brief periods, however, when he had someone around to think about things with. Playing *Magic* with Matt Nass was one; math camp was the other. After his freshman year in high school, he went to a summer camp for mathematically gifted kids, on the Colby College campus. (Joe drove him there and got lost—then saw an awkward-looking kid sitting under a tree, fiddling with a Rubik's Cube. "That's when I knew we'd found the place," said Joe.) For Sam, math camp was a revelation: here were kids with whom he had something in common. At math camp people didn't seem to care about his lack of facial expressions. At math camp he had conversations with other people that resembled the conversations he'd been having with himself. When other kids spoke about politics, it wasn't to express some dumb opinion. It was to figure out the best way to model elections and predict their outcomes. When they discussed their lives and how they might live them, they actually made sense to him. Math camp kids could think their way to a belief. "And if you can't think your way to a belief, how can you think your way to an action?" asked Sam.

At math camp Sam found people drawn to the flavor of utilitarianism that appealed to him. "For the first time I wasn't one of the smartest," said Sam. "Each of the campers was more interesting than the most interesting person in high school. They were smarter in every way. They were also more quantitative. But they had more distance from standard culture and felt less pressure or less ability to conform."

[*] Same sophomore college blog. In this case, the thoughts date back to the seventh grade.

At the center of math camp social life was not math but puzzles and games. Sam knew he loved games; after math camp he loved puzzles, too. When he got home he decided to create his own puzzles, for others to solve. Math camp had alerted him to the existence of people not entirely different from himself. He used these puzzles to seek them out. He'd put out an APB on every nerd site on the internet. Some weekends, one hundred socially awkward humans of every age from all over the Bay Area would turn up on the Stanford campus to find Sam waiting with a puzzle. Solving the first puzzle led them to some other place on campus, where, if they ever reached it, they'd find another puzzle, also created by Sam. Solving that puzzle would lead them to yet another place on campus, and yet another puzzle, and so on. On and on this went, for hours, until some genius arrived at, in essence, Sam's horcrux. Sam's puzzle hunts were seriously complicated. But he also created some simpler puzzles and put them online. Like this one:

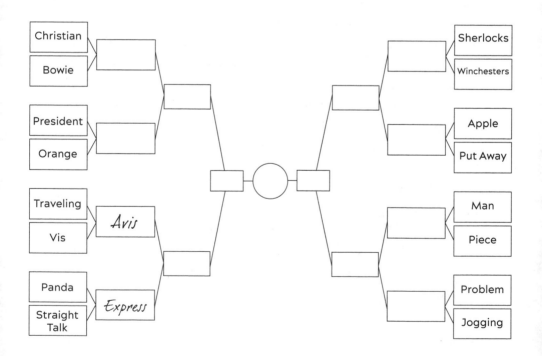

Sam's biggest puzzle remained himself. Before math camp, he'd told himself that he was smarter than other people. Math camp disproved that theory. "This feels like the place for me more than anyplace I've ever been," he said. "But I'm below average. I didn't think there was anything about me that made me special, and it bothered me. Nothing I did—no pieces of knowledge I had—set me apart at math camp." By math camp standards he was only mediocre at puzzles and games. But he also suspected that the sorts of games they played at math camp were too regular for his mind. "The place I am strongest is the place where you have to do things other people would find shocking," he said. He still had no idea where in the world, if anywhere, he might find such a place. Or if it existed.

3

META GAMES

After not much happening in the life of Sam Bankman-Fried for a very long time, two big things occurred in the fall of 2012, at so nearly the same time that it would soon be hard to remember that they had nothing to do with each other. Sam had entered his junior year at MIT as just another physics student who had lost his interest in physics. Approximately zero of MIT's physics majors became physicists anymore. Most went to work for Google, or for high-frequency trading firms. Jump Trading, Tower Research Capital, Hudson River Trading, Susquehanna International Group, Wolverine Trading, Jane Street Capital: all these Wall Street companies Sam had never heard of came to the job fair that year inside the MIT gym. And he became just a little curious about them.

Even a few months earlier his curiosity would have surprised him. He'd never had the slightest interest in money. He neither knew nor cared about finance. Apart from a firmly held idea that he should evaluate his actions by their utilitarian effects, he had no clue what to do with his life. He'd always just thought that he'd wind up being some kind of professor, like his parents. "I had sort of implicitly assumed that academia was the center of morality," he said. "It was where people were at least thinking of how to have the most impact on the world." Two years of college classes and the previous summer's internship, during which he'd helped MIT researchers with their projects, had killed that assumption. During college lectures he'd experienced a boredom that had the intensity of physical pain. He had no ability to listen to a canned talk. He'd figure out where the professor was going with whatever he was saying and, bang, he was out. The more Sam saw of academic life, the more it felt like one long canned talk, created mainly for narrow career purposes. "I sort of started to look at it from a different perspective, and I got a little bit disillusioned," he said. "There was very little evidence that they were doing much of anything to change the world. Or even thinking about how to have the most impact on the world."

Newly aware that he had no plan for the future, he'd gone to the job fair, where he found all these booths run by Wall Street firms. He'd never heard of any of them, but right away he could see that, whatever they did, they weren't all doing the same thing, because they were looking for different kinds of people. Some advertised for "core developers," or "programmers," while others were looking for "traders." Sam had no talent for coding—the two closest friends he'd made at MIT were both coders, but he still couldn't tell a good coder from a bad coder. About trading all he knew was that he was not obviously unqualified to do it. He dropped his résumé with the firms looking for traders. It still felt like a lark. "Someone told me that a lot of physics majors go to work on Wall Street, and I thought, Eh, maybe, but probably not."

He was surprised when three different high-frequency trading firms emailed him to invite him to interview for their summer internships: Susquehanna, Wolverine, and Jane Street Capital. "It turned out that this was a real thing," he said. Exactly what *it* was remained a mystery, even after the firms had reached out to him. You couldn't just google "Jane Street Capital" and learn anything useful about the place. There was hardly anything about Jane Street Capital on the internet.* "I had no idea what to expect," said Sam. "I didn't even know what types of interviews these were going to be."

He had three phone interviews with Jane Street traders, and they were like no interviews he'd ever heard of. Something about his résumé must have caught these people's attention, but they didn't seem to care about anything on it. They didn't ask him about what he was studying, or how he'd spent his summer vacations. They didn't ask for references or inquire into his hobbies—or really attempt to learn anything about his life thus far on earth. The Jane Street traders seemed to believe that no evaluation of him other than their own was of any use in determining whether he was suited to do what they did. But their questions were mostly just mental math. The first ones were so trivial that Sam figured they must just be trying to see how his mind responded when he was nervous. "What's twelve times seven?," for example. And: "How sure are you of your answer?" The more correct answers Sam supplied, the more complicated the mental math became. *If you roll two six-sided dice, what are the odds you get at least one three?* The odds of rolling a three with one die were obviously 1 in 6. If you didn't stop and think, you might guess the odds of rolling a three with two dice were 1 in 3. The error in that answer could be seen if you reframed the question: What are the chances of NOT rolling a three with two dice? You had a 5-in-6 chance of *not* rolling a three with a single die; to get the odds with two dice, you multiplied five-sixths by five-sixths. So: 25/36ths. There was an 11-in-36 chance that, with a roll of two dice, you'd get one three.

The in-person interview, in mid-November, was different. Jane

---

* Jane Street Capital, like the other high-frequency trading firms, felt very strongly that it was better off if the public did not know what it did. "The first time a *New York Times* piece appeared about them, there was like a nuclear meltdown," recalled one former Jane Street employee—who, like the other ten current and former Jane Street employees who helped me to understand what went on there, prefers to remain unidentified.

Street sent him a train ticket to New York City and provided a car and driver to take him out to a disaster relief site in Totowa, New Jersey. Hurricane Sandy had swept Jane Street out of its lower Manhattan offices. The disaster site had an eerie industrial feel—the desks were all the same, you needed a key to use the bathroom—but Sam hardly noticed. What preoccupied him was what Jane Street wanted him to do for an entire day: solve puzzles and play games. These games came with a warning label, however. The Jane Street selection process was designed to minimize the amount of valuable time the traders spent evaluating applicants. The moment any interviewer disapproved of Sam's play, the games would end, and he'd be sent packing. The Jane Street trader who handed him a stack of a hundred poker chips explained that this was his stake for the day—and that no one who had lost all their chips playing the games he was about to play had ever been given a job at Jane Street.

For the first game, Sam was grouped in a room with two other applicants and a Jane Street trader. The trader dealt out a hand of poker, then asked them each to reveal a single card. Then he started suggesting all these weird wrinkles on poker. For example: *You can pay four chips to exchange one of your cards for a new one. Does anyone want to do that?* After each new card, the trader would stop play and try to provoke Sam and the other two guys into making side bets with each other. *Does anyone want to make odds on the next card being a heart? How many clubs do you hold, collectively, in your hands?* This wasn't poker. This was some kind of meta poker. Or a jousting tournament, but with playing cards. Sam saw right away that the key to the game was to make quick judgments about the expected value of bizarre situations, and act on them. Yet none of the decisions actually felt all that strange to him. "The thing that was surprising about them to me was the lack of things that were surprising," said Sam.

Of course, it was impossible to know just how accurately these games identified great traders, because no one who played them poorly was given a chance to trade. Still, at the end of that first round Sam was sitting on a lot more chips than the other two applicants.

At which point his interviewers separated him from the other two applicants, whom he never saw again, and put him through five more rounds of forty-five minutes each. All of the games turned out to be as peculiar as the card game. The coin-flipping game, for instance:

Here are ten coins, each differently weighted. One is a normal, evenly weighted coin, and thus has a fifty percent chance of landing on heads (or tails). The other nine coins are all unevenly weighted, though no two in exactly the same way. We're not going to tell you how they are weighted, except to say that some are weighted to land more often on heads and some on tails. One coin might land on heads sixty-two percent of the time, for example, while another coin might land on tails eighty percent of the time. You'll be given thirty minutes to flip any coin you wish. You'll be allowed to flip one hundred times in total. For every heads that you flip, you win one poker chip.

The Jane Street trader who was interviewing him finished explaining the game and then asked: *How much are you willing to pay to play?* As you could simply pick the evenly weighted coin and flip that a hundred times, the expected value was at least fifty chips. Sam guessed he should be willing to pay roughly sixty-five chips to play, though there was no way to know, as they gave you no idea of the exact weighting of the coins. That must have been, at worst, not an entirely wrong answer to the trader's question, as the trader allowed him to play. Once he began flipping the weighted coins, the trader interrupted again, to offer him even more weird gambles: *Want to bet on what that next flip will be? Want to bet on the true weighting of the coin you've now flipped five times that came up heads four of them?* Sam could see that there was no exactly right way to play, just some wrong ones. Unless you were simply giving up, there was no point in flipping the evenly weighted, 50-50 coin, for example, as it gave you no new information. A lot of very smart people wasted flips searching for the optimal coin—that is, the one most heavily weighted toward heads. They'd flip each coin five times, say, to gather the data they needed to make decent statistical calculations. As a strategy it wasn't totally dumb. But their desire for greater certainty led them to waste a lot of flips on inferior coins. Sam's instinct was to pick an unevenly weighted coin and flip it until it came up tails. Based on how many flips that took, and some dirty math, he'd then decide whether to proceed with the coin or move on to another. He started the game willing never to find the optimal coin so long as he found a good enough one. The game, he sensed, was testing his relationship to information: when he sought it, how he sought it, how he updated his beliefs in response to it.

Jane Street poker wasn't normal poker, and Jane Street coin flipping wasn't normal coin flipping. None of the Jane Street games were even games, exactly, so much as games within games, or games about games. The most difficult part of each game was seeing exactly what it was. "A median American would take twenty minutes to just figure out what the game was," said Sam. "A Harvard student could understand the game, and a Harvard math student could understand the game and the mathematical structure underlying it. It's a lot of quantitative information but not perfect quantitative information. The idea is to give you partial knowledge and relationships that can be only partially understood. And there's time pressure." Sam thought time pressure favored him. It wasn't that he thrived under pressure; it was that he didn't feel it. He wasn't better than usual when he was on a clock; he just wasn't worse—and most people were. Other people felt emotions; he did not. Most people, facing a complicated problem and a ticking sound, had trouble seeing quickly what mattered and what did not, especially if the problem had no perfect solution. Few of the Jane Street traders' questions had perfectly correct answers. They were testing him for an ability to make messy judgments and act quickly on them—and not to be too bothered about questions to which he did not, and could not, know the answer. "It was all the intuitive decisions you make in *Magic*, condensed down but even more complicated," said Sam. "Even *Magic* does not get you there."

The puzzles that the Jane Street traders gave Sam to solve were designed, like the betting games, to expose blind spots in his mind. The one about baseball was the simplest example. *What are the odds that I have a relative who is a professional baseball player?* one of the Jane Street traders had asked him.

Sam's first thought was to define the problem. If you didn't define the problem, you couldn't solve it. "That was one thing he was testing for with the question," said Sam. "Did I realize that the question was ambiguous?" *What counted as a "relative"?* he asked the trader. *What did he mean by "professional baseball players"?* Every human being is related to every other human being, in some sense. And lots of people who are not in the major leagues are paid to play baseball. "Relative," the Jane Street trader said, was any second cousin or closer, and "pro baseball player" included both major and minor leagues but nothing else. Sam guessed there were roughly one hundred baseball teams that fit that definition, and that each had roughly thirty players. So: three thousand active pro baseball players, plus maybe another seven thousand retired ones. Ten thousand players in a population of three hundred million Americans. So: one in thirty thousand Americans had played or were playing pro baseball. Sam didn't know off the top of his head how many relatives the average American had, but he thought thirty was a reasonable guess. Thus the odds this guy had a relative who played pro baseball were roughly one in a thousand.

The numbers were obviously not exactly right, merely a good enough start. But it was here that Sam paused his mental math and said, *I think there's a decent chance you are asking me this question because it is salient for you—because you have a relative who plays professional baseball.*

Here things became tricky. The trader might have anticipated that Sam would have this thought. The trader might have intentionally asked a question that he had no special reason to ask, just to trick Sam. Here was just another aspect of the puzzle: you had to figure out how many levels down you should go before you should stop thinking. Sam decided, as he nearly always did, that more than one level down was too clever by half. It was far more likely that the guy had some reason to ask the question than that he did not. He didn't know by exactly how much, but the mere fact the trader had asked the question shifted the odds that he had a relative who played pro baseball to something better than one in a thousand. "That was the other thing he was testing for," said Sam. "Did I realize that there was information in the question I was asked?"

In the end Sam put the odds at one in fifty. And it turned out that the Jane Street trader did indeed have a second cousin who had played professional baseball. But none of that was the point of the problem. The point was how Sam framed it, or failed to. "There were no right answers," said Sam. "There were only wrong answers."

By the end of the day of interviews, Sam felt he'd discovered something about himself. "I thought, This is correctly testing for something that matters quite a bit, even if I find it hard to articulate what it is," he said. Nothing in normal life—not even the games and puzzles that had sustained Sam through childhood—could serve as a proxy for whatever "traders" did at Jane Street. "Childhood doesn't give you a version of this that would tell you that you are good at it," said Sam. Childhood had given him math, at which he'd been very good but not great. Childhood had given him various strategic board and card games, at which he'd also been very good but not great. The Jane Street traders had tested his mind for qualities it had never been precisely tested for. And it appeared to Sam that God had tweaked trading in various ways, or at least games intended to simulate trading, to make it different from math and board games. Each of those tweaks had made the games more congruent with his mind. "By the end of the day it was clear that it was by far the best I'd ever done at anything," he said.

Jane Street offered him a summer internship. So for that matter did the other high-frequency trading firms that had invited him to apply. One firm had halted their interview process midway through and announced that Sam had done so much better at their weird games and puzzles than every other applicant that there was no longer any point in watching him play. Later, on the Jane Street trading floor, one fellow trader still enjoyed dreaming up games and puzzles and putting them to Sam, just to watch him play. Other people would have no idea what she was talking about—would not even see what the game was. Sam would not only instantly understand the game but would play it beautifully.

Perfume in the mail, she'd once said to Sam.

Sent scent, he'd replied.

Britney Spears is no longer working.

Idle idol.

A Goldman Sachs analyst discovers a cash flow model that predicts the future.

Profit prophet.

In the presence of strange new games, the relevant thought processes just seemed to come to Sam.

One other oddly big thing happened to Sam at the beginning of his junior year. Completely out of the blue, a twenty-five-year-old lecturer in philosophy at Oxford University named Will Crouch[*] reached out and asked to meet with him. Sam never learned how the guy had found him—probably from the writing Sam had been doing on various utilitarian message boards. MacAskill belonged to a small group inside Oxford that had embraced ideas hatched long ago by an Australian philosopher named Peter Singer. He wanted Sam to join him for coffee, then attend a talk he was about to give down the road at Harvard. Just then Sam was maybe the least likely person in Cambridge, Massachusetts, to voluntarily attend a talk by some random academic. But the fact that this professor had sought him out (signaling, to Sam, a justifiable lack of self-importance), coupled with the mention of Peter Singer's name, caught his attention. Peter Singer was at least partly responsible for the ideas Sam had about what to do with his life.

---

[*] He'd later change it to Will MacAskill, so I'll do that here too.

Those ideas, in their modern incarnation, dated back to 1971, when Singer was himself a twenty-five-year-old lecturer in philosophy at Oxford University. The trigger for them had been an oncoming famine in Bangladesh. The sight of people dying of hunger who might have been saved if only other, richer people had sent food bothered Singer enough for him to think about it. In an essay, called "Famine, Affluence, and Morality," he groped for a way to dramatize the nature of this moral failing. "I was trying to think of an example when it would be wrong not to help even though you are in no way responsible for the problem," he said. The example he came up with was of a person out on a walk coming upon a child drowning in a pond. What, asked Singer, would *you* do in this situation? *You* wouldn't even think about it. *You* would leap into the pond and save the child, even if it meant ruining your expensive new shoes. Then why, asked Singer, were we so slow to send the equivalent of those expensive new shoes to prevent a Bengali child from starving? "The whole way we look at moral issues—our moral conceptual scheme—needs to be altered, and with it, the way of life that has come to be taken for granted in our society," he wrote, in that first of what would be a lifetime of similar salvos. We needed to go way beyond ruining our new shoes. Eventually he came to the view that we needed to give what we had to others until the cost to ourselves outweighed the benefits to them. We needed to stop thinking of charity as a thing that was nice to do but okay not to do, and begin to think of it as our duty.

Singer himself proceeded to do just this, and gave away more and more of his own earnings. His essay naturally launched a thousand rebuttals from other philosophers. "Teachers would assign it to students and say, 'Your task is to find where the argument is wrong,'" Singer recalled. There were many obvious complaints: His story was about a single child: it was not practical to save them all. Once you start down this road of giving away everything but the bare minimum of what you need to survive, where do you draw the line at what is enough? ("Sometimes There Is Nothing Wrong with Letting a Child Drown" was the title of one rebuttal.) Beneath much of the criticism was the feeling that Singer was making it too difficult for ordinary affluent people to live a moral life. "It has been argued by some writers . . . that we need to have a basic moral code which is not too far beyond the capacities of the ordinary man, for otherwise there will be a general breakdown of compliance with the moral code," wrote Singer, in one of his own rebuttals to this idea, in his original paper. "Crudely stated, this argument suggests that if we tell people that they ought to refrain from murder and give everything they do not really need to famine relief, they will do neither, whereas if we tell them that they ought to refrain from murder and that it is good to give to famine relief but not wrong not to do so, they will at least refrain from murder."

The academic debate turned out not to matter very much in the real world, as ordinary affluent people simply ignored Singer. For nearly forty years, whenever Singer's ideas came up, no one did much of anything except squirm in discomfort. At Princeton, the school brimming with ordinary affluent people where Singer wound up teaching, he was permitted to introduce a course in practical ethics only after students clamored for it. But then, in 2009, a small group of young philosophers at Oxford University set out to put Singer's ideas into practice. A graduate student and research associate named Toby Ord kicked it off by announcing that he would donate a third of his salary to charities proven effective in poor countries, then explained his reasoning. (At little inconvenience to himself his money would save, over the course of Ord's lifetime, eighty thousand African children from blindness.) Will MacAskill followed with a charm offensive to recruit young people on college campuses to join the cause. "The thing that Toby and Will did was to say, 'No, we think the argument is sound,'" said Singer. The new social movement sprang directly from Singer's forty-year-old argument. *Effective altruism*, the Oxford philosophers called their movement, after trying and failing to think of a better name.

The argument that MacAskill put to Sam and a small group of Harvard students in the fall of 2012 went roughly as follows: you, student at an elite university, will spend roughly eighty thousand hours of your life working. If you are the sort of person who wants to "do good" in the world, what is the most effective way to spend those hours? It sounded like a question to which there were only qualitative answers, but MacAskill framed it in quantitative terms. He suggested that the students judge the effectiveness of their lives by counting the number of lives they saved during those eighty thousand hours. The goal was to maximize the number.

He then showed the students a slide listing the sorts of careers they might pursue, were they to use their careers to save lives. He'd grouped these into four broad categories and offered examples of each: Direct Benefiter (doctor, NGO worker), Money-Maker (banker, management consultant), Researcher (medical research, ethicist), and Influencer (politician, teacher). Eventually, he told the students, you were going to have to choose which sort of career you would pursue. Each career type came with the opportunity to save lives, but the math was different for each, a bit like the math for which hero to play in *Storybook Brawl*. A Researcher or an Influencer stood a chance of saving some massive number of lives. The agronomist Norman Borlaug (Researcher), for instance, had invented disease-resistant wheat, which had saved roughly two hundred fifty million people from starvation. Researcher and Influencer, however, were tricky career choices: it was difficult to predict who would be good at them, and even harder to forecast their effects. The odds of any given Researcher or Influencer saving vast numbers of lives were vanishingly small.

The clearer choice—the choice MacAskill dwelled on in his talk—was between Direct Benefiter and Money-Maker. Put bluntly: Should you do good, or make money and pay other people to do good? Was it better to become a doctor or a banker? MacAskill made a rough calculation of the number of lives saved by a doctor working in a poor country, where lives were cheapest to save. Then he posed a question: "What if I became an *altruistic banker*, pursuing a lucrative career in order to donate my earnings?" Even a mediocre investment banker could expect sufficient lifetime earnings to pay for several doctors in Africa—and thus would save several times more lives than any one doctor.

Then he pushed his point a step further, in the direction of the investment banker. "Making a difference requires doing something that wouldn't have happened anyway," he said. If you didn't become a doctor, someone else would take your place and the doctoring would still get done. Of course, if you didn't become a banker, someone else would also take your place—but that person would spend his money on houses and cars and private schools for his kids and perhaps some non-life-saving donations to Yale. Very little of the replacement banker's earnings would find its way to doctors in Africa. All those people you might have saved if you had become a banker and given away your money would die. Thus anyone with the ability to go to Wall Street and make vast sums of money had something like a moral obligation to do so—even if they found Wall Street faintly distasteful. "Many lucrative careers are really pretty innocuous," said MacAskill, helpfully.

Earn to give, MacAskill called his idea. His final slide was an invitation: "If you are convinced to any extent by the arguments given above, please come up and speak with me afterwards." Even before he was done, he knew the sort of person who'd be coming up to speak with him: the sort of person who scored an 800 on their math SAT, and understood that the test was too crude to capture their full aptitude. Like Jane Street Capital, the effective altruism movement had come to Cambridge, Massachusetts, for a reason. Roughly three in four of the people who approached MacAskill after one of his talks were young men with a background in math or science. "The demographics of who this appeals to are the demographics of a physics PhD program," he said. "The levels of autism ten times the average. Lots of people on the spectrum."

A few days later MacAskill wrote an email to another newly minted effective altruist, whom he hoped to introduce to Sam.

I met Sam in Cambridge MA the other day—he's a junior phys-
icist at MIT. Despite having the geekiest email address ever* I
was super impressed by him. He was brought up as a utilitarian
by his parents, two Stanford professors, is serious, dedicated,
and committed to doing good, and seems really smart and sensible too (i.e. takes some of the weirder ideas seriously, but isn't
fanatic about them). He's thinking about earning to give or
going into politics.

Sam was only a step behind the first people responding to this new
call to arms. That fall of 2012, a student of Peter Singer's at Princeton
had just become the first college student, to Singer's knowledge, to
take a job on Wall Street for the express purpose of making money
to give away. His name was Matt Wage, and he'd been hired by Jane
Street Capital.

*In the presence of strange new games, the relevant thought processes just
seemed to come to Sam.* In the presence of strange new people, not so
much—though it took Jane Street Capital a bit longer to figure that
out. That's something they hadn't tested for in the interviews. But
at the end of the summer of 2013, nine months after they'd hired
him, Jane Street executives sat Sam down to discuss his performance.
The strengths he'd revealed in the interviews were still clearly
strengths. He'd been better at all the trading games than most of
the other interns. His mind was clearly well suited to modern financial markets—so obviously so that, just a few weeks into the summer internship, the Jane Street executives had taken him aside and
offered him a full-time job.

Sam's weaknesses were the news. At the point of intake, no one at

---

* Sam's email address was a Fibonacci sequence, a set of numbers each of which,
beginning with the third number, is the sum of the preceding two. 0 1 1 2 3 5 8 13,
and so on.

Jane Street had tested Sam for his social abilities. None of his interviewers had cared how he related to other people. The Jane Street
executives now told Sam that more than a few people inside the firm
were asking the question that people had often asked about him: *Who
is this guy?* They'd compiled what amounted to a rap sheet. Several
things had occurred that summer to cause the Jane Street executives
to be a bit less sure of their feelings about Sam. All had involved
social interactions. Some Jane Street full-timers had found Sam's
constant fidgeting annoying, especially the way he compulsively shuf-
fled playing cards. One senior Jane Street executive had been seriously offended by the bluntness with which Sam had revealed the
stupidity of a question the executive had posed to a class of interns.
Maybe most alarmingly, more than a few Jane Streeters were dis-
turbed by Sam's indifference to other people's feelings. As an example, the Jane Street executives cited what Sam had done to a fellow
intern, here called Asher Mellman.

Jane Street's interns had been encouraged to gamble with each
other and with the full-time employees. All summer the interns had
made bets with each other, on anything they could think to bet on—
which team would win some game, how many jelly beans some intern
could eat in forty-five seconds, which interns would receive full-time
job offers, and so on. To keep things from getting out of hand, Jane
Street set a loss limit of a hundred dollars per day per intern. The
gambling was a teaching tool. It taught interns to turn gambles that
most people would not make at all, or make by the seat of their pants,
into numbers that could be analyzed. It compelled them to think
quantitatively about qualitative things. To think rigorously about
everything—even a jelly-bean-eating contest. After all, what Jane
Street was looking for were traders who could think faster and better
than everyone else in global financial markets.

On the day in question, Sam hadn't been looking for trouble. It
was Asher Mellman who approached him. Which surprised him,
because Sam could not stand Asher. Asher had come to Jane Street
from Harvard, and Sam had decided, fairly quickly, that he was "fake

and stuck-up and unimpressive." ("He half had some maybe gig with Nate Silver and he made sure everyone knew.") Sam realized that his feelings were a reflection more of his own tastes than of some universal loathsomeness of Asher's. "It's not that he's an unlikable guy in general," said Sam. "Much of the world likes him. But if you don't like Asher, you really don't like Asher." Sam especially didn't like the way Asher tried to impress other people, because what Asher found impressive about himself were precisely the qualities Sam most disliked in others. Asher was pretentious about the food he ate, and he put more thought than most Jane Street interns into the clothes he wore. "He had opinions on what sweater was a nice sweater, and what were not nice sweaters." Sam knew that a lot of people, himself included, were bad at distinguishing their pet peeves from legitimate criticism. "It triggered me in specific ways that I know I'm sensitive to," said Sam. "Part of me is like, Jesus Christ, Sam, why do you care why he cares what sweaters he's wearing?" A bigger part of him cared.

And Asher had approached him. In the conference room, one morning. Before Jane Street's intern class.

Let's make a bet, Asher had said.

On what?

On how much any one intern will lose gambling today.

Sam's first thought was about adverse selection. Adverse selection was a favorite topic at Jane Street. In this context it meant that the person most eager to make a bet with you is the person you should be most worried about betting against. When people wanted to bet—or trade—with you, there was usually a reason: they knew something you did not. (That they had a second cousin who had played in the minor leagues, for instance.) The first thing you did when someone offered you a bet was to make sure you weren't missing what they might know. Some piece of information. Some non-obvious angle to the problem. Lots of bets looked stupid after the fact because the person on the receiving end hadn't thought about why a bet had been proposed in the first place. Jane Street hammered this bitter fact into you every day, and these gambling games were the tool.

A full-time Jane Street trader might approach a group of interns and say something like: *I got some dice in my pocket. Anyone want to make a market how many?* The interns, primed to gamble, were also eager to impress full-time Jane Street traders. And so some less savvy intern might actually do it. He'd think it over and (because he'd read the Jane Street guide on how to make markets) say something like, *Two at five, one up.* (That is, he'd "buy" at two dice or "sell" at five dice.) Some other intern who "sold" to the less savvy intern would be betting that the full-time Jane Street trader had fewer than two dice in his pocket—and the smarter intern would win one dollar for each die fewer than two the trader actually had ("one up"). If the trader had zero dice in his pocket, the intern who had made the market would owe the savvier intern two bucks. Anyone who "bought" from the intern at five was betting that the trader had more than five dice in his pocket—and would win a dollar for every die over five. Thus if you "bought" at five, and the trader had only two dice in his pocket, you would owe the intern three dollars. On the other hand, if the trader had nine dice in his pocket, the intern owed you four dollars.

The full-time trader was not testing for an ability to make intelligent guesses about the greatest and least number of dice held by a person who walked around with dice in his pocket. He was testing to see if the intern had the sense to ask meta-level questions: *Why is this trader asking me how many dice he has in his pocket? What risk might he be disguising?* "Two at five, one up" seemed reasonable—if you didn't ask those questions. After all, the trader probably had *some* dice in his pocket—otherwise why would he be asking? And if he had more than five dice in his pocket, surely you'd see a bulge. *Two at five, one up* was not reasonable, however. *Two at five, one up* was all you needed to hear to know that the intern should never be offered a full-time job as a Jane Street trader. This became obvious to all after the intern said *two at five, one up*, and the other, smarter intern had "bought" at five. And the trader pulled from his pocket sacks that contained a grand total of 723 extremely tiny dice.

I just want to be clear, Sam had said to Asher Mellman. *This cannot settle above one hundred or below zero, right?* (That is, the most that any intern might lose in a day is one hundred dollars, and the least is zero.)

Right, said Asher.

You really want to bet against me? asked Sam.

Yes.

Why?

It'd be fun.

You a buyer or a seller?

Depends on the price, said Asher.

Sam now knew most of what he needed to know—that Asher had not thought hard enough about this bet he'd dreamed up. "If I were a more mature person, I would not have taken the bet," said Sam. Instead, he said, *I'm a buyer, at fifty.* (As a "buyer" Sam was betting on an intern loss of more than fifty dollars that day. If the biggest loser that day lost only forty dollars, Sam would owe Asher ten dollars. If the biggest loser lost sixty dollars, Asher would owe Sam ten dollars.)

Sixty-five, countered Asher. Sam promptly accepted, then turned to the other interns in the room and shouted: *Who wants to flip a coin with me for ninety-eight dollars?* The day's lecture hadn't started, but the conference room was filling up. A bunch of interns already were hanging around, waiting. *I'll pay a dollar to anyone who will do it!* shouted Sam. ("By then the interns are all addicted to gambling, and to positive expected value gambling more than anything in the world.") To the Jane Street way of thinking, Sam was offering free money. A Jane Street intern had what amounted to a professional obligation to take any bet with a positive expected value. The coin toss itself was a 50-50 proposition, and so the expected value to the person who accepted Sam's bet was a dollar: $(0.5 \times \$98) - (0.5 \times \$98) + \$1 = \$1$. The expected value of Sam's position was even better, thanks to his side bet with Asher that paid him a dollar for every dollar over sixty-five lost that day by any intern. After the coin flip, either Sam or some other intern would have lost ninety-eight dollars: win or lose the coin flip, Sam would collect thirty-three dollars from Asher (the difference between ninety-eight and sixty-five).

Only Asher had negative expected value. Asher lost whatever happened. And Asher was now clearly deeply embarrassed.

Sam won the first coin flip. But that was just the start. To maximize Asher's pain, some intern needed to lose one hundred dollars. *I'll pay a dollar to anyone who will flip me for ninety-nine dollars,* Sam shouted.

Now he had a machine for creating wagers in which both parties enjoyed positive expected value. That machine was named Asher. Interns were lined up to take the bet. "People get so obsessed with free dollars when you frame it correctly," said Sam. He was by then in full obsessive gaming mode. "There was nothing that was going to stop me. If I'd have spent the rest of the internship flipping that coin, I'd have been satisfied." And for a while it appeared that he might, as he won the second coin flip too.

I'll pay a dollar to anyone who will flip me for ninety-nine fifty, shouted Sam.

The other interns clearly felt obligated to take the bets, but the mood in the room was shifting in response to Asher's feelings. Plus the Jane Street trader who was meant to deliver the lecture had arrived and was watching the whole thing. But Sam won the third coin flip too, so to his way of thinking the gambling wasn't yet over.

I'll pay a dollar to anyone who'll flip me for ninety-nine seventy-five, he shouted.

It wasn't until the fourth flip that Sam lost—and by then everyone except Sam was unsettled by Asher's humiliation. And yet Sam was ever so slightly taken aback, a few weeks later, when his superiors expressed their dismay at what he'd done. "They said the second coin flip was already one too many," said Sam. He wasn't surprised to learn that Asher Mellman felt wounded. What surprised him was that his Jane Street bosses thought that he somehow missed the effect he was having on other people. He'd known exactly what he was doing. What he'd done to Asher was no more than what Jane Street was doing to competitors in financial markets every day. "It was not like I was unaware I was being a piece of shit to Asher," he said. "The relevant thing was: Should I decide to prioritize making the people around me feel better, or proving my point?" Sam thought his bosses had misread his social problems. They thought he needed to learn how to read other people. Sam believed the opposite was true. "I read people pretty well," he said. "They just didn't read me."

4

THE MARCH OF PROGRESS

The Jane Street trading floor was one big room with lots of weird sounds. The sound effects were selected to alert traders that there might be some problem or issue that they should attend to. The shriek of glass shattering warned traders that their machines had done some trade at a weirdly bad price, for instance. The "1-Up" sound from *Super Mario Bros.*, Homer Simpson saying "D'oh!," a voice from the original StarCraft game that boomed, "You Must Construct Additional Pylons!"—if you didn't know what was going on, it sounded like an arcade. In busier moments the din reached the point that one job candidate, being interviewed by phone, complained that her Jane Street interviewer was playing video games. After that, Jane Street instructed its traders to explain before all phone interviews that they weren't playing video games. "The sound drives some people crazy," said Sam. "I loved it. It immersed you in the trading."

There was a dance between financial markets and the people who worked in them. The people shaped the markets, but then the markets in turn shaped the people. The markets that were about to shape Sam Bankman-Fried had themselves, over the previous decade or so, been reshaped in ways that mostly reduced the sounds they made. The 2008 financial crisis wasn't exactly responsible for what was going on, but it had played a role. Investment banks like Goldman Sachs and Morgan Stanley that had once taken the most interesting trading risks had become clunkier and more heavily regulated. They were being shoved into the boring Wall Street role once played by the big commercial banks. The trading action had moved into a new class of private trading firms shrouded in secrecy. By 2014, when Sam started as a full-time trader at Jane Street Capital, the financial institutions at the center of markets—those setting the prices of global assets—were not the old investment banks but opaque high-frequency trading firms, like Jane Street, that basically no one had ever heard of. The sums of money made by the people who ran these places were orders of magnitude greater than what the people who ran the big investment banks had ever made. In 2013, the guy who'd created Virtu Financial, Vinnie Viola, shelled out a quarter of a billion dollars for the Florida Panthers hockey team. The guy who created Citadel Securities, Ken Griffin, was worth $5.2 billion, according to *Forbes*. Jane Street didn't disclose profits, even to employees, but Sam could see the full record of its trades and guessed that in each of the previous five years it likely had made profits of at least a couple of billion dollars for its handful of partners. "By 2014 you just had to look at the average IQ of the people going to Morgan Stanley and the people going to Jane Street to know what was happening," said Sam.

The new financial markets had some peculiar properties. For a start, they were increasingly automated. People didn't trade directly with people. People programmed computers to trade with other computers. Removing humans enabled financial trades to happen faster and more frequently than ever before. Speed became maybe the single most valuable attribute in a trading system. The markets were engaged in a kind of information deforestation—an attempt to reduce to zero the amount of time it took for any piece of information to be registered in the prices of financial assets. "It's the most complex and efficient game in the world," said Sam. "More effort has

gone into optimizing the game than has gone into anything else."
From the sums of money being extracted from the game—and the
sums of money being handed by high-frequency trading firms to US
stock exchanges for faster access to their data—you could see that
an advantage of a few milliseconds was clearly worth billions a year
to whoever possessed it. Whether the speed added anything of value
to the economy was another question: Did it really matter if asset
prices adjusted to new information in two milliseconds rather than
a second? Probably not, but the new technology definitely made it
possible for the financial sector to raise the rents that it charged the
real economy.

It also changed the kind of person who was extracting those rents.
As late as the summer of 2014 you could still see, in the shapes of
the bodies on the Jane Street trading floor, the changes that had
occurred in financial markets. The older traders, anyone over the
age of thirty, were built differently than the younger ones. They
were bigger and taller. Their voices were louder. The people who
had founded Jane Street back in 1999 were a motley crew of white
guys from all over the place. They'd come of age at a time when
trading was still done human-to-human, either on trading floors or
in trading pits. In a crowd their bodies needed to be seen and their
voices needed to be heard. They were also less obviously intellectually gifted. They tended to be quick at mental math but less good at
higher-order analytical thinking. On one of those "March of Progress" charts that dramatized the evolution from ape to man they
represented perhaps the penultimate stage of Financial Man: hair
mostly gone, nearly upright, but still carrying a club on their shoulder, which they used to impose a greater taste for hierarchy on the
more egalitarian younger traders.

The younger traders were full *Homo sapiens*. They'd been har-
vested from the tiny slice of the population identified early in life
as having a gift for higher-order thinking. Many had gone to math
camp in high school. Almost all had excelled in computer science or
math at MIT, Harvard, Princeton, or Stanford. They were less socially

adept than the older traders, because they could afford to be. Now that trading was done machine-to-machine, it mattered less how well traders negotiated with other people. What mattered was their ability to help the machine replace humans in financial markets—either directly, by writing code, or indirectly, by giving instructions that might be codified. To their minds it was silly not to just let the computer do all the mental math.

But there were limits to how socially off-putting a trader could be at Jane Street. Sam had tested them. After his summer internship, he'd set out to address his superiors' criticisms. He'd long since realized that his inability to convey emotion created a distance between himself and others. Just because he didn't feel the emotion didn't mean he couldn't convey it. He'd started with his facial expressions. He practiced forcing his mouth and eyes to move in ways they didn't naturally. "It's not totally trivial to fake things," he said. "It was physically painful. It felt unnatural. And I wasn't good at it. It didn't look right."

In the beginning he was unsure whether his efforts would be an improvement on the status quo, but he suspected they couldn't make things worse. An ability to smile would not have changed how he treated Asher Mellman, but it might have changed the way other people felt about it. An ability to signal to others how he felt about whatever they had said or done would, at the very least, avoid a lot of misunderstanding. Sure enough, on the trading floor he finally began to see a smoothening in the surface of his relationships with other people. "It wasn't until Jane Street that I got decent at it," he said. "It became easier. Like my muscles started to loosen up. And it made people like me more. It made me able to fit in better."

Jane Street had installed him on what was then the firm's most profitable desk, the one that traded international ETFs. Exchange-traded funds pooled assets (stocks, bonds, commodities) that might otherwise be difficult for investors to buy on their own. The first US-listed ETF ever, hatched in 1993, was still the biggest: a fund created by the American Stock Exchange and State Street Global Advisors that contained all the stocks in the S&P 500. Later there'd be ETFs for everything. ETFs that held only stocks of small Indian companies, or big Brazilian ones. ETFs filled with fishing industry stocks, or only the shares of marijuana companies, or only the companies Warren Buffett invested in. Any investment idea you could dream up could be expressed in the form of an ETF and sold to the investing public—in 2021 someone created an ETF that invested in companies whose products were beloved by upper-middle-class American women. Without ever tapping outside capital, Jane Street had gone from a few traders with a few million dollars, in 1999, to roughly two hundred traders working with several billion dollars, in 2014. One big reason was ETFs, whose global value had grown from less than $100 billion to $2.2 trillion (on its way to more than $10 trillion in 2022). When ETFs changed hands, Jane Street was often present to take an ant-bite-sized piece of the transaction.

The role of the Jane Street trader—one of the biggest sources of profits—was to keep the prices of all of these ETFs in line with the assets inside of them. The price of any pool of assets should always, in theory, be equal to the sum of the assets in the pool. Trading an ETF was like trading a ham and cheese sandwich, as one Jane Street trader put it. If you know the price of a slice of ham, a slice of cheese, and a slice of bread, you know what the price of the sandwich should be: the sum of the ingredients. If the cost of the ingredients exceeded the price of the sandwich, you bought the sandwich and sold the ingredients. If the price of the sandwich exceeded the cost of the ingredients, you bought the ingredients and sold the sandwich.

Part of Sam's day was spent bringing the price of lots of ham and cheese sandwiches into line with the cost of their ingredients. He spent the first ninety minutes of every trading day just figuring out what was inside the sandwich—as overnight the precise content of the ETFs would change. The least exciting part of his job, the sandwich game was not without its moments. The companies that created ETFs essentially exported the problem of pricing their creations to Jane Street and other high-frequency trading firms. If some investor showed up and said they wanted to buy, say, $100 million worth of some ETF filled with Indian stocks, they'd be directed to Sam, who would give them a price. To determine the price, Sam couldn't make some simple calculation, using the current prices of the stocks inside the ETF, once he'd figured out what those were. He'd eventually need to buy the individual stocks, and his demand would drive their prices up by some difficult-to-know amount. He'd also have to pay Indian financial transaction taxes—so he needed to take that into account.

The Indian stock exchange didn't open until 9:15 a.m. Mumbai time, or 11:45 p.m. New York time. Until it opened, Sam would be unable to buy Indian stocks and would remain exposed to any news that might affect the market. He'd need to consider the identity of the ultimate buyer, as some buyers were likely to have better information about Indian stocks than he did. He'd also need to consider the possibility that one or more of the other high-frequency trading firms asked to offer the stock were about to front-run the trade and drive Indian stock prices higher. On top of it all, he had maybe fifteen seconds to come up with a price—though if he were lucky he'd have a bit of warning and maybe a few hours to think it over. Either way, other traders were always competing to do the same trade. On any given trade, there was never a lot of fat.

And so these ETF trades weren't riskless. As a rule, Sam was always choosing which weighted coin to flip. And the real world seldom offered you coins weighted dramatically in your favor. You didn't get to flip an 80-20 coin; if you were lucky, you flipped a 60-40 coin; more likely you spent most of your day flipping a 53-47 coin. Of course, even a coin weighted in your favor would land on the wrong side on lots of flips, and so even if you did your job well you might lose money. The idea at the heart of Jane Street's business was to make sure no single flip, or flipper, made all that much difference. The firm's two hundred traders all had some unusual aptitude for identifying weighted coins. Collectively they flipped coins millions of times a day. The law of averages would eventually enforce itself. But Jane Street still had losing trading days, and losing trading weeks and even, rarely, losing trading months.* "The biggest risk was that we wouldn't find enough coins to flip," said Sam.

Like all the Jane Street traders, Sam was forever looking for ways to automate his trading decisions. As the writer Byrne Hobart put it, Jane Street traders were engaged "in a constant process of finding and extending the efficient frontier of where computers can replace humans in finance." The job of the Jane Street trader was not simply to optimize financial markets but to optimize himself, by keeping his attention focused on the most valuable decision he might make. Teach the machine to make certain decisions and you freed yourself up to go looking for new weighted coins to flip. To empower the machine, you needed only to identify the patterns in markets that could be captured in computer code. Do that and, when investors asked you to offer $100 million worth of the Indian ETF, you didn't need to sit and calculate the financial transaction taxes you'd pay, the degree to which the buyer was toxic, or even how much the prices

---

* Which told you something about Jane Street. In 2104, the year Sam joined Jane Street, Virtu Financial applied to the US Securities and Exchange Commission to sell shares to the public. Its prospectus revealed that in 1,238 days of trading, it had had exactly one losing day. It had just ended a year in which it had made money trading in the stock market every day. How does any firm do that? the reader might intelligently wonder. The answer is outside the scope of this story but is partly addressed in a book I wrote in 2014, called *Flash Boys*. The point here is that while the high-frequency trading firms appeared interchangeable from a certain distance—their trading was automated, they all acted as intermediaries in financial markets—they differed in how they made their money. Firms like Virtu and Citadel paid US stock exchanges for speed advantages that enabled them to trade against others in the market with very little risk, which explained why they never lost money. They ended each trading day without any positions in the market. Their skill, such as it was, was to create a faster picture of the stock market for themselves than others were able to—which was why, when they went looking for young talent, they wanted computer programmers who could speed their machines more than traders who could make risk decisions. Jane Street had never gotten seriously into the US stock market speed games, and perhaps regretted it. Its relative strength had always been in arguably fairer markets, where they couldn't simply buy the advantages offered to high-frequency traders by, say, the New York Stock Exchange. If firms like Virtu and Citadel were playing a speed game, firms like Jane Street were playing a brain game.

of various Indian stocks were likely to rise when the market opened. You could just hit a button, and the machine would make the judgments, and the trade would happen, or not.

Of course, you still had to keep one eye on it. If, say, a nuclear bomb had exploded in Mumbai after the close of the Indian stock market, you didn't want a pre-programmed machine buying and selling stock. The Jane Street trader treated the machines as robot arms; they allowed you to do a lot more than you could with your own naked arms, but you still had to stick your own arms into them for them to operate. Most of the time the machine was far better than the human at trading decisions, especially when the human only had fifteen seconds to think about them. "I felt most valuable when I was identifying areas where it hadn't been automated but could be automated," said Sam. "It was better than people, because the people had to do it so fast."

Jane Street made money in the sandwich business. Jane Street also made money by finding statistical patterns missed by others in the markets. Of course, traders have sought patterns missed by markets for as long as anyone has traded anything. The difference between what happened at Jane Street and what happened on, say, a Wall Street trading floor in the 1980s was one of degree rather than of kind. Data had fully replaced feel. The standard procedure at the firm was for the traders to watch the machines trading out of the corner of their eye while they ran little research projects. (The trading occupied roughly the same place in Sam's attention that video games later would.) A trader on the international ETF desk, for instance, might start with the following question: When the price of oil moves during US trading hours, what happens to the ETFs filled with stocks of companies in big oil-producing countries whose markets are closed? If oil prices pop higher during lunchtime in New York City, the shares of, say, Nigerian companies will probably follow them higher—but the Nigerian stock market is closed. ETFs filled with Nigerian stocks, however, are live and trading on US exchanges. Perhaps these US-listed ETFs did not respond as quickly as they should have to movements in oil prices? Perhaps there is a chance to anticipate the rise that will inevitably occur in Nigerian stocks when the Nigerian stock market opens tomorrow? Perhaps others had not thought of this? There was no way to answer those questions without running a study of the historical price movements. Jane Street's traders spent a lot of their time engaged in these financial research projects.

It wasn't enough for the trader to make money. You needed to be able to explain why you were making money. A great trader at Jane Street was not a great trader unless he could explain why he was a great trader—and why some great trade existed. As one former trader put it, "It was, Why are you great, and how do we replicate you? And if you could not answer the question, they doubted you." But these little research projects didn't need to begin in a dignified way, with some theory about why some market might be inefficient. Often they'd be triggered by some weird event the trader had observed while trading. For example, you might notice, as Sam once did, that exactly twelve hours after the price of certain South Korean stocks rose on the Seoul stock exchange, the price of certain other Japanese stocks rose on the Tokyo stock exchange. Your first thought might be that this is merely a coincidence. But then it keeps happening. You dig into some old data and find that the same thing has been happening in these stocks for several months. You might trade on it— and buy the Japanese stocks the instant the South Korean stocks rise. You might even make money.

You wouldn't have satisfied the Jane Street system, however, because you didn't know *why* the Japanese stocks were rising in price twelve hours after the South Korean stocks. And so you looked even further into it—as Sam had. And he found that the prices of both the South Korean and the Japanese ETFs were being driven by a single trader at a German bank. Every few days, the German bank trader had a bunch of buy orders to execute, in both South Korea and Japan. He'd make his South Korean purchases before calling it a day, passing the Japan orders off to his Asian colleagues to handle when they awakened in Tokyo. The Jane Street trader could now happily see the pop in the South Korean ETF and buy the Japanese ETF until the German died, retired, or figured out how much his laziness was costing him.

Sam found lots of trades whose success turned on the idiocy of some other trader or trading algorithm. Asher trades. For a two-week stretch, Canada's main stock market index behaved weirdly at the opening every morning. At 9:30 it would pop higher or drop lower with unusual violence and then, at 9:31, revert to its previous levels. That wasn't how a market normally behaved in response to news. Something else was going on. Sam made a study and discovered that a month earlier, someone had done a massive, multibillion-dollar-contract-sized trade in options on the Canadian stock market index. The trader who had done it needed to hedge his position whenever the price of the Canadian index moved. To do this, the trader had created a bot, which mindlessly bought the Canadian index when it went up, and sold the Canadian index when it went down, thus causing it to go either up or down more than it otherwise would have done. On days the Canadian stock market opened at a higher price than the day before, the bot would buy the index, driving its price even higher, requiring the bot to buy even more. It did the same thing in reverse when the index opened at a lower price than the day before. For two weeks Sam's trading desk made a small fortune simply by selling the Canadian index after the bot had bought it, and buying the Canadian index after the bot had sold it, until the trader who had created the bot wised up and turned it off. "It was essentially reverse engineering someone else's dumb algo," said Sam.

The constant hunt for statistical patterns in markets led to all sorts of strange insights. Every time Brazil won a World Cup match, the Brazilian stock market tanked, for instance, because the win was thought to increase the shot at reelection of Brazilian president Dilma Rousseff, perceived to be corrupt. A faster and better sense of the Brazilian soccer team's odds in the next match gave you a weighted coin to flip in the Brazilian stock market. In late October of 2016—to take another example—global stock markets were moving around noticeably in response to any news that seemed to alter Donald Trump's chances of becoming president. At that moment, the upcoming election seemed as if it might be the most consequential election for global financial markets in modern times. The traders on Jane Street's international ETF desk kicked around ideas about how to trade it. And someone pointed out just how slowly, by high-frequency trading standards, election results found their way into financial markets.

Sam took the lead on this particular research project. There was no standardized national system for reporting the vote in a US presidential election. Fifty states decided how and when to release their election data. Some states moved more slowly than others. Some states had decent websites to aggregate totals; others didn't. "Most states had like seventeen different websites," said Sam. Even if the states were somehow maximally efficient in their data collection, it seemed likely there was a lag before the results reached the financial markets. "At Jane Street almost everyone had the same intuition," said Sam. "That it would be surprising if you couldn't do this."

That is, it would be surprising if Jane Street couldn't learn the results of the presidential election before anyone else in the financial markets or for that matter the entire world. After all, the financial markets still learned whatever had happened the same way the general public did, by watching John King on CNN. John King wasn't built to maximize the returns for high-frequency traders. "They had commercials so John King couldn't be worried about a two-minute delay," said Sam. "Plus it took him fifteen seconds to walk across the room to his map." The Jane Street traders had grown so accustomed to acquiring information faster than others in financial markets that they just assumed they could do it in political markets, too.

In short order they'd built a model—similar to those used by the news networks and the FiveThirtyEight political forecasting website—to make sense of the information they were about to gather faster than anyone else. Sam recruited young traders from other desks to make themselves expert on local voting data. To each state, he assigned a Jane Street trader to locate the fastest source of election data. One trader took Michigan; another, Florida. And so on. Getting the voting data more quickly than everyone else, Sam and his fellow Jane Street traders assumed, was the hard part. The smart trading strategy seemed so obvious that they didn't give it nearly as much thought. In the weeks leading up to the election, there had been a pattern: stock markets everywhere tanked on good news for Trump, and rose on good news for Clinton. Good news for Trump had proven to be bad news especially in emerging markets, like Mexico. The Jane Street trading plan wasn't all that complicated. They'd get the voting results before everyone else, that data would shift the odds of the election in one direction or the other, and they'd buy or sell both US and emerging market stocks in response.

On the night of November 8, 2016, the machine Sam designed and supervised worked beautifully. The Jane Street traders were indeed able to get a jump on CNN, sometimes by seconds, usually by minutes, and occasionally by hours. "Trump up!" one Jane Street trader would shout, and some other Jane Street trader would sell stocks. Five minutes later John King would confirm the fact, and the market would move.

As the evening wore on, Jane Street's worries that other high-frequency trading firms might be doing the same trade eased. "Markets were moving at the speed of CNN, not the speed of data," said Sam. "We were confident we had better info than the market. We had a sense that if anyone else was doing this, they were very small." Seven times that evening voting results arrived that swung the odds by as much as 5 percent in one direction or the other, and seven times Jane Street was ahead of the market move. The results from the Florida Panhandle were the most dramatic. After the early votes were counted, it appeared that Clinton had won Florida—and thus probably the election. Florida was so important, and the Panhandle went so powerfully for Trump, that in Jane Street's model it swung his odds of winning the presidency from 5 percent to 60 percent. "We saw the Florida Panhandle before John King saw it," said

Sam. "We even had time to freak out, to think there must be a typo, to see that there wasn't a typo and say, *Fuck it, let's sell!*"

By the time they'd finished, Jane Street had placed a bet of several billion dollars against the S&P 500 and another quarter of a billion or so against the stock markets of other countries, especially Mexico, whose economies were most likely to be damaged by a Trump presidency. Around one in the morning, after twenty-four thrilling hours without a break, Sam left the trading desk to get some sleep. The markets seemed to have fully digested the news of Trump's victory. Jane Street was sitting on maybe the single most profitable trade it had ever done. "It was the most exhilarating day I ever had at Jane Street," Sam said.

Three hours later he returned to find that the markets had changed their minds about the likely effects of Donald Trump on the world's stock markets. "It was supposed to be Armageddon," said Sam. "And maybe it was. But it wasn't Armageddon for US markets." Markets in the United States actually had rallied, and most of the Jane Street bet was against the US stock market. "What had been a three-hundred-million-dollar profit for Jane Street was now a three-hundred-million-dollar loss," said Sam. "It went from single most profitable to single worst trade in Jane Street history." Plus Donald Trump was now president of the United States, a fact that did not please Sam or anyone else he knew at Jane Street. "The universe was a cruel joke," he said.

He was struck by what Jane Street did next: not much. There was no big firm-wide formal postmortem. No one was punished, or even questioned. On the one hand, Sam admired the way the firm distinguished process from outcome. A bad outcome, in and of itself, did not suggest anyone had done anything wrong, any more than a good outcome suggested anyone had done anything right. "Jane Street really didn't like blaming people," said Sam. "They sort of asked, 'Did anyone do anything contrary to what they were being told?' When the answer was no, they said it could just as easily have been the CEO who did it."

On the other hand, this opaque and secretive trading firm had been in possession of the results, before anyone else in the world, of maybe the most consequential presidential election in modern times, and they had lost a fortune. In retrospect, they had spent too much time getting their information and not enough time thinking about how to use it. They'd just assumed that a Trump victory was a global financial disaster. In retrospect, the trade they should have done was obvious (in retrospect it always was): bet on the damage to small foreign markets being greater than the damage to US markets. They should have bought the S&P 500 and sold bigger amounts of, say, the Mexican stock market. "There was an extremely good trade in it that we fucked up," said Sam. "I thought the postmortem should be we almost nailed this. Everything we put a lot of thought into we did quite well."

Instead of trying to figure out how they might do such a trade better the next time, Jane Street's bosses decided they'd made a mistake by trying to do such a trade at all. "It was, We have no intuition for this, and we're not going to do it, and we're going to all not talk about trading on elections for a while until this isn't seared into our memory." This bothered Sam. It made him wonder if Jane Street was indeed set up to maximize its expected value.

It was striking how few people left Jane Street for other Wall Street firms, or really for anything else. "When a sort of senior person left to go to a competitor, there was a crying and drinking session because it was so traumatic," said Sam. The firm enticed young people who at any other time in human history were unlikely to have found their way to Wall Street and kept them sufficiently interested and engaged and well paid that they couldn't imagine doing anything else with their lives except trade for Jane Street. They turned math people into money people without any obvious loss in human happiness. Even the employees who weren't all that good at their jobs were kept on and made to feel a part of things. "Jane Street never fired people," said Sam. "It was cheaper to pay them to do nothing than to allow them to take trades to a competitor."

The firm had bent over backward to make Sam happy. They'd interviewed the two closest friends Sam had made at MIT and hired one of them. They even hired Sam's younger brother, Gabe, who had just started on the Jane Street trading floor. They'd allowed Sam to play a central role in cooking up and pulling off a trade on the 2016 presidential election that had lost the firm more money than any single trade in its history without anyone saying even a mean word to him. In his annual reviews, his bosses let him know that they had him ranked at the top of his Jane Street class. He wasn't the firm's most profitable trader, but he was still young, and doing very well. They'd paid him $300,000 after his first year, $600,000 after his second year, and, after his third year, when he was twenty-five years old, were about to hand him a bonus of $1 million. In his reviews, Sam pressed his bosses to paint a picture of his financial future at Jane Street. It would depend, of course, on Jane Street's overall performance, they said, but ten years in, if he kept on doing as well as he had been doing, he'd be making somewhere between $15 million and $75 million a year. "Jane Street's idea was to make people so happy they wouldn't leave," said one former trader.

And yet Sam was not happy. His unhappiness was not a simple matter; he was unhappy in so many ways that it would have helped him to create new words for the emotion, the way the Inuit supposedly create all sorts of words for ice. Every now and then, usually while he was taking a shower, Sam's thoughts about himself and his situation would coalesce, and he would write them down. The tone of these private writings, in which he was in effect presenting himself to himself, were wildly different from the tone in which he presented himself to others. "I don't feel pleasure," he wrote one day, late in his Jane Street career. "I don't feel happiness. Somehow my reward system never clicked. My highest highs, my proudest moments, come and pass and I feel nothing but the aching hole in my brain where happiness should be." He knew he should feel grateful to Jane Street for finding value in him that no one else had, but he also knew that he didn't. "To truly be thankful, you have to have felt it in your heart, in your stomach, in your head—the rush of pleasure, of kinship, of gratitude," he wrote. "And I don't feel those things. But I don't feel anything, or at least anything good. I don't feel pleasure, or love, or pride, or devotion. I feel the awkwardness of the moment enclosing on me. The pressure to react appropriately, to show that I love them back. And I don't, because I can't."

Jane Street was the only institution Sam had ever had anything to do with that he did not feel at some level disapproving of. He was surrounded all day by hundreds of people joined by a common purpose, playing the best board game ever invented. And yet he still felt cut off from other people. He'd learned to simulate responses to whatever other people had just done or said, so that they might read him better. All he'd really done was create a better mask, one that perhaps made it even more difficult for others to know whatever was actually going on behind it. "I enjoy my co-workers," he wrote, "but they show no interest in seeing who I really am, in hearing the thoughts I hold back. The more honest I try to make our friendships, the more they fade away. No one is curious. No one cares, not really, about the self I see. They care about the Sam they see, and what he means to them. And they don't seem to understand who that Sam is—a product of thoughts that I decide people should hear. My real-life twitter account."

He thought of himself as a thinking machine rather than a feeling one. He thought of himself as a person who thought his way to action. About this, he wasn't completely wrong. The big changes he made in his life tended to come after some other person had made an argument to him that he couldn't refute. Days after his arrival at MIT, for example, he'd met another freshman, Adam Yedidia—the friend whom Jane Street eventually hired. They'd fallen into a conversation about utilitarianism. Sam argued that it was life's only sensible philosophy, and that the main reason people didn't see this was a fear of where it would lead them. ("What scares people most about utilitarianism is that it encourages selflessness.") Adam had listened to Sam go on about his beliefs until he finally said, *If you really believed all that, you wouldn't eat meat. At little cost to yourself you reduce a lot of suffering.* Sam was serious about minimizing suffering. Sam also liked his fried chicken—but that wasn't really an argument. "Whatever he said had been rattling around in my head, but I had been avoiding it because of a thought I did not want to have," said Sam. "The thought was: *I spend thirty minutes enjoying chicken and the chicken endures five weeks of torture.*" There was nothing to do but overhaul his diet, and he did. "There are easy vegetarians and there are hard ones, and he was a hard one," said Adam. "It's unusual to change something like that when it's difficult."

A similar thing had happened to Sam when he'd met Will MacAskill. The Oxford philosopher's argument struck Sam as simply right. He'd long ago already decided that a person should judge his life by its consequences. MacAskill had made those consequences both dramatic and quantifiable: he should maximize the number of lives he saved. Sam had bought in, instantly. "It was very fast and matter of fact," said Sam. "What he said sort of seemed obviously right to me. It gave me a practical course of action: There are actual things to do. I can do this. There are people that do this." Three years into his career at Jane Street, he remained fully committed to generating as many dollars as possible and channeling them into the causes that saved lives most efficiently. He'd given away most of the money he'd made on the trading floor to three charities identified by the Oxford philosophers as being especially efficient at saving lives. (Two of those charities, 80,000 Hours and the Centre for Effective Altruism, the Oxford philosophers had started themselves. The third was the Humane League.)

And yet somehow Sam had committed his life to maximizing happiness on earth without feeling any of his own. Between the summer of 2014, when he started at Jane Street, and the summer of 2017, he'd taken no vacation. He'd actually worked ten days when US markets were closed—the action in foreign markets was especially great when US traders weren't paying attention—and so on the Jane Street books he had taken negative vacation days. On the trading floor, he'd found himself asking himself a question: What is the likelihood that this job I stumbled into by accident yields my highest value? He thought it implausible on the face of it. He'd even made a list of things he might do other than trade for Jane Street: *work in politics, write journalism, sell other people on becoming effective altruists, start some random tech company (even though I don't have an idea for one), set out to trade on my own.* "There were like ten of these things," recalled Sam. "I tried to estimate the expected value of each, and they were all very similar. A choice between Jane Street and any of them was a close call, but a choice between Jane Street and *all* of them is not. I was asking, *What is the likelihood that Jane Street is the best option?* Low. But it was pretty clear that I wasn't going to figure it out at Jane Street. The only way to figure it out was to fuck around and try some of these things."

Late in the summer of 2017, he finally took a vacation. Once he was free to experiment, it took him little time to see that one of the options on his list was not like the others. In 2017, cryptocurrency had gone from being this bizarre hobbyhorse in which he had zero interest to a semi-serious financial market, entirely separate from other financial markets. That year alone, the value of all crypto boomed, going from $15 billion to $760 billion. Jane Street didn't trade crypto. Neither, so far as Sam could see, did any of the other high-frequency trading firms. Jane Street was so skittish about crypto that it wouldn't even allow its traders to trade it in their personal accounts. (Sam had asked.) Yet each day roughly a billion dollars' worth of crypto traded, in such primitive fashion that you'd have thought high-frequency trading had never been invented.

Sam did a back-of-the-envelope calculation: if he could capture 5 percent of the entire market (a modest number, by Jane Street standards), he could make a million dollars a day or more. As the market never closed, that meant profits of $365 million a year or more. "That was my ballpark estimate," he said. "It seemed crazy. So I just cut it by a factor of ten. I was thinking thirty million a year. But I felt embarrassed showing that number to anyone else. They'd say, 'Fuck off, Sam.'"

He didn't feel all *that* embarrassed, however. Before he returned to Jane Street to quit his job, he spoke to his college friend who had provoked him into giving up meat. "Sam was unlike anyone else, in that when he stated his opinion he did it with exactly his level of confidence, which is often very high," recalled Adam Yedidia. "Before he left Jane Street, he said with a high level of confidence, 'I could make a billion dollars.' And I said, 'You're not going to make a billion dollars.'"

ACT II

5

HOW TO THINK ABOUT BOB

t took only a couple of weeks of working for Sam before Caroline Ellison called her mother and sobbed into the phone that she'd just made the biggest mistake of her life. She'd first met Sam at Jane Street, in the summer before her senior year at Stanford, after he'd been assigned to teach her class of interns how to trade. "I was kind of, like, terrified of him," she said. Like Sam, she was the child of academics—her father, Glenn Ellison, had been the head of MIT's Department of Economics. Like Sam, she was someone for whom math had played an important role early on—she'd first heard of Jane Street from the math competitions that the firm sponsored to meet young people just like her. Like Sam, she had discovered effective altruism in college, and found in it an intellectually coherent sense of purpose. Maybe even more than Sam, she had allowed math to pull her to a moral place. "I was attracted to people thinking about what to do in a quantitative, rigorous way," she said. "Before that, I don't think I had much of an impulse to do good in the world."

And like Sam, she'd been hired by Jane Street as a full-time trader.

But unlike Sam, she was unsure of herself and susceptible to being swayed by the opinions of others, especially men with whom she was involved. Unlike Sam, she wanted a normal life, with emotions and children and maybe even a sport utility vehicle in which to drive them around. After a year at Jane Street, she sensed that she was at best average at her job and in any case didn't have anything like Sam's feeling for the place, or share his fanaticism about work. "I did feel a bit, like, unsatisfied," she said. "There was something missing. I wasn't sure I was doing that much good." At the same time, she'd formed an unsettling attachment, at once full of promise and absent of hope, to another Jane Street trader, Eric Mannes. "Looking back on my relationship with Eric Mannes really makes me cringe," she wrote later, in an attempt to explain her emotional journey, which, because she was writing to Sam's attention span, she reduced to bullet points:

- he told me that he would probably never love me
- this made me feel really sad and really bad about myself
- I didn't want him to know how bad it made me feel, since I was worried it would cause him to break up with me
- so instead I hid my feelings and tried to act cheerful and chill about everything
- I tried to avoid talking or thinking about things that made me feel bad
- eg hearing about his exes made me feel jealous and insecure, so I never asked about them

"With Eric I had a feeling that if he really knew me deeply, he wouldn't want to be with me, and thus I needed to hide myself," she added.

In the fall of 2017, she'd been sent by Jane Street back to Stanford, to recruit to high-frequency trading the mathematically gifted friends she'd left behind. Upon arrival she'd called Sam and asked him to meet. Over coffee in Berkeley,* Sam was cagey about what he was up to. "It was, 'I'm working on something secret and I can't talk about it,'" recalled Caroline. "He was worried about recruiting from Jane Street. But after we talked a while, he said, 'I guess maybe I could tell you.'" By the end of their chat, Caroline thought that maybe she should quit Jane Street and join the crypto trading firm Sam was secretly building. The work felt familiar: she'd be doing the same sort of research in crypto for Sam's new quant fund that she was doing in equities for Jane Street. Asking questions like: Does the price of bitcoin vary significantly with time of day? Or: How does the price of bitcoin move in relation to the prices of all the other coins? But the underlying purpose of the work would be entirely different, because she would be doing it only with other effective altruists. Jane Street, as Sam put it, was "just a place where people come to work each day to play some games and increase the number in their bank account, because what the fuck else are they going to do with their lives?" Alameda Research, as he was calling the new firm, was going to be different: a vessel to save some vast number of lives.

Caroline told Sam that she'd need to think about it. Thinking about it meant returning to Jane Street and asking Eric Mannes one final time if he loved her. As it turned out, Eric Mannes did not love her— which, though sad in its way, freed up Caroline to quit Jane Street and join Alameda Research.

Quitting Jane Street wasn't as painless as Caroline thought it would be. First-year traders whom Jane Street had just paid $200,000 didn't simply up and quit—especially not to go work for a fly-by-night crypto

---

* By late 2017, Berkeley had replaced Oxford as the financial capital of effective altruism. One reason for this was that Facebook cofounder Dustin Moskovitz and his wife, Cari Tuna, signaled their intent to give away most of their multibillion-dollar fortune to effective altruist causes—but there were others. Oxford was still the movement's intellectual center, but the Bay Area had become the most likely place to raise the money needed to start what amounted to an effective altruist hedge fund.

trading start-up. Caroline sensed, rightly, that her departure alerted Jane Street to an alarming new threat. Jane Street and the other high-frequency trading firms had been fishing for traders in the same ponds as Will MacAskill and the other Oxford philosophers fished for effective altruists. People able to calculate the expected value of complicated financial gambles were the same people drawn to the belief that they could calculate the expected value of their entire lives. By Wall Street standards, Jane Street was not a greedy place. Its principals did not flaunt their wealth in the way that the guys who had founded other high-frequency trading firms loved to do. They didn't buy pro sports teams or hurl money at Ivy League schools to get buildings named for themselves. They were not *opposed* to saving a few lives. But Jane Street was still on Wall Street. To survive, it needed its employees to grow attached to their annual bonuses, and accustomed to their five-bedroom Manhattan apartments and quiet, understated summer houses in the Hamptons.

The flood of effective altruists into the firm was worrisome. These people arrived with their own value system. They had their own deep loyalties to something other than Jane Street. They didn't have the usual Wall Street person's relationship to money; they didn't care about their bonuses in the ways Wall Street people were supposed to care. Sam Bankman-Fried had been able to leave his lucrative Jane Street job for a nutso plan to try to make even more money on his own because he had no material attachments. "It wasn't going to cut into his lifestyle, because he didn't have a lifestyle," as one former Jane Street trader put it.

Caroline was the second effective altruist to quit Jane Street's New York office in a matter of months, by telling them, on her way out the door, that she was leaving to maximize her expected value. This time they were ready for it. Her manager, a Jane Street partner, pulled her into his office. "He was pissed off," she said. "Just cold." He then proceeded to challenge her deepest beliefs. Effective altruism made no sense, he said, then laid out the many senseless things about it: there was no accurate way to measure the consequences in the distant future of your present actions; if such measurement did exist, it would likely be done best by the market; no one would pay you as much as Jane Street paid you, ergo, your highest value was at Jane Street. And so on. This was a first: a Wall Street trading firm whose business was premised on its ability to hire the brightest mathematical minds was now compelled to make arguments about the limits of math in life. "It was this hour-long conversation with the partner where he tried to convince me to stay because utilitarianism was flawed," recalled Caroline. "I thought, *This isn't something we're going to solve in an hour.*"

She was surprised by the Jane Street partner's lack of sentiment after his argument hadn't landed as he imagined it might. "Once he saw I wasn't going to change my mind about utilitarianism, my stuff is in a box," she said. No one on the trading floor offered her so much as a hug. With her box of stuff, Caroline Ellison walked out onto the streets of lower Manhattan. Once there and on her own, her first thought was: *God, I've made a huge mistake.*

But the thought passed. And in March of 2018 she moved to the Bay Area and took some time for herself before reporting to her new job. On her blog she described her feelings of liberation.

> *me after living in the Bay Area for a week: monogamy is hopeless and dying. might as well be a plate for alpha guys while I'm still young/hot enough and freeze my eggs for later*

In late March she started the job. The situation inside Alameda Research wasn't anything like Sam had led her to expect. He'd recruited twenty or so EAs, most of them in their twenties, all but one without experience trading in financial markets. Most neither knew nor cared about crypto; they had just bought into Sam's argument that it was this insanely inefficient market in which they might use his Jane Street–like approach to trading to extract billions. They were now all living in Sam's world, and they weren't hiding their unhappiness. "He was demanding and expecting everyone to work eighteen-hour days and give up anything like a normal life, while he would not show up for meetings, not shower for weeks, have a mess all around him with old food everywhere, and fall asleep at his desk," said Tara Mac Aulay, a young Australian mathematician who was, in theory, running the company with Sam. "He did zero management and thought that if people had any questions, they should just ask him. Then in his one-on-ones with people, he'd play video games."

The firm's finances were already in a state of chaos. They'd started small a few months before, with the half million left over after taxes from Sam's Jane Street bonus, but within a few months they'd persuaded other, richer effective altruists to lend them $170 million to trade crypto. They'd lost millions of it already, though how many millions no one could say for sure. In February their trading system had lost half a million dollars *per day*. On top of the trading losses, some additional millions had simply vanished. No one seemed to know where the money had gone—but the employees were in full panic mode. "It's not that virtually the entire management team wanted to leave," said Ben West, one of its five members. "The *entire* management team wanted to leave." The four others held a series of increasingly tense meetings with Sam. In the first of these, Ben asked Sam what his ideal role was in the company. "He says that it was being the nerve center—the spider in the center of the web," recalled Ben. "That people would come to him with ideas and he would decide if they were good or not." Sam saw his job as listening to what others had to say, and yet the members of the management team, along with pretty much everyone else in the new company, felt that he wouldn't listen to a word they said.

Amid the turmoil, Sam inhabited what amounted to his own reality. His attitude toward the missing money was, *Eh, it'll probably turn up somewhere. So let's fucking trade!* His first stab at an automated trading system was losing money at an alarming clip, but he'd created another, supposedly better one. Modelbot, it was called. Modelbot had been programmed to scour the world's crypto exchanges for inefficiencies to exploit. If for even a few seconds it was possible to buy bitcoin on some Singaporean exchange for $7,900 and sell it for $7,920 on an exchange in Japan, Modelbot would do it over and over again, thousands of times per second. But that example made Modelbot sound simpler than it was. Modelbot was programmed to trade roughly five hundred different crypto coins on thirty or so different crypto exchanges, most of them in Asia, all of them basically unregulated. The tulip-bulb-like explosion in crypto over the previous year had encouraged the creation of hundreds of new coins. Modelbot made no distinction between the better-known coins with deep markets, like bitcoin and ether, the Ethereum blockchain's token, and the so-called shitcoins that hardly traded at all, like Sexcoin and PUTinCoin and Hot Potato Coin.* Modelbot just hunted for any coin it could buy at one price in one place and sell in another at a higher price.

Modelbot was maybe the biggest point of disagreement between Sam and his management team. Sam's Release-the-Kraken fantasy was to hit a button and let Modelbot burn and churn through crypto markets twenty-four hours a day, seven days a week. He had not been able to let Modelbot rip the way he'd liked—because just about every other human being inside Alameda Research was doing whatever they could to stop him. "It was entirely within the realm of possibility that we could lose *all* our money in an hour," said one. *One hundred seventy million dollars that might otherwise go to effective altruism could simply go poof.* That thought terrified the other four effective altruists in

---

* According to CoinMarketCap, 2,177 different coins were in circulation by the end of 2018. In value they ranged from bitcoin, with a market cap of around $60 billion, to a token called SHADE, with a market cap of just under twenty dollars. The different coins at least pretended to serve some special purpose or project: their creators usually issued what amounted to a mission statement. Sexcoin, for example, claimed to want to make it easier for people to buy sex toys. PUTinCoin said it was supporting the Russian economy and "was created to pay tribute to the Russian people and their president." Hot Potato was the best and, in a way, the most honest. A pure gambling mechanism, it self-destructed in thirty days.

charge of Alameda Research. One evening, Tara argued heatedly with Sam until he caved and agreed to what she thought was a reasonable compromise: he could turn on Modelbot so long as he and at least one other person were present to watch it, but should turn it off if it started losing money. "I said, 'Okay, I'm going home and go to sleep,' and as soon as I left, Sam turned it on and fell asleep," recalled Tara. From that moment the entire management team gave up on ever trusting Sam.

Once she'd started, Caroline heard the gory details from Sam's disaffected partners. "They told me, 'You should know for your own good that there are problems here,'" she later recalled. At the end of Caroline's second week, they called a meeting to announce that they had persuaded the rich effective altruists who had lent them the $170 million to demand its return—which meant that in a few weeks Alameda Research would have no money to trade with. Caroline did not know whom to believe. She felt deceived that Sam had not warned her of how poorly Alameda Research was doing before she quit her job at Jane Street. And yet she didn't know any of these other people. She thought she knew Sam, but she also thought that if the entire management was talking about quitting in protest, and the investors were taking their money back, someone must know things about Sam that she did not. It was at this point that Caroline called her mother and cried.

The business hadn't even really been Sam's idea but Tara's. Tara had been running the Centre for Effective Altruism, in Berkeley, and Sam, while at Jane Street, had become one of her biggest donors. Through the spring and summer of 2017, the two of them were on the phone constantly. At some point Sam revealed his romantic interest in her; at some other point Tara revealed that she was trading crypto in her personal account. Tara was no one's idea of a crypto trader—before moving to run the Centre for Effective Altruism, she'd modeled pharmaceutical demand for the Red Cross. She had no financial background and no money to speak of and yet was generating tens of thousands in profits trading crypto. The more Sam spoke with Tara, the more his interest drifted from her romantic appeal to her trading skills. Tara wasn't just buying bitcoin and watching it rise. She was exploiting the same sorts of inefficiencies in the market for cryptocurrencies that, to exploit in other financial markets, required Jane Street–level talent and speed and expertise.

Sam wrote her a check for $50,000 and sent it to her, no strings attached, so she might increase the size of her bets. She never cashed it. The money made her uneasy—and not because it had come from Sam. "I kept saying, 'What if I just got really lucky?'" recalled Tara. Sam finally put her mind to rest with some math that showed how statistically improbable it was that her rate of success was just luck. Tara's trades were sort of like the trades Jane Street did on everything else, bets on the relative values of different crypto coins. Her success led Sam to his secret belief that he might make a billion dollars by creating a hedge fund to trade crypto the way Jane Street traded everything.

But he couldn't do it by himself. Crypto trading never closed. Just to have two people awake twenty-four hours a day, seven days a week, he'd need to hire at least five other traders. He'd also need programmers to turn the traders' insights into code, so that their trading could be automated and speeded up. Tara had been making a handful of trades a week on her laptop; what Sam had in mind was an army of bots making a million trades a day. He'd need to hire some lower-IQ people to do the boring stuff, like finding office space and getting food for the traders and paying utility bills and probably lots of other things he hadn't thought of.

His access to a pool of willing effective altruists was his secret weapon. Sam knew next to nothing about crypto, but he did know how easy it was to steal it. Anyone who started a crypto trading firm would need to trust his employees deeply, as any employee could hit a button and wire the crypto to a personal account without anyone else ever having the first idea what had happened. Wall Street firms were not capable of generating that level of trust, but EA was.

Up to that point in his life, Sam hadn't led much of anything or even been vaguely responsible for other people. He'd managed puzzle hunts out of his parents' home in high school. He'd spent a year as "Commander" of a twenty-five-person living group at MIT. It crossed his mind, now that he was starting his own business, that he should read up on how to manage people. But every time he flipped through books or articles on management or leadership, he had roughly the same reaction he'd had to English class. One expert said X, the other said the opposite of X. "It was all bullshit," he said.

On the other hand, he had a nose for talent. His judgment of other people was always far more acute than their judgment of him. His first call, made even before he left Jane Street, was to Gary Wang. Sam had met Gary at math camp in high school but hadn't really gotten to know him until college. Born in China but raised mainly in the United States, he was a year behind Sam at MIT and had lived in the same nerd house. Even there he stood out: among shy, socially awkward introverts, Gary was always the most shy, the most socially awkward, and the most introverted. He had this clear, untroubled face and the smile of an angel but . . . no words. People who worked side by side with him for months would come away convinced that he simply didn't speak. Some found his silences rude, but they were mistaken. They were inevitable. In response to the attempts of others to engage him, the best he could manage was an apologetic smile. Otherwise, he kept his back to the world and his eyes fixed on his computer screen.

With Sam for some reason he made an exception. Sam had watched Gary win coding competitions at MIT and listened to people who knew a lot more about coding than he did talk about Gary's coding genius. Sam had also played board games with Gary, endlessly. Board games turned out to be maybe the only way to get to know Gary. "I ultimately saw him for what he was and didn't just dismiss him, and a lot of people did just dismiss him," said Sam. "Despite being very quiet, he seemed not terribly scared of the world.

He was very smart. He was good at games, so he could work on things that were not super literal."

After a while, when it was just the two of them, Gary spoke to Sam. Whatever had come out of Gary's mouth had impressed Sam enough that he'd tried to get Jane Street to hire him. Gary had flubbed the interviews, however, by not speaking. Following graduation from MIT, he'd stayed in Boston, working as a programmer for Google Flights. During his final weeks at Jane Street, Sam traveled to Boston just to tell Gary about his plan to make a billion dollars trading crypto for effective altruistic causes. (Sam had converted Gary to effective altruism.) "He was bored as shit at Google Flights," said Sam. "After a few hours he says he's probably in." Sam then called Tara and told her that he'd found their chief technology officer, and that she needed to talk to Gary. Tara called Gary and . . . well, it was a strange experience. It was tricky getting through a phone call with someone who didn't speak. Tara told Sam as much, and Sam said, *You're just, like, missing something. Wait until you meet him in person.*

That happened in October 2017, when Sam and Tara and Gary gathered in a house in Berkeley and used Sam's Jane Street bonus to make their first trades—with Sam doing all the talking. By then word was spreading through the growing community of effective altruists of this strange new adventure in altruistic moneymaking. All sorts of people with no experience of trading, and no particular interest in money, began to turn up and offer their services. Among the first was another person who would wind up with a central role in Sam's world: Nishad Singh.

Nishad was twenty-one years old and newly graduated from the University of California at Berkeley. He was also Sam's younger brother's best friend from high school. As classmates at Crystal Springs Uplands, Gabe and Nishad had gone vegan together, and then, in college, they had become effective altruists. After college, Nishad had taken the EA path sold far and wide by Will MacAskill and found the highest-paying job he could, so that he might donate his earnings to causes that saved lives. He'd been on a starting salary of $300,000 a year at Facebook when, after only five months, he'd lost his stomach for the work. "There was just some truly retarded stuff," he said. Word reached him that Sam Bankman-Fried had quit Jane Street to generate even more money for effective altruism, and Nishad was all ears. He called Sam and asked what he was doing. "I show up at their apartment," recalled Nishad. "It's just Sam and Gary and Tara. They show me this thing. Sam was like, *Watch me make these trades.* He makes a few clicks and says, *I just made forty thousand dollars.* I was like, 'Holy shit! This is *real?*'"

Like Gary, Nishad was the child of immigrants. His parents had come to Silicon Valley from India with little, turned themselves into upper-middle-class Americans, and never stopped charging forward. It bothered Nishad when they went back to India on a visit and ignored the people starving on the side of the road, and he let them know it. It bothered Nishad even more when he learned how animals were treated on their way to becoming his family's dinner, and he let them know that, too. "You're not jaded as a kid. You can feel how horrific it is. There's not much you can control as a kid, but I could control this." By high school he was reading Peter Singer and on a moral journey that his parents regarded as faintly ridiculous. "My parents' attitude was, *No one cares about this stuff; that must mean there is nothing to care about.* The truth is, I stopped talking about it, because they'd just leave the dinner table." They'd been especially bewildered by their son's turn toward effective altruism in college. "They thought giving away things is insane," said Nishad.

Maybe for this reason, Gabe's parents, Joe and Barbara, had become important to Nishad. "They were the first grown-ups who took me seriously," he said. "And it made me take myself seriously." Gabe's older brother, on the other hand, might as well have not existed. In high school, Sam didn't seem to have much to do with Gabe or anyone else; he seldom even emerged from his bedroom. "I just thought of Sam as a reclusive genius," said Nishad. "It's like he doesn't belong in childhood."

Face-to-face as a young adult with the reclusive genius, Nishad now had some questions. The first was: *How the hell did the crypto market let you just take forty thousand dollars out of it?* Sam explained how Jane Street made money, and added that the crypto markets were dominated by retail traders who didn't pay much attention to price discrepancies from one crypto exchange to the next. To which Nishad responded: *Why is it not the case that Jane Street or some other high-frequency trading firm will come along and take over the crypto markets?* Sam explained that Jane Street—and likely others—were waking up to crypto, but that it would take them months to ease their concerns that it wasn't all one vast criminal enterprise. *I'm an engineer,* Nishad said. *I don't even know the difference between a stock and a bond: How could I possibly be of use?* Don't worry, said Sam, it doesn't matter that you've never traded. It's just another engineering problem, and once you acquire even a little knowledge, you'll be able to help code the trading system.

Then what are the risks? asked Nishad.

That we blow up, said Sam.

They didn't blow up, not at first. Those first few weeks, they made no real money, but then they had only a few people and Sam's bonus money. By the end of December, they'd hired a bunch of people and raised $25 million in capital. Gary, basically all by himself, had written the code for an entire quantitative system. That month they generated several million dollars in profits. In January 2018 their profits rose to half a million dollars *each day*, on a capital base of $40 million—whereupon an effective altruist named Jaan Tallinn, who'd made his fortune in Skype, handed them $130 million more to play with.

The trading from the start was chaotic. Much of the money they made in their first two months came from just two trades. The frenzied demand for bitcoin created weird distortions in global crypto markets. By December 2017, retail speculators in South Korea were driving bitcoin to prices 20 percent higher than they were on US exchanges, sometimes more. Anyone who could find a way to sell crypto in South Korea and at the same time buy it outside of South Korea could lock in vast profits. It wasn't trivial to do, however. To open a crypto account on a South Korean exchange, just for starters, you needed to be South Korean. "We found a graduate student friend in South Korea and traded in his name," recalled Nishad, who now saw why maybe it would take Jane Street a while to export radical efficiency to crypto markets. Jane Street would smell legal trouble; Jane Street would at the very least be embarrassed if it wound up as news in the *New York Times* that they'd hired a South Korean grad student to front their business. "It was borderline illegal, but in practice, who goes after you when you do this?" said Nishad later. "No one." This was the very beginning of Nishad's financial education: there were laws that, in theory, governed money; and then there was what people actually did with money. "That's where I learned what the law is," said Nishad. "The law is what happens, not what is written."

Pretending to be South Korean was the easy part. It was illegal for South Koreans to sell more than ten grand worth of won without the permission of the central bank. Even if you could find a South Korean grad student to front your trades, you still had to find a way to turn won into dollars. Otherwise, you ended up with a bunch of won in South Korea (from the bitcoin you sold on the South Korean exchange) and a bunch of bitcoin you'd bought on some US crypto exchange. You couldn't complete the trade. Ideally, all at once, you'd sell the bitcoin in South Korea for won, then sell the won for dollars, use those dollars to buy the bitcoin (at a 20 percent discount) in the United Sates, and ship that bitcoin back to South Korea, leaving you with no bitcoin and a 20 percent profit on the trade. But the South Korean government wouldn't let you sell the won.

It wasn't Sam's first thought, but he considered buying a jumbo jet and flying it back and forth from Seoul, filled with South Koreans carrying suitcases each holding $10,000 worth of won, to a small island off the coast of Japan. "The problem is that it wasn't scalable," said Sam. "To make it worthwhile, we needed like ten thousand South Koreans a day. And we probably would have attracted so much attention doing it that we would have been shut down. Once the South Korean central bank saw you with ten thousand South Koreans carrying suitcases full of won they'd be like, *There's going to be a new direction here.*"

Still, he was tempted. There were moments when the price of bitcoin in South Korea was 50 percent higher than the price of bitcoin in the United States. At that point you didn't even need currencies. All you needed was to buy a huge amount of *something* with the won that you could then sell outside of South Korea for a huge number of dollars. Briefly, Sam considered creating an import-export company for Tylenol. Buy the pills with won in South Korea, and sell them for dollars in the United States.

Sam and his fellow effective altruists had a dozen ideas like this before they settled on Ripple. RippleNet was a platform created by some crypto entrepreneurs back in 2012 that was making a pitch to play the useful role in everyday financial life that Bitcoin had been meant to play. A big part of the theoretical appeal of Ripple's coin, XRP, was that, unlike bitcoin, which took vast amounts of energy to maintain, it was carbon-neutral. Ripple's actual appeal was the same as Bitcoin's: the price of its coin moved up and down a lot, and so it was fun to gamble on. By late 2017, lots of people traded XRP on every major crypto exchange. On South Korean exchanges, XRP was trading at an even greater premium to XRP on American exchanges than South Korean bitcoin was to American bitcoin.

If a bitcoin cost 20 percent more in South Korea than it did in the US, Ripple's coin cost 25 percent more. Ripple offered a path to exploit the insanity of the South Korean crypto markets: sell XRP in South Korea, use the won to buy bitcoin, ship the bitcoin to the US, where you could sell it for dollars, and use the dollars to buy XRP, which you could then send back to South Korea. The bitcoin still cost 20 percent more in South Korea than it did in the United States, but the 25 percent gains from Ripple's tokens more than paid for that. The 20 percent you might have made on each trade shrank to 5 percent, but the profits were still outrageous, even by, say, Jane

Street standards. The only risk was the five to thirty seconds it took to make the trades.

Or at least that's how it seemed when Alameda first made the trade. Then one day in February, someone—not Sam, who was frantically trading—noticed the missing Ripple. Four million dollars' worth of it had vanished. In fairness, it was not then clear whether it was gone forever. Sam and his traders, using the system Gary had built, were making a quarter of a million trades each day. So much Ripple and Bitcoin was flying around at any given time that it was at least possible that any missing Ripple was simply in transit. Sam suspected that the $4 million worth of Ripple had been sent from the exchange in the United States (and debited from Alameda's account) and had arrived at the exchange in South Korea, but that the South Korean exchange was just dragging its feet in crediting it to Alameda's account. The other members of the management team were unconvinced. They insisted that Sam stop trading so that they could figure out where their Ripple had gone.

At length Sam agreed. He stopped trading for two weeks. The other members of the management team confirmed that millions of dollars' worth of Ripple was indeed missing. At which point everyone except Sam, and perhaps Gary, became upset. "We thought we needed to tell investors and tell employees so they could reconsider their options, but Sam hated that idea," said one of the firm's managers. Sam continued to insist that the missing Ripple was no big deal. He didn't think anyone had stolen it. He didn't actually believe that it was lost, or that they should account for it as lost. He told his fellow managers that in his estimation there was an 80 percent chance that it would eventually turn up. Thus they should count themselves as still having 80 percent of it. To which one of his fellow managers replied: *After the fact, if we never get any of the Ripple back, no one is going to say it is reasonable for us to have said we have eighty percent of the Ripple. Everyone is just going to say we lied to them. We'll be accused by our investors of fraud.*

That sort of argument just bugged the hell out of Sam. He hated the way inherently probabilistic situations would be interpreted, after the fact, as having been black-and-white, or good and bad, or right and wrong. So much of what made his approach to life different from most people's was his willingness to assign probabilities and act on them, and his refusal to be swayed by any after-the-fact illusion that the world had been more knowable than it actually was. The missing Ripple reminded him of a favorite thought experiment. "You have a close friend, Bob," he explained. "He's great. You love him. Bob is at a house party where someone gets murdered. No one knows who the murderer is. There are twenty people there. None are criminals. But Bob is less likely in your mind than anyone else to have killed some-one. But you can't say that there is a zero chance Bob killed someone. Someone got killed, no one knows who did it. You now think there's like a one percent chance Bob did it. How do you see Bob now? What is Bob to you? And there is no updating: there is no new information about Bob."

One answer was that you should never go near Bob again. There might be a 99 percent chance that Bob is the saint you always thought him to be, but if you're wrong, you're dead. Treating Bob's char-acter as a matter of probability felt problematic. Bob was either a cold-blooded killer or he wasn't. Whatever probability you assigned before you found out the truth about Bob would appear, after the fact, unfair and even absurd. "There doesn't exist a guess you can make that is overwhelmingly likely to be roughly correct," said Sam. "Bob is either completely blameless or far more guilty." And yet assigning a probability to Bob's character was, in Sam's view, the only way to think about him, or indeed any uncertain situation. "It's not good enough to say, 'Bob's not the kind of guy I want to be around.' So what is the probability at which you say, 'Okay, I'm going to just stay away from Bob until this is resolved'?" said Sam. "It's sort of mind-bending. There is no way to deal with Bob right now that is just." Life's uncertainties often made a mockery of a probabilistic approach, but in Sam's view there was really no other approach to take. "A lot of things are like Bob," said Sam. "I thought that the Ripple was like Bob. We'd either get it back or not."

By early April, the other executives at Alameda Research had ceased to be interested in Sam's thought experiments. "After the trading pause, I expected Sam to update and he didn't update," said one. "Like, *Hey, we have a big problem. We don't know where the money is. But we know we don't have as much as we thought we did.*" They'd all wearied of Sam's stubborn unwillingness to manage anyone. They'd all grown to fear how little he worried about where exactly their money was. They were making two hundred fifty thousand trades a day and their system had somehow lost, or failed to record, some large number of them. Among the many problems their shoddy recordkeeping caused was the difficulty of filing an honest tax return. "How are we going to pass an audit if we're missing ten percent of our transactions?" asked Tara. The missing Ripple was the final straw. "The prospect of losing a couple of hundred million dollars that would have otherwise gone into solving the world's problems felt pretty high stakes," said Ben West. Under the circumstances, they thought it was insane to continue trading, but Sam insisted on trading. Crypto markets would not remain inefficient for long. They needed to make hay while the sun shone.

The sun unfortunately took that moment to hide behind the clouds. After crypto prices tanked in February, the Asian frenzy subsided and the gaps in crypto prices between Asian and US exchanges vanished. At the same time the Ripple went missing, the trading profits turned into trading losses. In January they'd made half a million dollars of profits a day trading $40 million in capital; in February, with four times as much capital, they'd lost half a million dollars a day. Apart from a shared alarm at his recklessness, the members of the management team were not perfectly unified in their opinions of Sam. Tara had long since decided that he was dishonest and manipulative. Ben still thought him well-intentioned—but terrible at his job. But all felt themselves on a suicide mission. "I had a conversation with Tara and Peter [McIntyre, another executive]," recalled Ben, "and we were talking about how to help Sam and the conversation changed to: *How do we get rid of Sam?*"

Like everything else about Alameda Research, this bid by the firm's other managers to get rid of Sam proved complicated. For a start, Sam owned the entire company. He'd structured it so that no one else had equity, only promises of equity down the road. In a tense meeting, the others offered to buy him out, but at a fraction of what Sam thought the firm to be worth, and the offer came with diabolical fine print: Sam would remain liable for all taxes on any future Alameda profits. At least some of his fellow effective altruists aimed to bankrupt Sam, almost as a service to humanity, so that he might never be allowed to trade again. "He seemed to feel very sorry for himself," Ben wrote of Sam after the meeting. "I reminded him that everyone else at the company has sacrificed a huge amount."

Enter Nishad. In his treatment of others, Nishad was almost painfully considerate—the sort of person who, after he offers up an opinion, qualifies it four different ways to make sure he hasn't caused offense. He could see merit in both sides of any argument. And, young as he was, he now drifted into the uneasy role of human buffer between Sam and people who perhaps did not fully understand Sam—basically everyone except Gary. "I think it was because I prioritize the person over the work and Sam is exactly the opposite of that," said Nishad. "In spite of being emotionally inattentive, I'm much more emotionally attentive than Sam." Nishad would have been the first to admit at that moment that he knew nothing about how to manage people—especially people so fixated on their careers as tools for maximizing the expected value of their lives. "I tried to think about how to role-play a good manager," he said. "I thought it would involve like maybe a one-on-one meeting every week to check on their feelings, and giving good feedback and some other things like that. And Sam didn't meet any of those criteria. People kept complaining about that thing where he is looking at his computer while he's talking to you and giving you half answers. And he's resistant to the idea that someone is going to tell him something he doesn't know."

As the dispute between Sam and the other higher-ups turned ugly, Nishad was dragged in to mediate. "I basically agreed that Sam was a very bad manager. He was genuinely a terrible manager." But while Sam was sullen and withdrawn, the other members of the management team, in Nishad's view, were excessively outraged. "The conversations we had were absolutely fucking nuts," he recalled. "Like to what extent Sam should be excommunicated for deceiving EAs and wasting EA talent. And like 'the only way Sam will learn is if he actually goes bankrupt.' They told our *investors* he was faking being an EA, because it was the meanest thing they could think to say." Ruining Sam wasn't enough, however: they expected to be paid on their way out the door. "They wanted severance, even though they were quitting and it was a money-losing operation in which they didn't have a stake," said Nishad. "They were saying that Sam needed to buy them out and they were worth more than one hundred percent of the value of the entire company because Sam was a net negative."

It occurred to Nishad that the effective altruist's relationship to money was more than a little bizarre. Basically all of Alameda Research's employees and investors were committed to giving all their money away to roughly the same charitable causes. You might surmise that they wouldn't much care who wound up with the money, as it all would go to saving the lives of the same people none of them would ever meet. You would be wrong: in their financial dealings with each other, the effective altruists were more ruthless than Russian oligarchs. Their investors were charging them a rate of interest of *50 percent*. "It wasn't a normal loan," said Nishad. "It was a shark loan." In what was meant to be a collaborative enterprise, Sam had refused to share any equity with anyone. And now all these unprofitable effective altruists were demanding to be paid millions to quit—and doing whatever they could to trash Sam's reputation with the outside world until they got their money. "It felt super weird," said Nishad. "It felt wild for money to be the object of our focus rather than something else. I thought caring about money itself was morally bankrupt."

In the end, for Sam to leave he had to want to leave, and Sam did not really want to leave. And so, on April 9, 2018, his entire management team, along with half of his employees, walked out the door, with somewhere between one and two million dollars in severance. At that moment, the outside investors were in the same uneasy position as Bob's friend. They heard two radically different stories about Sam, one from the management team, the other from Sam. But as one put it, "There was no smoking gun." No one thing Sam had done for which they could easily condemn him. It was, as Tara said, "one hundred small things." The investors had no real idea whom or what to believe, or even how to figure out whom or what to believe. "There may be ways in which I shouldn't trust Sam, but it felt nuanced," said one. They'd all made their money in start-ups; they all knew that start-ups were chaotic. Now they had to decide: Was Sam a reckless, phony effective altruist who was going to steal or lose all their money, or were these other people simply unsuited to working in a start-up hedge fund? It was one or the other, an either/or question, to which they responded probabilistically. Just about all of them kept money invested in Alameda, but just about all of them reduced the size of their investments. The capital at Sam's disposal plunged from $170 million to $40 million. He wouldn't be able to trade as much as he had before, but he could still trade.

The remaining employees were also in the position of Bob's friend, in that most of them didn't understand what had happened. Sam had fully absorbed the Jane Street management technique of letting the rank and file see only their tiny piece of the puzzle, reserving for himself a view of the whole. Gary, though unintentionally, had done something similar with the computer code, which was indecipherable to everyone but him. "Gary was the only person who understood how to code it, and Gary didn't talk to anyone," said Nishad. The company was a bit of a black box to nearly everyone still inside it. Nishad was briefly on the fence about staying but decided that, as inept as Sam was with other human beings, and as little as he understood what Gary had built, he'd rather throw in his lot with Sam and Gary and see what happened. He'd do what he could to teach Sam about other people's feelings. "One thing I think would make people feel heard in the one-on-ones," he wrote to Sam, soon after half the company had quit, "is if you asked about their emotional states in general and their emotional takes."

What happened next, in retrospect, seems faintly incredible. With no one left to argue with him, Sam threw the switch and let Modelbot rip. "We turned it on and it instantly started making us lots of money," said Nishad. And then they finally found the $4 million worth of missing XRP. First they figured out its travel itinerary: it had been sent from Kraken, a US crypto exchange, to an exchange in South Korean called Bithumb. Then they figured out that the computer languages used by the two exchanges were not perfectly compatible. Bithumb was able to receive the XRP from Kraken but not the name of the person who owned the tokens. The South Korean exchange had failed to detect the problem because it was specific to Ripple's coins—it occurred with no other cryptocurrency—and there had only been one big player in the market shipping massive amounts of them from Kraken to Bithumb. Inside Bithumb in South Korea, the employees saw huge amounts of XRP piling up without any indication of who it belonged to. Once Sam figured out where the missing XRP was meant to be, he telephoned the Bithumb exchange directly. The call was transferred around the company about three times before a voice finally came on the line and said, "Are you the fucker who sent us like twenty million Ripple tokens? How the fuck are you only calling us now?" In the background Sam heard someone shouting, "Holy fuck, we found them!"

They'd even paid their taxes. (Sam had brought in his dad to help with that.) And they resumed making millions of dollars a month in trading profits. They weren't the same company, however. They were no longer a random assortment of effective altruists. They were a small team who had endured an alarming drama and now trusted Sam. He'd been right all along! To those who remained—and even to some who had quit—Sam went from someone they weren't quite sure about to a leader to be followed even if they didn't completely understand what he was doing, or why. ("Ex post I was wrong and we should have been willing to have a higher risk appetite," one of the departed members of the management team later said.) An odd company from the start had just become even more odd. The people inside were those most able to tailor their thoughts and feelings to those of its creator.

"To Sam: Sorry I wrote all of this in the third person," wrote Caroline, in late 2018. "I didn't decide to send it to you until the end." The turmoil had been stressful for Caroline; but she'd left her job at Jane Street and had no obvious place to go, and so, even though she wasn't sure whom or what to believe, she'd stuck it out. The dust had settled on what was being called The Schism, and only Sam was still ruminating on the meaning of it all. Alameda Research had righted itself and was consistently profitable. All was not right with Caroline, however. Which was why she was now writing to her boss.

"What is the problem?" she asked, in what at first glance appeared to be a business memo.

I have pretty strong romantic feelings for Sam.

Not a business memo! It was merely written in a businesslike manner.

Why is this a problem?

These feelings consume a ton of my brainspace

This prevents me from thinking about other important things and takes up a lot of my time

These feelings can often be positive or feel good but are on net unpleasant

They affect my ability to work
– Mainly by amplifying work-related feelings in unhelpful ways e.g. "I did a bad job on this thing"-> "now Sam will hate me"-> sad

The memo went on for four pages. She clearly wanted to be heard, and equally clearly sensed that her intended audience was likely to be playing a video game as he half listened. She pressed on anyway, sounding logical, or at least reasonable, about what were at bottom emotional needs.

I feel embarrassed because the current situation just seems like so the obvious result of all the choices I've made. I'm not sure what choices I should have made differently, though. It's possible I shouldn't have worked at Alameda in the first place, though at the time I honestly didn't think it would be an issue ("kinda attracted to my boss" was also an issue when I worked with Turner and it was a 100% nonissue.) Maybe I shouldn't have slept with Sam, though by that point it kind of felt like the feelings/desires were going to get worse over time and become unbearable unless I did something.

For Sam's benefit, she imagined what he might be thinking about her. ("The last thing he told me was that he feels 'conflicted.' I imagine the conflicting desires here are wanting to sleep with me, etc, vs. worry about negative professional consequences.") She listed the things Sam had done that bothered her, among them giving off "confusing signals, e.g telling me that he felt conflicted about having sex with me, then having sex with me, then ignoring me for a few months." She attempted an expected value analysis of their clandestine relationship, such as it was, starting with the costs:

- *scandal if it comes out*
- *conflict of interest stuff*
- *work-related tensions*

She ended by wondering if she might not be better off quitting her job at Alameda Research and cutting off all contact with Sam. On the other hand . . .

- *It would be ideal if Sam and I could have a discussion to understand each other's feelings and reach a conclusion about what to do.*

Ideal, perhaps. However, unlikely under the best of circumstances, and circumstances were soon less than best. Not long before Caroline was moved to write her memo to herself and then share it with Sam, Sam had left for what was meant to be a brief trip to Hong Kong. After he read her memo, he called the fifteen or so people still working for him in downtown Berkeley to say he wasn't coming back.

6

ARTIFICIAL LOVE

n late October 2008, someone calling himself Satoshi Nakamoto—
and who to this day, incredibly, has kept his identity a secret—
published a paper that introduced the idea of Bitcoin. It was mostly
a technical description of what would become the world's first cryptocurrency. A bitcoin was an "electronic coin"; it existed on a public ledger called a "proof-of-work chain"; each time it was transferred from
one person to another, its authenticity was verified by programmers,
who added the transaction to the public ledger; those programmers,
who would eventually become known as bitcoin "miners," were paid
for their work by being given new bitcoin; and so on.[*] (Interestingly,
the word "blockchain" is nowhere in the paper.) How Bitcoin worked

---

[*] That's it for crypto explanations for the moment, as that's about all that Sam
Bankman-Fried knew about crypto, or for that matter needed to know, to trade
billions of dollars' worth of it. Plus, so many writers have taken a crack at explaining to a lay audience what a bitcoin is that it's hard to see the point of doing it all
over again. See, for example, Matt Levine's excellent forty-thousand-word article in
Bloomberg Businessweek, "The Crypto Story." What *is* curious is how elusive Bitcoin
is, as a thing to understand. Bitcoin often gets explained but somehow never stays
explained. You nod along and think you are getting it but then wake up the next
morning needing to hear the explanation all over again.

was interesting chiefly to technologists; what it might do was interesting to a much broader audience. It might allow ordinary people to exit the existing financial system and never again rely on the integrity of their fellow human financial beings. "What is needed is an electronic payment system based on cryptographic proof instead of trust," wrote Satoshi.

Trust, or the need for it, bothered Satoshi, whoever he was. His paper doesn't mention the 2008 global financial crisis, but his invention was obviously a response to it. If Bitcoin had its way, banks and governments would no longer control money. Bitcoin could be owned and moved without the need for a bank. Its value could not be eroded by governments. It didn't require anyone to trust anyone or anything, except, of course, the integrity and design of the computer code. It was at once a plea for sound money and an appeal to mistrust. It was both financial innovation and social protest. Crypto was like the friend you'd made only because you shared an enemy. The sort of person drawn to it, at least in the beginning, was the sort of person suspicious of big banks and governments and other forms of institutional authority.

Zane Tackett was a good example of the type, though to call Zane a type was to miss both the joy and the point of Zane. "The OG," is how others often referred to Zane. In April of 2013, with the price of bitcoin hovering around $100, Zane, then a student at the University of Colorado, had come across a strange magazine article. The writer announced that he was going into hiding and offered a prize of $10,000 to anyone who found him. The prize would be paid in bitcoin—which payment, the writer explained, had the virtue of being irreversible and untraceable.* The article, oddly enough, caused Zane not to go looking for the writer but to want to know what a bitcoin was. He'd recently been ripped off, after he'd sold a Michael Jordan jersey card online and the guy who'd bought it had reversed

---

* True at the time. The opposite of true now, as crypto sleuths have built the tools to exploit the fact that every bitcoin transaction is preserved for all time on the blockchain.

the credit card transaction and kept the Michael Jordan jersey card. Zane was outraged that the financial system had allowed that to happen. At the same time, he wasn't much enjoying college, and was perhaps more open than most to certain people telling him what he should do with his life other than remain in college. "My grandpa had said you should go to China and learn Chinese, because they're going to take over the world," said Zane.

He'd taken the advice once and gone to China right out of high school for a year, before returning to attend the University of Colorado. Now he bought some bitcoin, dropped out of the University of Colorado, and moved to Beijing, where he landed a job at a crypto exchange called OKEx. He was the first non-Chinese person ever to work at the place. Chinese companies were private empires. Their employees were treated less as valuable assets than as vassals. "The employees can get screwed, because if you get screwed, what are you going to do?" said Zane. "There aren't any protections." His grandfather approved of his growing fluency in Chinese, even as his parents grew increasingly concerned that he'd gotten tangled up in something he shouldn't have. And Zane continued to acquire more bitcoin, and bitcoin continued to rise in price, and one day Zane was rich. "I got funny money, and then I got quoted in the *Wall Street Journal* and my parents decided I must be okay," said Zane.

By 2016, bitcoin's price had cracked $400, and Zane was not only wealthy but sufficiently well respected to cut deals with crypto exchanges to work from wherever in the world he wanted. Everyone in crypto knew Zane, and everyone trusted him. He had a gunslinger's name and a gunslinger's rail-thinness and now wandered, unattached to anything or anyone, from place to place, the way gunslingers supposedly wandered the Wild West. One month he might be in Indonesia; the next, Argentina. Zane, like bitcoin, became placeless. As a matter of principle, he lived his entire financial life in bitcoin. He was paid in bitcoin and paid others only with bitcoin. He enjoyed affirming his faith in the movement he had joined. "I did kind of want to take the power of money away from government," he said. Zane, like Bitcoin, had a code.

By 2017 there had been a shift in the spirit of the movement he'd joined. Bitcoin enthusiasts believed that Satoshi had created a replacement for government-backed money, but government-backed money wasn't what Bitcoin most easily replaced. Gambling was. The mad rise in bitcoin's price in 2017 pulled in a generation of new speculators. It wasn't like the stock market: anyone in the world who knew how to use a computer could trade crypto at any hour of any day of the week. The new demand for speculative objects encouraged people to create hundreds of new cryptocurrencies. Typically they were marketed to speculators as an investment in some new enterprise, but seldom was the enterprise of any real value. The initial sale of one new crypto coin, called EOS, raised $4.4 billion dollars. Having nothing useful to do with the money, the founders announced it would be used for "asset management." The money grab bothered Zane. "It was, 'Hey, you're telling me I can tell people I'm going to build this project and they'll give me money and I get to keep the money even if I don't build the project?' " he said. The money grab likely would have perplexed Satoshi—as, very likely, would the very idea of a crypto exchange. Bitcoin's original selling point was that it eliminated the need for financial intermediaries. It removed trust from trades. You could trade your bitcoin directly and easily with other people in a way that you couldn't trade Swiss francs, or shares in Apple, or live cattle. As it turned out, the people who set out to eliminate financial intermediaries simply created some new ones of their own, including, by early 2019, *two hundred fifty-four* crypto exchanges.

These early crypto exchange founders weren't typically financial experts. They were a grab bag of technologists and libertarians and idealists and high plains drifters, like Zane. Even more than, say, the New York Stock Exchange, the institutions they created required their customers to trust them. The New York Stock Exchange had regulators. If the New York Stock Exchange stole all your money, its executives would be sent to jail. In any case, the New York Stock Exchange would find it hard to steal all your money, as you didn't keep your money on the New York Stock Exchange but in a brokerage account, managed by a bank, overseen by other regulators. The new crypto exchanges had no regulators. They acted as both exchange and custodian: they didn't just enable you to buy bitcoin but also housed the bitcoin you'd bought.

The whole thing was odd: these people joined together by their fear of trust erected a parallel financial system that required more trust from its users than did the traditional financial system. Outside the law, and often hostile to it, they discovered many ways to run afoul of it. Crypto exchanges routinely misplaced or lost their customers' money. Crypto exchanges routinely faked trading data to make it seem as though far more trading had occurred on them than actually had. Crypto exchanges fell prey to hackers, or to random rogue traders who gamed the exchanges' risk management.

Here was one example of the games that were played: Several of the Asian exchanges offered a Bitcoin contract with one hundred times leverage. Every now and then, some trader figured out that he could buy $100 million worth of bitcoin at the same time he sold short another $100 million worth of bitcoin—and put up only a million dollars for each trade. Whatever happened to the price of bitcoin, one of his trades would win and the other would lose. If bitcoin popped by 10 percent, the rogue trader collected $10 million on his long position and vanished—leaving the exchange to cover the $10 million he'd lost on his short. But it wasn't the exchange that covered the loss: the exchange did not have the capital to cover the loss. The losses were socialized. The customers—usually those on the winning end of the trade—paid for them. And the losses could be huge. The Chinese-founded exchange Huobi had one loss so big that it docked all traders on the profitable end of trades nearly half their gains.

In traditional finance, founded on principles of trust, no one really had to trust anyone. In crypto finance, founded on a principle of mistrust, people trusted total strangers with vast sums of money. The situation was less than ideal—and just how much less than ideal became clear to Zane Tackett in August of 2016. That month, the exchange he was then working for, Bitfinex, lost more than $70 million worth of bitcoin to a pair of hackers working out of New York City. (By the time the couple was arrested, the bitcoin was worth $4.6 billion.) Zane, then living in Thailand, found himself responding to messages from the people whose money Bitfinex had lost. "I got a lot of death threats and suicide notes from it," he said. "The death threats felt empty, but the suicide notes did not. They were heartrending—*I had put the money for my new house with you and we will now be homeless.*" He hated it. Because it was a point of pride with him to be worthy of other crypto people's trust.

After that, Zane found safer work with a new kind of crypto firm. The firm specialized in over-the-counter trading—that is, privately buying and selling large blocks of crypto to speculators who for various reasons wished to avoid revealing their hand on public exchanges. The guy who started the company had worked for Goldman Sachs and knew what he was doing. For the next eighteen months, Zane made easy money in markets with fat spreads between the bids and the offers, of a percentage point or more. Toward the end of 2018 the markets suddenly changed again. Spreads tightened dramatically, going from 1 percent to *seven one-hundredths* of a percent. Some huge trader had entered the market. Whoever he was, he more or less instantly established himself as the official market maker of crypto. "It was pretty quick," said Zane. "And I was like, *What the fuck just happened?*" Zane's trading firm sat in the middle of the crypto markets and for the longest time had no idea who this new player might be. "Then someone says, 'It's some vegan dude who wants to give all the money to charity,'" said Zane. "Then someone else says this same vegan dude had moved to Hong Kong and is starting his own crypto exchange."

Zane became curious. He found a copy of the white paper the vegan dude had published, proposing a new kind of crypto exchange. It stunned him. And to his surprise, he found himself badly wanting to work for the vegan dude.

Sam later couldn't remember exactly why he'd agreed to fly to Asia in the first place. It wasn't to see sights in which he had zero interest. Flying frightened him so badly that, before takeoff, he had to medicate himself and listen to soothing music. "Viscerally I've never believed that a hunk of metal would fly," he said. The stated purpose of his trip was to attend a crypto conference in Macau, but once he'd arrived, he discovered reasons to stay. For the first time since he'd entered the market, he found himself in the same room with every major player in crypto—many of whom were Asian. Also for the first time, he let people outside his small circle of effective altruists know who he was, and what he'd been up to; and it had some powerful effects.

Up to that moment, in late November 2018, Alameda Research had operated in the shadows. They traded more than 5 percent of the total volume of crypto markets and were still a secret. Jane Street had left Sam with the view that there was no upside to publicity, and that the best thing to do was to avoid it. He'd traded billions of dollars in crypto but never in his own name, or in the name of Alameda Research (whose name itself had been chosen in part to hide the fact that the firm had anything to do with crypto). The Asian crypto exchanges had grown so accustomed to their customers not wanting anyone to know who they were that a few issued you a pseudonym when you started doing business with them. One of the biggest exchanges at the time, BitMEX, had bestowed fictitious names upon Alameda Research's trading accounts, each consisting of three seemingly randomly generated words. Shell-Paper-Bird was one. Hot-Relic-Fancier was another—and so weirdly funny that the Alameda traders had commissioned a painting of a Hot Relic Fancier. On BitMEX's leaderboard of the year's most profitable crypto traders, Shell-Paper-Bird and Hot-Relic-Fancier were both in the top ten. No one had any idea that they were all the same trader, or who that trader might be. That changed in Macau.

I'm Hot-Relic-Fancier, Sam would say, when he was introduced to someone at the conference he thought might be important.

No, you're not, was the typical reaction.

Even Sam knew that he wasn't credible: a twenty-six-year-old white guy with the hairdo of a lunatic, dressed in baggy shorts and a wrinkled T-shirt. He needed to pull out his phone and open the trading account and show them his money before these people believed him. Once he'd done that a few times, a lot of people wanted to meet Sam. He had never been big on face-to-face encounters, but he now had to concede that their effects were astonishing. Weeks before he flew to Asia, one of the big Chinese crypto exchanges had frozen Alameda's account with a bunch of money in it, for no obvious reason. Customer service hadn't returned their calls. After meeting Sam in person, the exchange's bosses handed him back his money. "All of a sudden I'm in a room with an important person from every single crypto company," said Sam. "My calendar is filled with meetings every one of which is more interesting than the most interesting meeting I'd have in the Bay Area." More often than not, the people he met hadn't known what to make of him, or of Alameda Research. "There was no one like us out there," said Sam.

At that moment, Sam himself wasn't quite sure what to make of the crypto trading firm he'd created. His civil war with his fellow effective altruists he now viewed as "the worst thing that has happened to me in my life." He'd pulled together a group of people he admired and who shared his values, and he'd wound up a pariah to half of them, who were still out there trashing him to their fellow effective altruists. "It made me question myself," he said. "It was the first time in my life I was surrounded by people I respected who are saying that I'm wrong and that I'm crazy. It made me question my sanity." When he flew to Asia, he was still writing and rewriting about the traumatic event. "I did damage to the EA community," he wrote. "I made people hate each other a little more and trust each other a little less . . . and I severely curtailed my own future ability to do good. I'm pretty sure my net impact on the world has, so far, been negative and that is why."

One of the curious things about Sam's writing, given that much of it was for his eyes only, was how evenhanded it was. He clearly felt sorry for himself, but recognized that others might feel even sorrier for themselves. He really didn't like to blame himself for anything; he didn't particularly like to blame anyone else, either. "I'm a utilitarian," he wrote. "Fault is just a construct of human society. It serves different purposes for different people. It can be a tool to discourage bad actions; an attempt to recover pride in the face of hardship, an outlet for rage, and many more things. I guess maybe the most important definition—to me, at least—is how did everyone's actions reflect on the probability distribution of their future behavior?"

How did everyone's actions reflect on the probability distribution of their future behavior. The sentence told you a lot about how Sam viewed other people, and maybe himself too. Not as fixed characters—good or bad, honest or false, brave or cowardly—but as a probability distribution around some mean. People were neither the worst nor the best thing they'd ever done. "I deeply believe and act as if people are probability distributions, not their means," he wrote. "It's pretty important to me that others engage on that level as well." His fellow EAs' behavior caused him to update his understanding of their probability distributions in ways that left him less willing to hire EAs. At the start he'd thought that hiring only effective altruists created a special advantage—everyone in the company would trust each other's motives, and so no one would need to waste time and energy doing the many things that people did to create trust among themselves. They could skip the one-on-one meetings, and the eye contact and the firm handshakes and, above all, the arguments about who deserved to be paid how much, and why. As it turned out, they couldn't.

After Tara and the others had left, Alameda returned to profitability and remained there. It wasn't making as much money as it had at the very start, but it arrived at the end of 2018 with an annualized return of more than 110 percent. Seeing the firm right itself, at least a few effective altruists, including the remaining employees, wondered if Sam had not known what he was doing all along. A few months after The Schism, one former female employee sent Sam a message with a leading question: *Why do you think there's been this theme of people thinking you're wrong about some EV [expected value] and you turning out to be right but people not knowing/understanding that?* Sam replied to her in three separate brief messages.

Because people decided that Sam is evil and then refused to acknowledge any evidence that contradicted it.

Because they were too emotionally invested in the belief, in decent part because it was a way for them to avoid assigning any fault or blame to themselves.

And also because it's a big social statement to try to destroy someone's life and really embarrassing to take it back.

To put it another way: people misread him, decided that he couldn't be trusted, and then refused to change their minds about him. He needed to do a better job of helping others to solve the puzzle. The facial expressions he'd gone to so much trouble to master had been insufficient: he needed to be more explicit.

Among the pages he wrote about the crisis were short documents addressed to his employees, with titles like "Some Notes About Working With Me" and "What it Means When Sam is Blocking You." Woven through his writings was advice to current and future employees about how to understand him. "I spent a while during, middle, after and way after trying to figure out what I should change about myself," he said later. "And that was a very frustrating experience. The thing that triggered me was that people didn't like my management and said I needed to learn management technique." He still didn't think there existed any management technique worth learning, just a lot of self-contradictory nonsense about it. "It's the blind leading the blind here," he said. "The only way is to teach yourself to see."

In the end, he decided that there was just one change he needed to make in himself: to become less off-putting to others. Even the people of whom he most approved had complained that he needed to be "more approachable," and "offer more constructive advice," and be "less negative." He was genuinely mystified by the criticism. He didn't think of himself as frightening. He didn't intend to intimidate. But he wasn't going to change human nature, and so he decided that, going forward, he would bury any negative reactions he had to any-thing anyone said or did. He would give human beings with whom he interacted the impression that he was far more interested in whatever they were saying or doing than he actually was. He'd agree with them, even if he didn't. Whatever idiocy came from them, he'd reply with a *Yuuuuuuppp!* "It comes with a cost, but it's on balance worth it," he said. "In most ways, people like you more if you agree with them." He went from being a person you'd be surprised to learn approves of you to a person you'd be surprised to learn that, actually no, he doesn't.

Sam didn't need to change himself as much as he needed to change his business. By early 2019, there was a yawning gap between his self-given goal to generate dollars to donate and the number of dollars that he was able to generate as a crypto trader. In 2018, trading $40 mil-lion in capital, Alameda Research had generated $30 million in profits. Their effective altruist investors took half, leaving behind $15 million. Five million of that was lost to payroll and severance for the departing crowd; another $5 million was lost to expenses. On the remaining $5 million they'd paid taxes, and so, after all was said and done, they'd donated to effective altruist causes just $1.5 million. It wasn't anything like enough, in Sam's view. "We needed to get a lot more capital, or way cheaper capital, or make much higher returns," he said. But at that moment, with his reputation in EA circles in tatters, it was not obvi-ous where any new capital would come from. The crypto markets were becoming more efficient every day. The big Wall Street high-frequency trading firms like Tower Research Capital and Jump Trading and even Jane Street were entering the markets and engaging in the same defor-estation they practiced in other financial markets. Even if Sam some-how found more capital, there'd be less money to be made with it.

The idea of creating a crypto exchange was at once obvious and implausible. Obvious because the crypto exchanges were money machines. They were the casinos that sat in the middle of a world-historic speculative frenzy and charged fees for every bet that was placed. The founders of the world's half-dozen or so biggest crypto exchanges were all likely already billionaires, even though the exchanges themselves routinely lost their customers' money. Implausible because of who Sam was, and how he related to people. He had no clue how to engage with ordinary people in the way ordinary people needed engaging with, when you ran an exchange. To create a successful exchange, you needed to attract a crowd; you needed to relate to a mass audience. You needed *customers*. And you only got them if they trusted you. And they only trusted you if they knew who you were or thought they did. Sam wasn't sure his own colleagues knew who he was, which was why he was writing memos to explain it.

Plus he'd already tried and failed to do it. Back in May 2018, in Berkeley, Sam had asked Gary Wang to write the code for a bitcoin exchange, and within a month Gary had done it. CryptonBTC, it was called. They put it out on the web without any idea how to attract attention to it. No one showed up to trade on it. It was as if it had never happened. The code Gary had written for the first exchange had been sweet, however. From the total nothingness that had been CryptonBTC, Sam had learned that if he asked Gary to create a crypto futures exchange, he could do it in a month, and it would be more reliable and less risky for its users than any existing exchange. Gary was a genius.

In Hong Kong, Sam and his small team began to pitch the billionaire founders of existing exchanges on the idea of paying Alameda Research (Gary) to create a crypto exchange, different in important ways from any that existed. Alameda would supply the technology; the existing exchanges would supply the customers, and the trust. The most likely buyer, and the person to whom Sam himself pitched the idea, was CZ.

CZ was Changpeng Zhao, CEO of the crypto exchange Binance. Born in Jiangsu province, he was raised, from adolescence, in Canada, and educated there, returning eventually to China, with Canadian citizenship. He'd run through some ordinary jobs on the fringes of high finance—including a stint as a developer at Bloomberg—before landing as the chief technology officer at OKCoin. He'd left OKCoin in 2015 and created Binance in 2017; two years later, he was being described in industry publications as "the most powerful man in crypto." It might not have been true at the time, but it was about to become so. In mid-2019, Binance was still just a spot crypto exchange—it did not trade crypto futures or other derivatives—no bigger than a handful of others, and handicapped by its inability to offer most of its customers the leverage they longed for. (Everyone in crypto wanted to bet more than they had.) Binance's customers traded various cryptocurrencies but generally weren't borrowing money from the exchange to do it. CZ preferred it that way. And he was a bit wary of what Sam was proposing: an exchange that traded only crypto futures contracts.

A futures exchange was different in important ways from a spot exchange. On a futures exchange, traders put up as collateral only a fraction of the bets they made. On a trade that was losing money, the exchange typically asked for more collateral at the end of the day. If a trade went bad fast, it could wipe out the collateral and leave the exchange on the hook for losses—whereupon the exchange turned to its customers to cover the losses, as crypto exchanges had, histori- cally. The design that FTX (Gary) had come up with solved the prob- lem, in an elegant way. It monitored customers' positions not by the day but by the second. The instant any customer's trade went into the red, it was liquidated. This of course was unpleasant for the cus- tomers whose positions went into the red. But it promised to do away with socialized losses, which had plagued crypto exchanges from the beginning. An exchange's losses would never need to be socialized, because the exchange would never have losses.

Sam had first met CZ not long after his move to Hong Kong at the end of 2018. Binance was looking for crypto companies to pay $150,000 apiece to sponsor its conference in early 2019 in Singapore, and Sam stepped in with the money. CZ had rewarded him by appearing onstage with him, and ever after, Sam was to say, "That's what gave us legiti- macy in crypto." He'd effectively paid CZ to be his friend. But even then Sam didn't have a good feel for CZ, except that they didn't have much in common. Sam lived in his head and thought his way to decisions, or at least believed that he did. If CZ ever had an original thought he never expressed it, and he seemed to feel his way to his decisions. Sam thought about the size of the pie, while CZ cared more about the size of his piece. Sam was gunning to build an exchange for big institutional crypto traders; CZ was all about pitching to retail and the little guy. Sam hated conflict and so was almost weirdly quick to forget grievances; CZ thrived on conflict and nurtured the emotions that led to it. CZ had a complex web of allies and enemies. In the pitch book he created to launch Binance back in 2017, much of what he listed as his qualifications for the task were social alliances with other crypto insiders. (Zane Tackett among them. In a brief biography, CZ described Zane, oddly, in relation to himself, saying that to Zane he played the role of "mentor and good friend.") Sam had no real social alliances at all. In his interactions with CZ, had he not trotted out his learned facial expressions, he would have spent a lot of time staring blankly while CZ spoke. "CZ sort of just says things," said Sam. "They aren't dumb. They aren't smart. I didn't have much of a sense of him until he had to make decisions."

The first decision CZ had to make was whether to pay Sam the $40 million he was asking for his cleverly designed futures exchange. After thinking it over for a few weeks in March 2019, CZ decided no—and then told his people to create a futures exchange on their own. Which struck Sam as such an ordinary and vaguely disappointing thing to do. "He's kind of a douche but not worse than a douche," said Sam. "He *should* be a great character but he's not."

Only after CZ turned him down did Sam decide to create an exchange himself. The idea was simple: the first crypto futures exchange that was well enough designed that it would serve the needs not just of crypto people but also of big professional traders, like Jane Street. Still, Sam was deeply uneasy about it. "We were going to build a product that is better than any product out there," he said. "If it works it is worth billions of dollars, but I thought there was a better than fifty percent chance it wouldn't work. I'd never done marketing. I'd never talked to media. I'd never had customers. It was just different from anything that I'd ever done." And so he started grabbing people who might do the things he didn't know how to do. People unlike any he had ever worked with, but who had strong ties with other crypto people. He grabbed Zane Tackett, for instance, and with Zane came a great deal of crypto trust. Even before he grabbed Zane Tackett he grabbed Ryan Salame.

If there was such a thing as the opposite of an effective altruist it was Ryan. Ryan was a freedom-loving, tax-loathing Republican. He had started his career as a tax accountant at Ernst & Young and been liberated from the misery and the tedium after the crypto trading firm Circle hired him to do their books. It had taken Ryan about two seconds to see that crypto trading was more fun than tax accounting. When Sam found him, Ryan was working as a salesman on Circle's trading desk in Hong Kong and had become a walking advertisement for worldly pleasure. Any guy in crypto who wanted what every guy in crypto wanted found in Ryan an ally in the pursuit: Ryan was who you called if you wanted to have fun.

Ryan was handsome; Ryan was also shrewd. When Alameda Research ramped up its trading in Hong Kong and collapsed the spreads for everyone else, Ryan was struck by just how much smarter it was than the rest of the market. He had no idea who Sam Bankman-Fried was, but he noticed that CZ seemed to want to keep him close— going so far as to allow Sam to set up a booth for Alameda Research at Binance's conference. Ryan also noticed that Sam and his traders lacked the usual crypto social graces. "They wouldn't respond to you in chats," said Ryan. "They wouldn't react to your jokes. It was not the experience you were used to in crypto. Sam wasn't part of the crowd. No one had seen him at anything."

Eventually Ryan visited Sam in his new Hong Kong office. "You talk to Sam for five minutes and you realize something's different," he said. Sam's disinterest in ordinary social interaction had spilled over into his company even more dramatically than Ryan had imagined it might have. "It was just a college dorm of nerds sitting at computer screens," as he put it. "They never left the office." Ryan could see that Sam could use him to establish social connections with crypto people, and to make them feel comfortable with him—which at that moment they were not. "Sam forgets how many people thought he was a scammer at first," said Ryan. "You'd expect to find a Sam behind any scam."

Sam did have one thing going for him, socially, with other crypto people. The higher crypto prices rose, the greater the flood into crypto of sober-minded people in suits that people like Zane found insufferable. Ryan might have counted as one such person, but Ryan was not sober-minded, so he got a pass. The Goldman guys and the venture capitalists and the corporate lawyers turned crypto bros— they were all part of this invasion of conventional people who wanted to make fast money without the kookiness that had made the fast money possible. The pseuds would seek common ground with the original crypto religionists by exhibiting their excitement about the technology. The blockchain! *The blockchain is going to change . . . everything*, they'd say, and hope that would suffice. A religion based on hating banks and government and any sort of institutional authority— well, for the pseuds, that was usually taking things too far.

The crypto religionists, the people who had been drawn to the cause for their own reasons, had, at best, mixed feelings about the people who came to it later, and just for the money. About Sam, Ryan thought, they might be a bit more inclined to suspend judgment. Sam shared an important trait with the crypto religionists: a dissatisfaction with the world as he found it. He did not have any particular hostility toward governments or banks. He just thought grown-ups were pointless.

Ryan was less a grown-up than the highest expression of a new species, the crypto bro, that Sam sensed he needed on hand. He hired Ryan without being totally sure what Ryan would do. "The job description was sort of *make it all better*," said Ryan.

To create a crypto exchange, Sam needed crypto people, but he also needed money to pay the crypto people. The normal, old-fashioned way to get it would be to go hat in hand to family and friends, or to raise the money from venture capitalists. Sam didn't have any friends with the kind of money he needed, and he didn't know any venture capitalists. What he had was a token. It belonged to the same general family as the thousands of other crypto coins that had been created since 2017 and shilled to the public. The FTX token was called FTT.

The most important feature of FTT was that its holders were collectively entitled to roughly a third of the annual revenues of the FTX exchange. Of the $1 billion in revenues the exchange generated in 2021, for example, $333 million would be set aside to "buy back and burn" FTT. FTX would remove tokens from circulation in the same way that a public company bought back its shares, and thus raise the value of all remaining shares. FTT was not merely like stock in FTX, it *was* stock in FTX—and even came with voting rights on certain decisions made inside the company. As it gave you a share of the gross, rather than the net, it was arguably even more valuable than the stock. "The crypto people would say, Why would I want your equity? I'd rather just buy the token," said Sam. "The venture capitalists would say, What's a token?"

One hitch to the tokens was that they were illegal to sell inside the United States. The explosion of new crypto tokens had spawned a new game of cat and mouse, between token creators and securities regulators. The world's most aggressive securities regulator, the US Securities and Exchange Commission, now devoted a meaningful amount of energy to arguing that a lot of these tokens were securities (which they obviously were), and so a threat to American investors, and banned from the US unless they first won SEC approval (which seemed highly unlikely). Crypto exchanges and token creators who wanted to sell to Americans insisted that these tokens weren't securities but more like, say, Starbucks Rewards points. As FTX was incorporated in Antigua, operated in Hong Kong, and in principle did not allow American investors to trade on its crypto exchange, and in principle did not sell its tokens to Americans, it was beyond the reach of the SEC.

At any rate, the buyers of the FTT would either be foreigners, or Americans living outside the country. And now that was who Sam was courting, in his own awkward way. Three weeks before he offered FTT to the public, he flew to a conference in Taipei. All the big crypto players turned up at a party thrown by one of the biggest exchanges. And so, mechanically, did Sam. "Tonight was a night about booze and women and lasers and loud booming music," he wrote in his journal afterward, "but there was an odd microclimate that seemed to follow me around as I wandered between the tables. It didn't start to crystal-lize until I walked by CZ a few . . . times and each time he broke eye contact with his eye candy and embraced me: *people were thinking about us, a lot.* This was the first time CZ seemed more interested in me than I was in him."

Out of thin air FTX minted three hundred fifty million FTT tokens. Sam offered a chunk of them to employees at five cents each, and another chunk to important crypto people, like CZ, who might be friends of the exchange, at ten cents. CZ initially declined, as did most of FTX's own employees—Ryan Salame was a big exception—but other outside investors bought up enough that Sam eventually raised the price, first to twenty cents and then to seventy. On July 29, 2019, FTT was listed on FTX and thus offered to the general pub-lic. ("That was the most nervous I'd ever seen Sam," said Nishad.) It opened at $1 and traded up to $1.50. Inside two months, Ryan Salame had made thirty times his money, and the outside buyers had made fifteen times their money. Of the original three hundred fifty million tokens minted, FTX had sold roughly sixty million at about a dollar less than they were now worth. Within a week or so, Sam's doubts about his ability to earn the trust of a mass audience had turned to regret for selling FTT way too cheap. Just how cheap became clear when, a few weeks later, CZ called Sam and offered to buy a 20 per-cent stake in FTX for $80 million.

It was as if a wildcatter had accidentally built his house on an oil field: Sam hadn't even really wanted to run a crypto exchange. He'd built a casino that offered gamblers the chance to make bets big-ger than their bank accounts justified, at seemingly no risk to the casino or to the other gamblers, and it was exactly what the crypto world wanted. His timing, though accidental, was perfect, as big pro-fessional traders like Jane Street were entering the crypto markets and in need of a professional-grade futures exchange. Sam's choice of location, also accidental, was perfect too: Hong Kong was maybe the only spot in the world where he and CZ would both feel at ease.

Hong Kong was like a chessboard with a voice embedded in it to shout rule changes in the middle of every game. The Hong Kong regulators gave a crypto exchange cover to do pretty much whatever it wanted to do but changed the rules often enough to keep it interesting.

On top of it all, Hong Kong, and Asia generally, teemed with ambitious young people with no particular qualifications who thought nothing of dropping whatever they'd been doing to go to work for a crypto exchange run by a person who was all but unknowable. Sam needed people just like that: right from the start, FTX should have hung a sign on the door that said No Experience Necessary. Sam hired Natalie Tien, who had little experience with media or marketing, and made her head of corporate public relations, for instance. He hired a young saleswoman from the Huobi exchange named Constance Wang and made her the company's chief operating officer. Faced with a necessity, Sam turned it into a virtue. "It's a moderately bad sign if you are having someone do the same thing they've done before," he said. "It's adverse selection of a weird sort. Because: why are they coming to you?"

The funny thing about Ramnik Arora was that all he'd really been looking for was a chance to walk to work. He'd grown up in India, completed a master's in computer science at Stanford, done a stint at Goldman Sachs, and was now married and settled in the East Bay. For three years he'd had a miserable commute, from Berkeley to a job at Facebook in Menlo Park. He'd started on a team working on real-time auctions for online ads—with the goal of showing the perfect ad to the perfect person at the perfect time—then moved to another team trying to launch Libra, Facebook's doomed bid to create its own cryptocurrency.

Somewhere between Goldman Sachs and Facebook, Ramnik had given up looking for passion in his work. If he seemed older than he was, it was because he was letting go of one of the things that defines youth: hope. "The smartest minds of our generation are either buying or selling stocks or predicting if you'll click on an ad," he said. "This is the tragedy of our generation." The effect of the tragedy had been to shrink his ambition. He was thinking less and less about changing the world and more and more about making himself and his wife comfortable within it. "I'd read a study that there was a fifteen percent happiness gain if you could walk to work," he said.

And so it was with domestic happiness in mind that, in the late spring of 2020, he'd plugged "crypto" and "Berkeley" into LinkedIn. He'd received a single result: Alameda Research. He'd never heard of it. He sent in his résumé. Within minutes he received a Zoom invitation from Sam Bankman-Fried—who wanted to talk to him not about Alameda but about a new crypto exchange that Alameda Research had launched, called FTX. The numbers coming out of Sam's mouth via Zoom shocked Ramnik, as did Sam's willingness to disclose them to a total stranger. FTX had existed for just a bit more than a year. In the final six months of 2019, it had generated about $10 million in revenues. In 2020, the number was going to jump to somewhere between $80 million and $100 million.

At some point during the conversation, Ramnik figured out that Sam was not in Berkeley but in Hong Kong, where it was three in the morning. People behind Sam were scurrying back and forth with all the hustle and bustle of people in the middle of their workday. Whatever Sam actually said on that first call, Ramnik heard mainly a sound he'd nearly forgotten. It was the sound of passion.

He took a job with FTX, at an 80 percent pay cut to what he'd been making at Facebook (and at a 95 percent discount to what TikTok was offering). Between Alameda and FTX, he was Sam's fiftieth hire. His title was Head of Product, which was weird, as Ramnik didn't know anything about the product. On the Zoom call, Sam had said that he actually had no idea what Ramnik might do for FTX but that they'd figure out something.

Once Ramnik moved to Hong Kong, his absence of a purpose became a problem. FTX clearly didn't need a Head of Product. There was no such job. Gary had written all the code. A tiny force of young Chinese women and crypto dudes were already out evangelizing the product, and they didn't need Ramnik's help. Nishad was basically managing the developers, who fixed any problems that arose with the product, and dealing with anyone who was unhappy with their job or Sam's management style.

For the first twenty-one days on the job, which he spent quarantined inside a dreary Hong Kong hotel room, Ramnik wasn't sure what he was supposed to do. He fiddled some with the exchange's computer code—the product—but every time he did, he had to let Nishad know what he'd done. He'd send Sam notes, but Sam would take two days to reply. Emerging from his quarantine, Ramnik asked Nishad, "Am I a net positive for the company or a net negative?" "Net negative," replied Nishad. "The amount of time I'm spending checking on your work is greater than the amount of time it would take for me to do the work myself." Ramnik actually appreciated the honesty. And decided he'd need to find something else to do.

Soon he found himself playing a role that had never existed either in the company or in Sam's life. "I quickly became the person Sam relied on for random things," said Ramnik. "The first thing he asked me to do was find an auditor, because we didn't have one." As Sam didn't care about titles, Ramnik's never changed. He was and would remain Head of Product, when he more accurately could be described as Sam's Handyman. "It was, 'Lots of stuff comes up, and you're going to handle what comes up,'" said Ramnik. Oddly, much of what came up was, in one way or another, about trust. As in: how could FTX get people to trust it?

Sam didn't hire grown-ups, but now he had Ramnik, and Ramnik had some grown-up-like traits. He hesitated before he spoke. He'd worked for years at Goldman Sachs and Facebook. He'd just turned thirty-three and could pass for thirty-five and his knee didn't bounce up and down when he spoke. He wore long pants. He had a wife and an almost Wemmick-like view, not shared by Sam or anyone who had thus far managed to survive Sam's management style, that private life was one thing and the office another. He had the ability to imagine what grown-ups might think if, say, they found you in bed with the wrong person. It was Ramnik who intervened when Sam went all in on the idea of FTX being the first to list the token of a Taiwanese porn business called Swag. Swag would cut them a big check in exchange for FTX creating a market for Swag tokens; FTX would thus become the financial engine for a Taiwanese porn empire. "I had to talk him out of that," said Ramnik. "In talking him out of it, I felt there was a fork in the road. There was no turning back. Sam was hell-bent on doing this. And I'm like, *No fucking way we're doing it.*"

Inside of crypto world, none of Ramnik's qualities made much of a difference and indeed they might have been a disadvantage. Outside of it, they were invaluable.

Ramnik noted that people didn't identify with companies; they identified with people. They might never trust this new crypto exchange, but they might trust its founder, odd as he was, if they thought they knew who he was. "The first thing we asked was can we get Sam on TV," said Ramnik. "That seemed like a long shot. But Natalie somehow did it." To help her in her new and unfamiliar role as head of FTX public relations, Natalie had called a New York public relations firm called M Group Strategic Communications. Its head, Jay Morakis, was at first wary. "I thought maybe it was some shady Chinese thing," he said. But then he heard Sam's pitch, and watched Sam's first big public appearance, on Bloomberg TV. "Whatever the closest thing in my PR experience has been to this, nothing is close," he said. "I'm fifty years old. I've had my firm for twenty years and I've never seen anything like it. All my guys want to meet Sam. I have CEOs calling me and asking: Can you do for us what you did for Sam?" He'd had to explain, back in 2021, that he actually hadn't done anything. Sam had just sort of . . . happened.

The effect of Sam's media appearances in the latter part of 2021 exceeded everyone's expectations. This person who had always kept the world at a distance, and from whom the world had mostly kept its distance, somehow, through media, came alive in people's imaginations. Inside of crypto Sam was becoming famous; outside of crypto he was still unknown and, therefore, untrusted.

Part of Ramnik's odd new job was to help fix that. "How do you determine something is credible?" he said. "It's by association. Trust comes from preexisting relationships." Sam had no preexisting relationships; before about the age of eighteen he'd hardly had any relationships at all; since then, he had come to know a bunch of effective altruists (a lot of whom were furious with him for creating a civil war inside their movement) and another bunch of Jane Street traders (who were massively irritated with him for leaving Jane Street to create a rival firm, and for poaching Jane Street traders).

And so, with Sam, Ramnik set out to create new relationships, starting with some venture capitalists. FTX didn't really need capital. But if they could find the right venture capitalist to form a relationship with Sam, it might help them ease their way into the minds of others outside of crypto. "We had this conversation about legitimacy and trust," said Ramnik. "It was, 'Can we raise money from a *good* VC?' No Chinese VC was a big thing. We wanted to be associated with US institutions."

The first conversations between the crypto people and the venture capital people were a bit awkward. "They wanted samples of what our internal controls are," said Ramnik. "We didn't have any." The venture capitalists could see how fast FTX was growing—that they were wildcatters sitting on a gusher—but were unsure if what they were seeing was closer to the last gallon of oil than the first. Was it just a big trade that would go away with the crypto craze, or was Sam building something enduring? If the latter, he'd need access to American investors, and for that FTX needed internal controls. They also needed to be licensed and regulated.

Therein lay the biggest problem, in earning the trust of the VC: there was no global license for a crypto futures exchange. Some countries, like Hong Kong, offered a license for a spot crypto exchange and agreed to turn a blind eye to futures trading. Most countries, like the United States, offered no license at all. The United States government wasn't even sure which agency should regulate crypto—the Securities and Exchange Commission or the Commodity Futures Trading Commission. The question of who regulates any given crypto product in the United States turns on whether the product is defined as a security or a commodity. Bitcoin was defined early on, in 2015, as a commodity, and so is regulated by the CFTC. FTT—or for that matter a leveraged Bitcoin token—would likely be defined as a security and so fall under the jurisdiction of the SEC.

At that moment, in early 2021, both agencies were sort of claiming authority, but neither was doing much with it. With no rules in place, the people who opened crypto businesses in the US were constantly at risk of lawsuits and fines over anything they weren't explicitly permitted to do—which, apart from buying and selling bitcoin, was basically everything. Crypto people would implore the regulators for permission to sell a new crypto token, or to pay interest on crypto deposits or create a crypto futures contract; the regulators would hem and haw; the crypto people would push ahead and actually do something, and the regulators would sanction them. "It's a game of twenty questions with the regulators, but if you ask the wrong question, you get fined," explained Sam.

As for the venture capitalists, Sam had no real experience with them: this was an entirely new game. Ramnik watched him figure out how to play it. In early 2021, Jump Trading—not a conventional venture capitalist—offered to buy a stake in FTX at a company valuation of $4 billion. "Sam said no, the fundraise is at twenty billion," recalled Ramnik. Jump responded by saying that they'd be interested at that price if Sam could find others who were too—which told you that the value people assigned to new businesses was arbitrary.

Selling a new business to a VC was apparently less like selling a sofa than it was like pitching a movie idea. The VCs' eagerness to buy turned less on your hard numbers than on how excited they became about the story you told. It was as if they spent their day listening to stories and picking the ones they liked best. There was no rhyme or reason to their evaluations: English class all over again. Sam quickly figured out that most of the stories these people heard were just not very persuasive. "Most people tell stories that are trivial to falsify," he said. The story he and Ramnik told was not that way. It went roughly as follows:

Global stocks traded $600 billion a day, crypto was now trading $200 billion each day, and the gap was closing. Inside of eighteen months, FTX had gone from nothing to the world's fifth-biggest crypto exchange, and every day, it was seizing market share from its competitors. They were now the only crypto exchange making a priority of obtaining licenses and going legit. They were also the only crypto exchange that hadn't in one way or another offended US financial regulators. Once licensed in the United States, a crypto exchange like FTX could also trade stocks or anything else people wanted to trade and challenge, for example, the New York Stock Exchange. To that end, Sam had already incorporated a business called FTX US—but was being careful about allowing customers to trade stuff on it of which the SEC might disapprove. "The argument was, 'Look how fast we're growing, the market is huge—and we're going to be the credible party,'" said Ramnik.

There was a circularity to their situation. To be the credible party, it would help to have money from fancy venture capitalists. To get the VCs' money, they needed to be the credible party. And yet it was all so loosey-goosey. After hearing their pitch, one fund sent them a term sheet and said, "We love you so much just fill in a number." Sam filled in a number: $20 billion. The fund went quiet for a bit and then, when Ramnik called, said they'd changed their mind. A British venture capital firm oddly named Hedosophia called and offered to pay what Sam asked—and hand over $100 million for a 0.05 percent stake in FTX. Ramnik hardly knew who they were and so arranged a call with them. "It was weird," he said. "I felt they didn't know enough about the business. Basic shit like they didn't know that FTX US existed."

Even so, the Hedosophia people sent Ramnik a term sheet—only to change their minds after a mini crash in crypto prices and withdraw it. A guy from Blackstone, the world's biggest private investment firm, called Sam to say that he thought a valuation of $20 billion was too high—and that Blackstone would invest at a valuation of $15 billion. "Sam said, 'If you think it is too high, I'll let you short a billion of our stock at a valuation of twenty billion,'" recalled Ramnik. "The guy said, 'We don't short stock.' And Sam said that if you worked at Jane Street you'd be fired the first week."*

Even if the VCs didn't all realize that Sam was playing a video game at the same time that he was talking to them, most sensed that he didn't care what they had to say. Ramnik came to think that Sam's indifference to their feelings actually heightened their interest in him. That FTX was profitable and didn't really need the money probably also helped. In the end, between the summer of 2020 and the spring of 2021, in four rounds of fundraising, they sold roughly 6 percent of the company for $2.3 billion. Roughly *one hundred fifty* different venture capital firms invested. All of them caved to Sam's refusal to give them a seat on the board (he had no board) or any other form of control over the business.

---

* There was the other point of view to consider, of course—how these venture capitalists viewed this odd new crypto entrepreneur. "I got on the phone with him," recalled Nick Shalek, of Ribbit Capital. "I asked him a question. And he talked for an hour. I asked him a second question, and he talked for another hour." Shalek was struck, as were many of the VCs, by Sam's seeming artlessness. "He says if he has a decision to make and the decision is a million-dollar decision, he'll make it in five seconds. If it's a ten-million-dollar decision, he'll take a few minutes, and if it's a hundred-million-dollar decision, he'll spend a couple of hours on it. And it's like he's serious? I'm thinking, God, you can't say that to a regulator, or a journalist . . . or anyone." This artless workaholic was plotting to take over the financial world—and had a plausible story about how he might do it. "For him to build the business he was describing, it would be the largest global crypto exchange and then go beyond that—to become the largest global financial institution," said Shalek. He, like everyone else, quickly saw that Sam didn't resemble most of the entrepreneurs he'd dealt with. "He's not a showman. He's not a salesman. He's got a nonconventional way of thinking about building his organization. Everything is probabilities, and he'd pull these probabilities out of thin air. And then he'd change them. He's sleeping on a beanbag. He's doing all of this by himself. And he doesn't seem particularly interested in our opinion on anything. Which is fine. But we were like, He's an unusual person. We have to spend time with him in person." But they couldn't spend time with Sam in person. The Hong Kong government had responded to the global pandemic by requiring anyone who entered the country to quarantine in a hotel for fourteen days. Sam was understood and interpreted by his original investors mostly via Zoom, and in the middle of one of the great venture capital booms in history.

And yet FTX was just a piece of a much larger puzzle of Sam's design. He owned 90 percent of Alameda Research. And the nature of Alameda Research was changing. It was still a quant trading firm, with its good months and bad months, but its traders were playing, in new ways, with bigger and bigger sums of money. Crypto world had created what were, in effect, unregulated new banks. People would deposit their crypto with, for instance, Genesis Global Capital or Celsius Network, and receive some rate of interest, and these pseudobanks would re-lend the crypto to traders like Alameda Research. In early 2018, rich effective altruists had charged Sam interest rates of 50 percent a year. Three years later, Genesis and Celsius were willing to lend billions to Alameda Research at interest rates that ranged from 6 to 20 percent. And there were other, even more mysterious billions inside of Alameda that no one knew about. "FTX is smaller than people think, and Alameda is bigger," said Ramnik. "Way bigger."

It was never clear where Alameda Research stopped and FTX started. Legally separate companies, they were both owned by the same person. They occupied the same big room on the twenty-sixth floor of an office building. They shared the same vista of the forest of high-rises surrounding Victoria Harbor and, twenty miles beyond that, China. Sam's desk was positioned at one end of the identical long trading desks used by both Alameda and FTX, with a clear view of both. It didn't occur to anyone that there was anything weird about Alameda covering the start-up costs of somewhere between $5 million and $10 million for FTX. Ditto FTX selling FTT and using the capital not to expand FTX but to trade inside Alameda. It seemed perfectly natural for Alameda to control all the remaining FTT, and use it as collateral in its trading activity. Sam didn't even try to hide what he was doing. FTT "has single-handedly fixed [Alameda's] equity problem," he wrote, in a memo to employees. He retained 90 percent of Alameda Research, with Gary owning the remaining 10 percent. Even after he'd sold stakes in FTX to the one hundred fifty venture capitalists, Sam still owned more than half the company. The third-largest shareholder, Nishad, owned a mere 5 percent of the company.

At the same time, Sam sort of ran both and neither. Much of his day was spent promoting FTX and himself to the outside world. And as FTX boomed, he found it harder to find people of whom he approved to work for Alameda. Qualified people might turn up looking for work at Alameda, but the moment they saw FTX's growth they would say that, no, actually, they'd rather work for FTX. "It became almost impossible to find smart people who wanted to work at Alameda," he said. To manage the place, he felt he was sort of stuck with the people already there.

He wasn't able to run the day-to-day trading operations at Alameda and also play this new and unfamiliar role as the face of the booming FTX franchise. Seeing no single person inside of Alameda qualified to run it, Sam handed the job to two people. The first was a clever but socially awkward trader named Sam Trabucco whom he'd known since high school math camp and hired away the year before from the high-frequency trading firm Susquehanna. Right away Trabucco had established himself as the only person who could rival Sam Bankman-Fried in his devotion to crypto trading: he could go weeks without ever leaving the Hong Kong office. The moment Sam promoted him, his interest in work collapsed, however, and he discovered a new taste for life's pleasures. The shocking shift inside Sam Trabucco in the late summer of 2021 was hard to explain but impossible to deny. "The moment he became co-head of Alameda he checked out," said an Alameda employee.

That left Sam's private hedge fund in the hands of its other co-CEO, Caroline Ellison. When he'd named her to the job, Sam imagined Caroline managing the people, while Sam Trabucco managed the trading risks. "People really liked being managed by her," he said. By the fall of 2021 Caroline was effectively managing both the people and the trading risk while herself being managed only by Sam. This created some complications. The two were now leading a secret life, and it bothered Caroline a lot more than it did Sam. She wanted to improve and expand their relationship; he wanted . . . well, not to. After he'd split for Hong Kong, Sam had replied to Caroline's first memo with a memo of his own, laying out the pros and cons of a sexual relationship. It began with a seriously compelling list, titled: ARGUMENTS AGAINST:

In a lot of ways I don't really have a soul. This is a lot more obvious in some contexts than others. But in the end there's a pretty decent argument that my empathy is fake, my feelings are fake, my facial reactions are fake. I don't feel happiness. What's the point in dating someone who you physically can't make happy?

I have a long history of getting bored and claustrophobic. This has the makings of a time when I'm less worried about it than normal; but the baseline prior might be high enough that nothing else matters.

I feel conflicted about what I want. Sometimes I really want to be with you. Sometimes I want to stay at work for 60 hours straight and not think about anything else.

I'm worried about power dynamics between us.

This could destroy Alameda if it goes really poorly PR-wise.

This combos really badly with the current EA shitshow I'm supposed to be, in some ways, adjudicating.

I make people sad. Even people who I inspire, I don't really make happy. And people who I date—it's really harrowing. It really fucking sucks, to be with someone who (a) you can't make happy, (b) doesn't really respect anyone else, (c) is constantly thinking really offensive things, (d) doesn't have time for you, and (e) wants to be alone half the time.

There are a lot of really fucked up things about dating an employee.

This list was followed by another, briefer list, titled "ARGUMENTS IN FAVOR."

I really fucking like you.

I really like talking to you. I feel a lot less worried about saying what's on my mind to you than to almost anyone else.

You share my most important interests.

You're a good person.

I really like fucking you.

You're smart and impressive.

You have good judgement and aren't full of shit.

You appreciate a lot of me for who I am.

She'd still followed him from Berkeley to Hong Kong and reentered their relationship. Two years later, its contours hadn't changed. Sam was better able to see the reasons why he might have feelings for Caroline than he was to experience those feelings. Caroline wanted a conventional love with an unconventional man. Sam wanted to do whatever at any given moment offered the highest expected value, and his estimate of her expected value seemed to peak right before they had sex and plummet immediately after. Caroline didn't like it and let him know, in a series of long, businesslike memos. "There are things I want out of our relationship that I feel like I'm not getting to the extent I want," she wrote, in early July 2021. The usual bullet points followed:

- Communication about our feelings and preferences
- Consistent affirmation/positive reinforcement
- Social affirmation of our relationship in at least some context

Sam had a list in his head of all the bad things that might occur if people knew they were sleeping together. Caroline thought that Sam's list masked his true motives. "I guess a lot of what bothers me is feeling like you're ashamed of me," she added, six days later, in a follow-up memo, before explaining how and why that bothered her.

- *I feel excited about people knowing we're dating; in past relationships I definitely haven't always felt that way, and it came down to*

whether I was embarrassed by that person, and whether I thought
people would think worse/better of me for dating them.

- *If I felt you also felt positively about people knowing we were dat-*
ing but just thought it was a bad idea to share, I think I wouldn't
mind as much.

- *Again, I feel like if I were better/more impressive, you wouldn't be*
embarrassed for people to know we were dating.

Their deep interests remained unaligned. Caroline sensed that, even as Sam promoted her to CEO of Alameda Research, he disapproved of her job performance—and she shared his opinion. "It feels like I'm doing a much worse job managing Alameda than you would if you were working on it full-time," she wrote, in a follow-up to the follow-up, "and I'm going to fuck up important things if you don't step in sometimes."

Eighteen months earlier, Alameda Research had been limping along with $40 million in capital from a handful of effective altruist friends. It now had billions in it, much of it borrowed from strangers at pseudobanks, and a stash of lesser-known cryptocurrencies, like FTT, worth between zero dollars and $80 billion, depending on who was doing the counting. The job had become more complicated. She clearly needed help. Once again she was thinking aloud to her boss about either quitting her job or breaking up with him, or both.

Before she could do either, Sam left again, in August 2021, on another trip—to the Bahamas, to see if maybe it might serve as host to a satellite office or a disaster recovery site if, say, the Chinese government shut them down. He liked the place so much that, pretty much on the spot, he decided to stay. For the second time in three years he messaged a group of people he was meant to be leading to say he wouldn't be coming back.

7

THE ORG CHART

It didn't take a psychiatrist to see a pattern in Sam's relationship with Caroline, but there happened to be one sitting in the middle of it. His name was George Lerner, and by late 2021 he might have been the world's leading authority on the inner life of effective altruists. The curious role had just naturally opened up to him, in much the same way psychiatry had in the first place. He'd been drawn to it by the instant intimacy it allowed him with others. "Honestly, it's kind of amazing to listen to other people's stories and get paid for it," he said. In his first days at Baylor College of Medicine, they'd asked students to raise their hands when their hoped-for field was called. When they called for surgeons, lots of the students raised their hands. When they called for psychiatrists, George's was the only hand in the air. He'd moved to San Francisco for his residency, at the University of California, and remained to teach and build a practice.

George was born in Russia but moved with his family at the age of eleven to California. He'd emerged from the experience a strange combination of the two places. His eyes, his hair, his unchanging five-o'clock shadow: all were part of the same picture, which might have been drawn by Dostoevsky. Everything about George was dark, except for his smile. While the rest of him frowned, his mouth would express mirth and even glee. It was as if California had gone to work on him to lift him out of a bottomless despair and stopped before finishing the job. His patients, as a result, could likely find in his demeanor whatever emotion they happened to need at the time.

The first group were all lawyers; one lawyer had wandered in and recommended him to another lawyer, and before George knew it he was spending all day listening to lawyers' problems. "The lawyers didn't have great boundaries," said George. "They'd all send over colleagues." The lawyers wanted to talk mainly about their failed relationships, which got old fast. But after the wave of lawyers came a second wave, of tech executives, who were far more interested than the lawyers had been in talking about their work. "The tech people didn't talk much about their relationships," said George. "They wanted me to really coach them to be better engineers."

The crypto people started turning up around 2017, the year crypto went boom. They came in two basic flavors. First to come were the originalists, who had been drawn to Bitcoin when it was still an old-time religion. "They were, like, libertarians who have always worked on their own and who didn't fit well in big companies because of their views," said George. "They had a lot of complaints about people at work pushing onto them pro-government views. They're a little paranoid. The world to them is a kind of conspiracy." George saw enough of these people to realize that it was no accident that they wound up in crypto. "There was a dog whistle coming out of Bitcoin that attracted these people," he said. "They worked in some regular company but on the side they had this interest. They wanted to talk about how they are afraid of government. A lot of times their spouse or their family didn't want to hear about it anymore."

They came to George because their bitcoin didn't have ears and they needed someone to listen. George was suited for the role, up to a point. He'd always found it shockingly easy to occupy another person's intellectual point of view. "In some ways it really hurt me in residency, because I couldn't spot psychosis," he said. "I'm like, *I can totally see from your point of view how you think your employers are listening to your phone.*"

The rise in the price of bitcoin ushered into George's waiting room a different type of crypto person. "The second crypto type is the person who is young, hip, and wants to make money," said George. This other crypto type was less interesting to George. They were just worried the government was going to tax their profits.

Then the effective altruists started showing up—and when they did, George took a new and keener interest in his patients. Gabe Bankman-Fried, Sam's younger brother, was the first, but hard on his heels came Caroline Ellison and others from Alameda Research. By the time Sam arrived, a year later, George was treating maybe twenty EAs. As a group, they eased a worry George had about himself: the limits to his powers of empathy. When ordinary people came to him with their ordinary feelings, he often found himself faking an understanding. The EAs didn't need his empathy; the EAs thought that even they shouldn't care about their feelings. In their single-minded quest to maximize the utility of their lives, they were seeking to minimize the effect of their feelings. "The way they put it to me is that their emotions are getting in the way of their ability to reduce their decisions to just numbers," said George. "They'd ask: Should I have an affair? Well, let's run the cost-benefit analysis. EAs love that approach." This approach also suited George. He wasn't able to feel his patients' feelings. But he could feel their thoughts.

He would never be one of them—he was himself unsure if altruism existed in human nature. But he adored them. It was fun, for starters, how young they all were—just kids, really, starting out in life. "Initially it felt like they were playing a game. They were all outliers in terms of their intelligence and the way they approached the world." Soon enough, he saw that it wasn't a game. They were all completely and utterly sincere. They judged the morality of any action by its consequences and were living their life to maximize those consequences. George accepted their premise, as he had accepted the premises of the crypto guys who thought the government was spying on them. "It wasn't my job to challenge them," he said. "They were internally consistent, and if they're internally consistent, I'm okay with it. And, you know, maybe it's a way of actually benefiting the world, even if it is a little bit of a weird way."

As a group, they were as likely to want to talk about their philosophy as they were their personal issues, and these philosophical discussions were more entertaining to George than anyone's issues. But George heard about the issues, too, and this allowed him to detect patterns in his new patients' behavior. For example, they all professed to care about "humanity," while at the same time often being a bit slow to love actual people. "It doesn't really start with people," said George. "It starts with suffering. It's about preventing suffering. They care about animals in the same way. They also care about not having the earth blown up by an asteroid. But it's not a longing for a connection."

They also cared about the logic underpinning their behavior; consistency was, for them, not the hobgoblin of a little mind but the mark of a big one. They brought logic and rigor to their most emotionally fraught decisions—for instance, the decision whether to have children. "A lot of EAs chose not to have kids," said George. "It's because of the impact on their own lives. They believe that having kids takes over from their ability to have impact on the world." After all, in the time it took to raise a child to become an effective altruist, you could persuade some unknowably large number of people who were not your children to become effective altruists. "It feels selfish to have a kid. The EA argument for having a kid is that kid equals happiness and happiness equals increased productivity. If they can get there in their head, then maybe they have a kid."

The fact that none of this came naturally to human beings—

that they had had to think their way into their way of life—was also important. "There are two parts of being EA," said George. "Part one is the focus on consequences. Part two is the personal sacrifice." On part one the EAs were in general agreement; when it came to part two there were serious differences among them. It was easy to talk the talk, but how far were you willing to walk the walk, in your commitment to saving other people's lives? Would you give up kids? Would you donate a kidney? Sam Bankman-Fried, George felt, lived on one end of the spectrum. Sam had an almost weirdly low tolerance for physical pain and so passed on donating his kidney. Otherwise, Sam was all in on the sacrifice.

Caroline Ellison wasn't like that. She lacked confidence in herself. "She was borrowing her ego from Sam because she lacked one," said George. "Sam gave her real inner strength." In George's EA patient population, Caroline defined the other end of the spectrum of willingness to sacrifice for her principles. When she'd first come to him, back in 2018, she'd had two issues she wanted to talk about: her attention deficit hyperactivity disorder and her new and emotionally complicated polyamorous lifestyle. Every subsequent session after the first, Caroline came with just one issue she wanted to discuss: Sam. She'd fallen in love with Sam, Sam didn't love her back, and that fact alone left her deeply unhappy. "I thought of her as an exception," said George. "I thought she might be willing to trade EA for reciprocation of love any day."

George didn't really see it as his job to explain Sam to Caroline or to dissuade her from her quest for his love. "If I was her friend—and not her therapist—I would have said you're never going to get what you want from this guy." It was still painful to listen to the steady drumbeat of her desire for Sam to publicly acknowledge their relationship. After nearly two years in Hong Kong, she'd let a few of their inner circle, their fellow EAs, know about it. "That's the highlight of the relationship for her," said George. "It was a big ask of him, and she seemed happy with that. It was an affirmation of the relation-

ship, and it showed some level of commitment. She never got anything that big from him before." After which Sam hopped on a plane
to the Bahamas and never returned. And then, just a few weeks later,
called George, and suggested that he move from San Francisco to
the Bahamas and serve as corporate psychiatrist to FTX.

After The Schism, and right before his flight to Hong Kong, Sam had
been in the market for a new therapist. Various former therapists
had failed to be useful, mainly because they could not bring themselves to believe that he was who he was, and instead insisted that
he must be someone else. "The previous therapists were incredulous
about various parts of me," he said. He'd explain, for example, what
he thought of as his perfectly rational decision made at a surprisingly
young age to never have children. Or he'd tell them of his absence
of feeling, or how he had never felt pleasure. (They had a term for
it: anhedonia.) They'd sort of nod for a bit but then mistrust his self-
diagnosis. "It was like, what about me are you disputing?" said Sam.
"There was not any clear way to break through with them. I know
that there are things that are unusual about me. They wouldn't just
accept them and move on." Add to the list of people who failed to
understand him his therapists.

What he liked about George was that George simply took him as
he was—and actually didn't seem all that interested in engaging in
pointless conversations about his feelings. Sam had long since decided
that any discussions about his inner life, and its consequences for others, were futile. "The social stuff was basically unsolvable," he said.
He didn't need a therapist to deal with his problems—though he did
need someone who could prescribe his medications. The problems
that interested Sam were *other people's* problems. He soon figured out
that George could be extremely useful with these. When, say, two
employees were squabbling, George could help Sam think through
ways to resolve their dispute. To most everyone else George was a
shrink. For Sam, he became something like a management consul-

tant. ("Sam never wanted to talk about himself," said George. "All we ever talked about was business.")

Caroline's insistence on going public with her and Sam's feelings for each other would not have made it onto any official, or likely conscious, list of the reasons Sam felt he'd be better off staying in the Bahamas than returning to Hong Kong. In his mind there was not one reason for the move; there were several. The Hong Kong government's imposition of quarantines of fourteen to twenty-one days for anyone entering the country made foreign travel all but impossible. The Chinese government's habit of arresting the heads of any crypto exchanges they could get their hands on and arbitrarily freezing their funds put everyone at FTX on edge. The lawyers, and a few of the Chinese employees, bothered Sam constantly about the risk. FTX employees had hatched an escape plan for Sam and Gary—of which Sam was oblivious—to be carried out if the Chinese police ever came for them. "The 007 plan," they called it. There were two large men guarding the front door of the office, a way out the back, and a fueled-up jet ready to take the two to safety at any moment. Still, scary as the Chinese police might have been, they were, to Sam, less worrisome than Caroline. "I feel bad dumping this on you now," he wrote to her, not long before he fled Hong Kong. Then he launched into his own business memo:

1. I *really really* don't like people knowing we're dating. The reasons are, basically:
    1. It makes it really hard for me to manage well because of worries about bias
    2. It's potentially really bad PR
    3. It makes me feel really uncomfortable
    4. It makes people more uncomfortable at work around you
2. I was really unhappy with the conversation around it leaking at the office:

1. I understand you might like it if it leaks, but I don't, and it's a borderline dealbreaker for me
2. I also think you are wrong to like it leaking; I think you're forgetting the second order effects here

3. This comes up in a lot of ways. Examples are:
   1. If I go up to you specifically and say goodbye at a mass event we're both at, that's not very subtle
   2. Being indiscreet about finding ways to meet up (this is at least as much my fault as yours)
   3. Telling people

4. I'm pretty wary of ending up in traps where a relationship really bends my life in shitty ways

5. Most of all—I really want to make you stronger, and I worry that in part I might be doing the opposite.
   1. I worry that the drive to impress me is too much on your mind.
      1. You don't have to; you already do.
   2. I worry that fear of judgement from me makes you find some things really aversive.

He ended with a single line: "I'm really sorry that I'm such a shitty person to date."

At any rate, by late summer 2021 the hard part wasn't leaving Hong Kong. It was figuring out where to go. It had to be somewhere with financial regulation that explicitly allowed a crypto futures exchange. That ruled out Europe and the United States. Taiwan was no good, as the Chinese might invade at any moment. Antigua had good laws but bad internet. Uruguay just felt weird. Dubai might have worked, but it would be hard on FTX's large and growing population of Chinese female employees, and Sam bridled at the idea of the government telling people what they could and could not wear. Singapore, Gibraltar, Israel . . . this list of places in which FTX would be legal yielded a bunch of names that didn't work for various reasons. Oddly, the Bahamas hadn't even made that initial list—but then Ryan Salame visited to look for a vacation house to buy, and happened to learn that the Securities Commission of The Bahamas was putting the finishing touches on new crypto regulations.* The Bahamas had great internet, piped in by undersea cable from Florida. It had a neutral tax system that gave you credit for taxes paid to other countries, empty office space, and a truly wild number of empty luxury condominiums waiting to be turned into worker housing. And it was sufficiently hungry for any kind of business that when Sam landed to

---

* This is a footnote. And so it will feel on the page as it did at the time in real life: like a distraction from the story. But there's a backstory, and a person, you need to know about to grasp the spirit of the enterprise and to understand what is to come. Back in the 1970s, the Bahamas had been slow to create regulations for the insurance industry, and had lost out on a massive potential economic opportunity when a booming reinsurance industry set itself up in Bermuda, whose regulators had moved more quickly. By remaining entirely dependent on cruise ship tourism, the Bahamas had paid a price and run a risk—which became a reality when Covid stopped all cruise ships and torpedoed the economy. Back in 2015, a woman named Christina Rolle took over the job of chief financial regulator: executive director of the Securities Commission of The Bahamas. Her defining trait was her lack of self-importance. She was quiet and thoughtful and curious about the world—and aware that financial services offered the Bahamas one of the few ways to expand its middle class. By late 2018, she'd heard enough PowerPoint talks from financial regulators at international conferences to realize that everyone was avoiding dealing with crypto. She set out to do what US regulators have so far not done: sit down and write the rules to legalize much of crypto finance. "The technology is not going to go away," she said. "And what is going to happen with it is going to disrupt financial services in ways we cannot see." She was aware of the risk: you write the regulation to allow some financial activity, and you never know who is going to show up or what they will do. "We had no one in mind, no one," she said. "We didn't know who was going to come. And I thought initially, Bahamas being so small, no one is going to be recognizing it right away, but at least we'd be a player in the market." Then, out of the blue, in the late summer of 2021, the founder of the world's hottest crypto exchange had turned up and made Christina Rolle look like a genius. She remained wary. "My fear is that I'll wake up one morning and there will be a big headline that I didn't see coming," she said, in early 2022. "Because there are so many people watching from the wings and waiting to say 'I told you so.' There are a lot of crypto skeptics out there." Hold that thought.

check out the place he found himself meeting with the newly elected prime minister. "Sam, we're broke," he'd confessed.

Sam wasn't broke. Just then Sam was the opposite of broke. Alameda Research was no longer paying loan shark interest rates to borrow tens of millions of dollars from effective altruists. The new crypto lenders like Celsius and Genesis were willing to hand Alameda Research collectively between $10 billion and $15 billion at rates as low as 6 percent. The rate of return inside Alameda was steadily declining, but with access to vast amounts of cheap capital, its raw trading profits kept rising: from $50 million in 2018, to $100 million in 2019, to $1 billion in 2020 and again in 2021. And those were just the trading profits; the numbers didn't include the seemingly vast unrealized gains on Sam's token stashes.

In March 2020, a Silicon Valley engineer named Anatoly Yakovenko launched a new and better blockchain that offered a solution to maybe Bitcoin's biggest weakness as a means of exchange: it was way too slow. Bitcoin could only validate seven transactions a second. The new Solana blockchain promised to process up to sixty-five thousand transactions a second. Sam had no independent ability to evaluate the thing, but he asked people who did and soon decided that Solana might be the crypto of the future. Even if it wasn't, Solana's story was good enough that other people might see it that way and drive up the price of its token. Eighteen months later, Alameda owned roughly 15 percent of all Solana tokens, most purchased at twenty-five cents apiece. The market price of Solana had gone as high as $249, a thousand-times increase on what Sam had paid for the tokens, and the face value of Sam's entire stash was roughly $12 billion. It was hard to know the resale value of such a huge stake. But there was a real market for Solana tokens. Two billion dollars' worth of the things traded each day. "I watched it in wonder," said Sam.

Solana was a microcosm of everything else Sam touched at that moment. It had a story that Sam amplified, by embracing the story. "It was the most complete proof we ever found of the hypothesis that we could have an insanely large edge on things like this," he said.

"It was self-fulfilling. The fact that we took a big position was part of what caused it to go up."

There was more like this in Sam's dragon's lair. Alameda had also hoovered up about half the existing FTT tokens, for instance, creating, in effect, a second stake in FTX for Sam, with a claim on about one-sixth of all FTX's revenues. In the past eighteen months, FTT's price had risen from roughly $3 to roughly $80. Again, it was hard to say how much Sam could unload FTT for, had he tried to sell his stake all at once. But the crypto lenders were happy to lend him billions of dollars against his FTT, so, to get his hands on cash, he didn't need to sell it.

Then there was Sam's equity stake in FTX, which was very real indeed. A large number of venture capitalists had paid $2.3 billion for a mere 6 percent of it. Sam had good reason to believe that he might now sell an even smaller piece for several billion more to an even bigger group. FTX underpinned his growing empire: a real business with booming revenues and profits. It hadn't even really needed venture capital. (As if to make the point, Sam, having taken $200 million from Sequoia Capital in exchange for a piece of FTX, turned around and invested $200 million from Alameda Research in one of Sequoia's funds.) FTX was now the world's fastest-growing crypto exchange, and the casino of choice for big professional traders. In less than three years, it had gone from 0 to 10 percent of all crypto trading. In 2021, it would generate $1 billion in revenues.

And yet it still obviously had lots of room to grow. Its biggest rival, Binance, had five times the trading volume of FTX, which meant that it likely had roughly five times FTX's revenues and five times FTX's market value. The experts who tried to determine the present value of rich people had trouble putting a number on CZ's. No one was sure how much of Binance CZ actually owned. In 2021, *Forbes* had listed CZ's wealth as less than Sam's, but neither Sam nor anyone else inside FTX believed the numbers. Sam thought CZ might be the richest person in the world. And CZ, to the people who supplied Sam with capital, seemed vulnerable. When *Forbes* looked at Sam in the fall of 2021, they saw the richest person in the world under the age of thirty. When the VCs looked at Sam, they saw the guy who might very soon replace CZ as the richest person in the world, period.

All of that explained what Sam was about to do at this moment— and what would later feel a lot harder to explain or even to believe. He set out to establish FTX as the world's most regulated, most law-abiding, most rule-following crypto exchange. To acquire as many licenses to allow him to operate legally and openly in as many countries as he could. To make a bet on the rule of law shaping the lawless crypto markets. By the end of 2021, 16 percent of Americans claimed to have dabbled in crypto. Across Asia the numbers were likely bigger. It was only a matter of time, Sam thought, before regulators engaged with crypto and banished the unlicensed exchanges.

The strategy was something like the opposite of Binance's. When FTX launched, in May 2019, Binance was merely one of a handful of crypto exchanges with roughly the same market share, of roughly 10 percent. One of those, BitMEX, soon ran afoul of the US Department of Justice, for "willfully failing to establish, implement and maintain an anti-money laundering program," and its founders, two American and one British, were variously fined, given probation, and placed under house arrest. Two other exchanges, OKEx and Huobi, reportedly watched executives being hauled off by the Chinese police, and saw their assets frozen. CZ had left China three years earlier, in late 2017, before that year's government crackdown, one of several before and after. He'd landed first in Singapore but finally settled in Dubai, which, among its charms, had no extradition treaty with the United States. Which was useful, as CZ's first response to new rules and regulations was often to ignore them, and count on the regulators to lack the nerve or the resources to take action.

That had been the smart thing to do, so far. In two years, Binance's share of crypto trading had boomed, from 10 percent to 50 percent. It offered financial products that local regulators either had banned or had yet to approve, and the regulators did not seem willing to do much about it. Binance's own exchange token, called BNB, was an example. BNB was to Binance what FTT was to FTX: a claim on the revenues of the enterprise. You could make a reasonable argument that bitcoin wasn't a security and the Commodity Futures Trading Commission had made it, and declared it a commodity. There was no similar argument to make for BNB or FTT. They'd been created and sold to investors to raise money for profit-making enterprises. They paid dividends to their owners, in the form of lower fees on the exchange and the buyback-and-burn agreements. There was no definition of a security that they didn't meet. If you tried to sell them to American investors inside the United States, it was hard to imagine the Securities and Exchange Commission simply turning a blind eye. And yet Binance sold BNB—and much else—to Americans inside the United States. In the immortal words texted by Binance's *chief compliance officer* to a colleague in 2018: "we are operating as a fking unlicensed securities exchange in the USA bro." (This and other similar morsels turned up in a lawsuit filed by the SEC against Binance five years after the fact, in June 2023.)

In their willingness to court the wrath of US financial regulators, the crypto exchanges fell into one of at least four categories. A small group of tiny US exchanges listed only bitcoin and ether, the two oldest coins, blessed by the SEC as commodities and openly regulated by the CFTC. (A bit oddly, the older the coin, the more people thought of it as a commodity.) FTX's new US exchange listed those two coins, plus maybe eighteen other, newer ones, none of which had the most obvious properties of a security. None of them had buyback-and-burn features, for example, or were solely intended to raise money for some for-profit enterprise. Coinbase, the exchange that serviced the greatest number of US customers, appeared willing to take more regulatory risk. It listed roughly five hundred coins, including some that the SEC pretty clearly viewed as securities, and its CEO, Brian Armstrong, took to Twitter to criticize the regulators for "sketchy behavior." Coinbase itself had no exchange token akin to FTT, however, and so wasn't in the most brazen position of using its exchange to sell its own unregulated securities to US investors. Only Binance did that, with BNB.

Selling what were in effect shares in itself to US retail investors on its own new US crypto exchange, Binance lifted the biggest middle finger to the US regulators. In the bargain, it juiced the value of BNB incredibly. When Binance formally opened its US exchange, in September 2019, the market cap of BNB was a bit shy of $3 billion. By the fall of 2021, it topped $100 billion. How much of the rise was driven by demand from US investors was hard to guess, but Sam guessed anyway: $20 billion. The ire of US regulators seemed, by comparison, a small price to pay.

Which is why, when Sam took in the situation, he decided that Binance's strategy was unsustainable. That the smart thing to do was to be the world's most law-abiding and regulator-loving exchange. FTX could use the law, and the regulators, to drive crypto trading from Binance and onto FTX. If countries did not yet have the laws, a small army of FTX lawyers would help them to create them. In the country that mattered most—the one country whose financial regulators chased people outside of their borders, and enforced its rules around the globe—Sam would personally take the lead. He'd set out to persuade the United States government to regulate crypto and punish those who violated the new rules, leaving FTX alone as a kind of teacher's pet of crypto. (Maybe the best thing about the Bahamas, from Sam's point of view, was how close it was to the United States.)

The US was now, in Sam's mind, the holy grail. It had an incumbent crypto exchange, Coinbase. But Coinbase's CEO had already written insulting tweets about the SEC. And Coinbase, compared to FTX, was a boring and bloated casino. It had *fifteen times* the number of employees FTX did, and only about a fifth of FTX's volume. Charging retail investors fees between five and fifty times what FTX charged, it was still running big losses. Even so, it was a public company, with a market capitalization of more than $75 billion. If FTX was granted a license to offer crypto futures in the United States and was given full access to US investors, it might steal Coinbase's customers, along with its market cap. Or so Sam thought—which is why he also thought that the license might double or even triple FTX's value overnight.

Before he could do any of this, he needed to get rid of CZ. CZ still owned the stake in FTX that he had bought in late 2019 for $80 million. Relations between Binance and FTX had since deteriorated into simmering resentment. Binance was the class bully, FTX the class nerd, and each took pleasure in using its special powers to torment the other. The Binance futures launch was a case in point. It had taken the Binance internal team three months longer to create their crypto futures trading platform than it had taken Gary, working by himself, to create FTX's. Once it was up and running, it attracted little interest. Or, rather, as Sam instantly noticed, what trading there was in Binance's new futures contract was fishy: instead of the spasmodic flows of naturally occurring market activity, there was a regular tick, tick, tick of trades. He guessed that Binance had created bots to trade its new contract with itself, to create the illusion of activity.

Wash trading, as it was called, would have been illegal on a regulated US exchange, though the sight of it did not bother Sam all that much. He thought it was sort of funny just how brazenly many of the Asian exchanges did it. In the summer of 2019, FTX created and published a daily analysis of the activity on other exchanges. It estimated that 80 percent or more of the volume on the second- and third-tier exchanges, and 30 percent of the volume on the top few exchanges, was fake. Soon after FTX published its first analysis of crypto trading activity, one exchange called and said, *We're firing our wash trading team. Give us a week and the volumes will be real.* The top exchanges expressed relief, and gratitude for the analysis, as, until then, lots of people assumed that far more than 30 percent of their volume was fake.

Sam was less surprised that Binance was wash trading than by how badly they were doing it. "They were doing a B-minus job at market manipulation," he said. One Binance bot would make a wide market in Bitcoin futures, and another Binance bot would enter and lift its high offer. If, to keep the numbers simple, the fair value of bitcoin was $100, the first Binance bot would insert a bid at $98 and an offer at $102. No normal trader would trade against either—why sell for $98 or buy for $102 on Binance what you could buy or sell on some other exchange for $100? But then, at regular and predictable intervals, the second Binance bot would enter the market and buy at $102. It looked as if a trade had occurred between two different parties, but it hadn't. It was simply Binance buying from Binance.

Sam loved this sort of thing: it was Jane Street trading all over again. In response, he had his traders at Alameda Research build their own, faster bots. Alameda's bots inserted offers a tiny bit cheaper than the offers from Binance bots. The Binance bot would offer to sell a Bitcoin future at $102, and, moments before the second Binance bot showed up to buy, the Alameda bot would leap in and offer it at $101.95. Instead of buying bitcoin from itself at an inflated price, Binance was buying it from Alameda Research at a price nearly as high.

Selling to Binance bots for $101.95 what they could buy elsewhere at $100 was found money for Alameda. But then the futures team inside Binance began to notice that their wash trading was losing money—and complained to CZ. That they hadn't told CZ the full story, or that they had not fully grasped what had happened, was evident in CZ's confusing response:

CZ Binance ✔
@cz_binance

Follow ⌄

The attacker is a well-known account that trades with @binance, and started their own futures exchange a few months ago. This was the 2nd attempt they tried. Shame!

7:10 PM - 15 Sep 2019

"It was very Chinese not just calling me up and saying, 'Hey, can you stop?'" said Sam. After that he'd called Binance's chief financial officer, Wei Zhou. It was a weird conversation—the CEO of one crypto exchange calling the CFO of another to inform him that, if he didn't want to lose money on his new futures contract, he'd need to improve his market manipulation. Wei Zhou spoke to CZ, who called Sam for a brief though not unfriendly chat, after which Sam concluded that CZ still had not been told by his traders what had actually happened. Whatever he'd been told led him to tweet a retraction that didn't make much more sense than what he'd originally written:

CZ Binance ✔
@cz_binance

Follow ⌄

Had a chat with the client. It was an accident, due to a bad parameter on their side. Not intentional. All good now.

8:55 PM - 15 Sep 2019

In the first eighteen months of FTX's existence, there had been several other dustups with Binance of this sort. CZ developed what three of his employees at the time described as an obsession with his new rival. He'd ask staff for regular reports about FTX, and speak of FTX in ways he would not of the other exchanges. "CZ is super astute," said one. "He'll never talk about any exchange. He thinks it's free marketing. But FTX worried him. From 2019 on, he only spoke of FTX. He thought FTX was the only real threat to his position." A threat in which he was, weirdly, the second-largest shareholder, after Sam.

By the middle of 2021, Sam saw that he could not sweet-talk regulators and at the same time have CZ as a big investor. If you wanted to be the teacher's pet, you couldn't sit in the back of the classroom with the badass in the leather jacket. The first thing every regulator asked for was a list of your investors, and personal details about them. "They were asking CZ what his family situation was and where he lives, and CZ didn't want to say," said one former Binance employee. In the end, Sam told CZ that he wanted to buy him out of his FTX shares. For the stake he'd paid $80 million to acquire, CZ demanded $2.2 billion. Sam agreed to pay it. Just before they signed the deal, CZ insisted, for no particular reason, on an extra $75 million. Sam paid that, too. Whatever gratitude CZ felt about his two-billion-dollar windfall he hid. "From then it was a cold war," said Sam.

The buyout of CZ occurred against a backdrop of the bigger public relations assault. Sam was now a regular on television and had appeared on the cover of *Forbes* magazine. He still had no idea how to create a brand, and, as ever, zero interest in expert opinion about how to do it. He decided to figure it out from scratch, by talking it over internally, hurling some money around, and seeing what worked. With one hand he was handing CZ $2.275 billion; with the other he was writing memos to people inside FTX in which he ruminated, as might a Martian, on what caused ordinary Americans to like and trust a product. "We're currently ahead in tech and favorability ratings, and behind in name recognition," he wrote. "We need to get 50m low engagement users to decide to switch from Coinbase to FTX. This will take a fairly forceful nudge!"

He began by noting how few marketing campaigns had had the effect that he hoped to achieve with FTX's. He counted only three:

1. Yes we can: Barack Obama
2. Just do it: Nike. Lots of athletes but there are two who made the brand what it is: Michael Jordan and Tiger Woods
3. Think different: Apple. Albert Einstein, John Lennon, MLK, Muhammad Ali, Rosa Parks, Gandhi, Alfred Hitchcock etc.

The crypto crowd was overwhelmingly young and male, and so it seemed obvious to use sports celebrities to win their love and trust. But even within the narrow world of sports, what people paid attention to struck Sam as arbitrary. For example, in the United States, everyone knew and cared about the names of the companies on their stadiums, but no one knew or cared about the names of the companies on their players' jerseys. There was no rule of human behavior that made this so: in Europe everyone knew and cared about the names on the players' jerseys but not about the corporation the stadium was named for. There was no moment at which Americans had agreed on the importance of the stadium sponsors: it had just somehow happened. "And once everyone agrees on what matters, it gets repeated," said Sam.

The initial general wariness of crypto money made it a bit trickier than it otherwise would have been to buy the naming rights for a professional sports arena. FTX tried and failed to sponsor the stadiums used by the Kansas City Chiefs and the New Orleans Saints. And so when someone from the Miami Heat reached out to them to suggest that FTX buy their naming rights, for $155 million for the next nineteen years, Sam leapt at the chance. That the deal required the approval not just of the NBA but also of the Miami-Dade Board of County Commissioners, a government body, was a bonus. After that, they could point to a government entity that had blessed FTX.

Once their name was on an American stadium, no one turned down their money.* They showered money across US pro sports: Shohei Ohtani and Shaquille O'Neal and LeBron James became spokespeople. They paid Major League Baseball $162.5 million to put the company name on every umpire's uniform. Having the FTX logo on the umpires' uniforms, Sam thought, was more useful than having it on the players' uniforms. In basically every TV shot of every Major League Baseball game, the viewer saw the FTX patch. "The NBA put us through a vetting process," said FTX lawyer Dan Friedberg. "Major League Baseball just said okay!"

Still, the idea that a person might find a product more desirable simply because some famous person lied and claimed that they used it struck Sam as dubious. "If you're buying something, do you really care what Baker Mayfield or Dak Prescott think?" he wrote to the random collection of FTX employees deputized to help him stew on the subject, as if no one had ever thought about it before. "If I told you that Baker Mayfield really liked some home insurance company, you'd probably update not at all."

It wasn't that celebrities didn't make a difference but how unpredictable were their effects: there was some mysterious interaction of person and product that, very occasionally, penetrated the public imagination. "Kevin Durant is a really good basketball player!" wrote Sam. "But you probably don't care which car he drives. But what if LeBron James drives a Tesla? I mean, sure you're probably not about to go out and get one, but I have to say that it would probably make me slightly more likely to eventually."

With some products, he decided, no celebrity could help. ("Could

---

* Steph Curry had at first declined but then changed his mind. Much later, it would be reported that Taylor Swift had turned down FTX's money. That wasn't quite true. FTX had an agreement with Swift to pay her between $25 and $30 million a year, but Sam dragged his feet on the deal. "She wanted to do it," said Natalie Tien, "but Sam kept postponing on response to her team." Another person intimately involved with the negotiation between Swift and FTX said, "Taylor did not turn it down. They were waiting for Sam to sign it when he didn't."

any endorsement deal make you much more excited to buy a Nissan? I'm not sure any could for me.") With others, it was a matter of who exactly was doing the endorsing. He came to see the problem as one of finding "one of the few people or things in the world that really move our imagination." And of all the things they did to promote the brand, only three things really mattered, he thought, and one mattered more than all the other things combined: Tom Brady.

You would think—Sam had initially thought—that if you were going to pay some NFL quarterback to stand up and say he used FTX, it would make little difference whether it was Tom Brady or Aaron Rodgers or Dak Prescott. You might see that Brady would be a bit better but think Rodgers's endorsement must be worth, say, half of Brady's. But everywhere Sam went, people mentioned that they had heard of FTX because of Brady. Hardly anyone mentioned any of the other endorsers. "It was very clear which things had an effect and which did not," said Sam. "For the life of me, I can't figure out why this is. I still don't know how to verbalize it." The Martian had discovered another weird but true fact of modern human life: at any given moment there were only a few people inside the collective imagination. "No one cares if Coinbase gets Russell Wilson as a spokesperson after we get Brady," Sam wrote in a memo to his team.[*]

From the outside, FTX appeared to be creating a brand around an oddly charismatic and possibly self-absorbed leader. The truth was even stranger. FTX was spending a fortune learning how to market a

---

[*] There was a price to hiring Tom Brady, over and above the $55 million they paid him, but at the time it seemed trivial: the bundled $19.8 million deal with Gisele Bündchen. With Gisele came a celebrity campaign, complete with a fashion marketing consultant, who quickly spun up her own ideas without a whole lot of supervision. It was through the consultant that, without Sam quite understanding how it happened, he found himself on the Zoom call with Anna Wintour, trying to figure out which Met the gala was in. Soon his face was plastered in fashion magazine spreads and at bus stops around the country—after which he fired the fashion marketing consultant. "It was all part of the celebrity deal with Gisele," said Natalie Tien, who by then was running Sam's media life. "Very cringe. No one at FTX liked the idea, including Sam himself."

product on the fly, without much input from anyone who had done it before. In one way, the approach clearly worked: in the mind of the American consumer, FTX became better and better known, and Sam Bankman-Fried became more and more famous. In another, it made little sense: FTX didn't really yet have much use for the American consumer. They'd opened a small exchange in the US on which American investors could do very little. The exchange's most important products, crypto futures, were illegal to sell to Americans. They were spending a lot of money on a business that might or might not happen.

Except for the psychiatrist, and a lawyer or two, there was still no one inside FTX who had much experience doing whatever it was they were doing, other than the experience they were gaining by doing it for FTX. No one saw any reason to make an exception for the architects. On a bike trip across the United States to raise money for a good cause, Ryan Salame had met an architect in her late twenties named Alfia White. One thing led to another, and before Alfia knew it, Ryan was asking her to design a vacation home for him in Bali. After Sam surprised Ryan by calling for the whole company to follow him to the Bahamas, Ryan scrambled for a place to put it. Not finding anything suitable as a permanent home, he hired Alfia to design FTX's new corporate headquarters. Alfia had never done anything like it.

She brought in a friend from architecture school named Ian Rosenfield to help. The curious thing about Ian, apart from the fact that he'd never designed office buildings either, was that he'd been a high school classmate of Sam's. He was shocked to discover that not only was Sam Bankman-Fried now one of the world's richest people, but he was also somehow working together with, and even managing, other human beings. Ian still had an image in his head of the brainiac no one knew chugging along by himself with the wheels of his rolly backpack clattering across the Crystal Springs Uplands School cobblestones.

Alfia and Ian traveled to the Bahamas, set themselves up inside an FTX conference room, and tried to figure out what to do. Sam had handed Ryan his checkbook and told him to buy office space and as much worker housing as fast as possible without worrying about the cost. No man was ever so good at not worrying about the cost as Ryan. In a matter of weeks, he had snapped up between $250 and $300 million in real estate, including $153 million worth of condos in an expensive new resort called Albany. To serve as temporary headquarters, he'd acquired a depressing office park of a dozen small buildings. They'd been planted on six acres of asphalt surrounded by a dense foliage that a scientist or a real estate developer would call a subtropical forest but which anyone stuck inside of it would call a jungle.*

Along the way, Ryan had paid $4.5 million to acquire, as a site for a new corporate headquarters, 4.95 acres of the jungle itself, on a narrow West Bay beach. He handed the land and a budget of several hundred million dollars to the young architects and basically said, "Have at it." A project that size normally called for a project manager and an owner's representative and assorted other wizened adults, but Ryan left the two young architects to handle it all on their own. "We were supposed to design a mini city," said Ian.

Before they could design a space to accommodate FTX, they needed to understand its structure and its rituals and its habits. To be FTX's architects, they'd also need to be FTX's anthropologists. Ian hadn't really known Sam in high school; now he and Alfia tried to figure out this enterprise he'd built. Sam himself, they soon realized, would be of no practical use. "Sam has no time," said Ian. "Sam delegates all this stuff to other people. From the start we tried to engage him, but he didn't engage. He said, 'You're the architects, I don't have any idea.' "

The mini city creators obviously had some questions needing answers. For example: "How many people will occupy this city?" Or:

---

* FTX also bought a fleet of maybe sixty vehicles. "I'd bought Sam a BMW," said Ryan. "He made me return it. I was like, 'Sam you're worth forty billion dollars. And these are bumpy roads.' But whatever."

"What does Sam want his mini city to look like?" But Sam wasn't interested in their questions, and by the time they arrived neither was Ryan. Ryan had moved back to the United States to help his new girlfriend run for Congress. The architects found themselves handed off to Nishad Singh's girlfriend, Claire Watanabe—who had assumed Ryan's role as spender of money and manager of support staff in the Bahamas. "We said just give us a list of the employees, give us anything," said Ian. "Claire said, 'I know it's weird, but we don't have any of that—even the number of employees.'"

Lacking direction from above, the architects set out to observe FTX's employees in the makeshift jungle huts they now occupied. Every now and then, they'd pull one of these incurious creatures aside to ask them how they had used their old Hong Kong offices. "They kept saying, you don't need to interview us, just design it how you want to design it," said Alfia. That was obviously a dumb idea; even people who said they didn't care about the spaces they inhabited ended up caring, sometimes without realizing that they did. "They don't care what it looks like until they see it," said Alfia. There'd been a knock-down, drag-out argument in the old Hong Kong office about the placement of a single door, for instance. "A woman said it needed to be removed for feng shui, and a guy said no, he wanted it, and the argument escalated," said Ian. Eliminating the doorway in a Hong Kong office building to satisfy one employee, and adding another to satisfy another, had cost a million dollars. "It was the million-dollar door," said Ian.

The architects watched and listened and learned. They could see that these FTX people, like their leader, essentially lived in the office. Sam famously slept on the beanbag chair beside his desk in Hong Kong, but Nishad, too, had made a bed under his desk. Ordinary employees who thought that to be as successful as Sam was they must live as Sam did were starving themselves of sleep and occupying the workspace in unhealthy ways. One employee had gone thirty days without once leaving the Hong Kong office. The office needed showers and sleep spaces; food, clothing, and other material needs must be satisfied as efficiently as possible, to minimize the downtime. "They get anything they want," said Ian, "but it gets delivered to their desk. The Amazon box storage room hardly gets used." That half the employees of the company were East Asian had to be taken into account (everything would be subject to feng shui), but the off-the-charts nerd factor mattered even more. "What they want is power outlets—all over the place," said Alfia. If the building had windows, it must also have good blinds, to prevent the glare from obscuring their computer screens. "They love their shades down," said Ian. They were either all alone at their desks or all together in a big space, engaged in nerd recreations, and seldom anything in between. They needed a big space for LARPing (live-action role-play) but told the architects that they could really do that anywhere.

And they pretty much all shared, or said they shared, their boss's utter indifference to grace or beauty. "I've observed other tech employees, and these people are different," said Ian. "They care even less about aesthetics and amenities." The only sight that the FTX employees all wanted was of their boss. Status in the company was measured by proximity to Sam. Even from their jungle huts people jockeyed for a view of him. The architects schemed the main building with glass walls and mezzanines that offered unlikely interior views of Sam. "It gives you an opportunity to catch glimpses of Sam no matter where you are sitting," said Ian.

In their quest to understand this strange new company, the architects nagged enough people that finally someone sent them a note with what they'd asked for in the first place: a list of what Sam Bankman-Fried wanted in his corporate mini city. "There were only three things on it," said Ian. Sam wanted the building shaped like an *F*, for the benefit of the people in the planes descending into Lynden Pindling International Airport. He wanted the side of the building to evoke his unruly hair. Unlikely as that sounded, Ian thought that it was just possible—they could use CNC cut aluminum to abstractly mimic what he was now calling "Sam's Jewfro." "It wasn't actually a bad idea," said Ian.

The third and final item on the list of Sam's desires was the tungsten cube. The tungsten cube was a bit of a head-scratcher. The imaginations of crypto people everywhere, it turned out, had been gripped by tungsten cubes. Tungsten, the architects now learned, was the planet's trendiest dense metal. Crypto people were then memeing about "the intensity of the density." A company in the Midwest had supposedly created the world's biggest tungsten cube. A mere fourteen inches, it had cost a quarter of a million dollars and weighed two thousand pounds. Sam had apparently ordered up such a cube, flown it into the Bahamas, and wanted it displayed on a plinth in his mini city. The architects never were shown Sam's dense and precious cube, but they nevertheless incorporated it into their drawings. "We designed a space for it," said Ian. That space was the big atrium in the city's main building. The tungsten cube would be the first thing a visitor to the global crypto empire would see. Rising from the sea of abstraction, the earth's most concrete object.

Other than Sam's list, the architects had no guidance. This puzzled the architects, as the decisions they were making would be set in stone. These were, after all, buildings. Once erected, they would be unresponsive to any new thoughts Sam might have about their expected value. Twice inside of three years, he'd moved his entire company nine thousand miles. Their mini city was meant to serve as the headquarters for a global financial empire, but the most likely way for FTX to become a global financial empire was for the US regulators to give it permission to set up shop in the United States. In which case Sam almost certainly would move the company to the United States—and this mini city would be, at most, some satellite office. "It has to feel comfortable if it's for six hundred people or for ten people," said Ian delicately.

Instead of guidance, what the architects were given was a deadline. They were to prepare the five acres of jungle, together with a slide-show of photos of the imagined buildings, for a big public announcement. Incredibly, they were ready for it when it happened, on April 25, 2022. They'd cleared the jungle without a permit and sketched out their designs without help. Beside the freshly shaven five-acre bald patch of jungle, they'd erected a billboard, with a picture of the mini city and a slogan, FTX: GROWTH IN PROGRESS. The Bahamas media assembled. The new prime minister arrived, with an entourage. A big group of FTXers appeared, carrying shovels, likely for the first time in their lives, with which to break ceremonial ground. And from a car that also carried FTX's COO, Constance Wang, Sam emerged, looking as if he had fallen out of a dumpster: cargo shorts, wrinkled T-shirt, droopy white socks. *Same guy*, thought Ian.

From the moment he had started on the project and begun to observe Sam from afar, Ian had found the same thought often crossing his mind: how shockingly just like he'd been in high school Sam still was. When the oddball in your high school class became one of the richest people in the world, you sort of assumed the oddball must have changed. Sam hadn't changed. The world around him had.

Before the groundbreaking ceremony, Sam was meant to give a speech. Ian thought he might need some help, and so before the proceedings, he pulled him aside.

What have you seen of the design? asked Ian.

I've seen nothing, said Sam.

Have you at least seen the plans?

Nope.

Huh, thought Ian. How would Sam give a speech about his new mini city if he knew nothing about his new mini city?

What are you going to say?

I'll just wing it, said Sam.

Which he did. By changing the subject. He did this a lot. Tossed a question he didn't want or know how to answer, Sam simply turned it into one that he was happy to answer. The question he wanted to answer that day was not "What is this mini city, and why does it look as it does?" It was "Why did you come to the Bahamas?"

At some point the architects realized that Sam had no clue what they'd designed, or that they'd designed anything at all. That they'd made all the decisions about FTX's new headquarters, projected to cost hundreds of millions of dollars, without the slightest input from the person who was paying for it. Soon they'd learn that even the list of Sam's desires they'd been given had not come from Sam— and that Sam himself wasn't aware that he had stated any desires. The list had been created by someone else inside FTX who'd tried to imagine what perhaps he himself might want in his new office buildings, were he Sam. Sam didn't want his Jewfro on the side of the building. This other person had just imagined that "Jewfro on the side of the building" was the kind of thing Sam might find amusing. The tungsten cube had been a cool idea, but, really, what were the odds that Sam or anyone else bought and shipped into the Bahamas a one-ton cube? If the cube existed, why hadn't the architects ever seen it? "I don't even know if it was ever actually bought," said Ian, of this thing he had designed a building around. Only in the context of FTX was this not bizarre. "Everyone was always making decisions for Sam," said Ian.

At the end of the ceremony, Sam lingered a bit. Ian seized the moment to finally ask him directly the question he'd been trying for months to ask.

What's one thing you want out of these buildings, other than work?

For the first time, Sam thought about it. *Badminton courts*, he said. That was it. That was all he wanted. Badminton courts.

How many courts? asked Ian.

Three, said Sam. Then he left.

"That was the first and only question we got to ask him," said Ian.

It was, of course, George Lerner's job to listen to people's problems. Really, he tried. By the spring of 2022, he'd set up his small office inside one of the jungle huts. A simple desk, a red sofa across from it, and, in the corner, a baby blue beanbag chair, which everyone understood was Sam's spot. George's door was open to anyone who wanted to talk, but it wasn't long before he was weary of how many people wanted to talk to him, and why. "There were a bunch of people unhappy in the Bahamas," he said. The Asian guys wanted more Asian women to date. The Asian women didn't like the Asian guys available. "Everyone is complaining about the lack of dating opportunities," said George. "Except the EAs. The EAs didn't care."

The non-EAs thought the EAs thought they were smarter than everybody else. A lot of people were unhappy with Sam's radically hands-off approach to management. The Asians especially were confused by the lack of an organization chart. A surprising number of people who were meant to report directly to Sam had discovered how little Sam wanted to be reported to by them. "There are a lot of people Sam would avoid," said George. "People thought they could use me to get to him. Other people talked to me because they couldn't talk to Sam. This was super annoying."

The Bahamas hadn't granted George a medical license. His title was Senior Professional Coach. This was actually the role he'd always played for Sam—who would inevitably prefer to talk through his business problems rather than his psychological ones, which he viewed as intractable and thus pointless to discuss. Now, in the Bahamas, George took to his new role as management consultant. From employee therapy sessions he absorbed information about the company whose CEO he was now advising. Complaints from the employees suggested that Sam either wasn't managing the people he was meant to manage or was doing it so badly that he might as well not be doing it. "I felt there were way too many people reporting to Sam," said George.

A few months into his new job, George had seen one hundred of FTX's three hundred something employees. He enjoyed maybe the single best view of its corporate architecture, with a clarity not available to its investors, its customers, its employees, and, possibly, the person who had created it. "Sam didn't like people to have job descriptions," said George. "Everyone knew that he hated org charts." Everyone also knew that, as much as they might long for an important-sounding title for themselves, Sam hated those too. He had written a memo to explain why. "Thoughts On Titles," he called it. "In the past few years, we've found that titles can make people sub-stantially worse at FTX," it began. Sam then listed some reasons why this might be so:

a) Having a title makes people feel less willing to take advice from those without titles.
b) Having a title makes people less likely to put in the effort to learn how to do well at the base-level jobs of people they're managing. They end up trying to manage people whose jobs they couldn't do, and that always goes poorly.
c) Having titles can create significant conflicts between your ego and the company.
d) Having titles can piss off colleagues.

Be that as it may, George felt he needed to know where his patients stood in the organization. "I didn't understand the different relation-ships, and I needed to, because a lot of people were coming to me with conflicts," he said. "I needed to see if what I was hearing made sense." Sam had turned his organization into a puzzle; his psychiatrist set out to solve it.

In the end, George drew up the only internal org chart ever made of Sam's sprawling creation. (See inside of dust jacket.) By the time he was done, he'd discovered many interesting things. Twenty-four differ-ent people thought that they were reporting directly to Sam, for exam-ple. The group included Sam's father, Joe, and Sam's childhood friend Matt Nass, whose game, *Storybook Brawl*, Sam had for some reason just bought. This group did not include the chief financial officer, because FTX did not have a chief financial officer. There was no chief risk offi-cer or head of human resources, because they had none of that, either. "It seems like a clubhouse more than a corporation," said George.

It did have a chief technology officer, Gary Wang, but Gary was socially isolated, with no one reporting to him. "Gary was off in his own little box," said George. In an ordinary tech company, a bunch of programmers would be reporting to the chief technology officer.

In FTX they apparently all reported to Nishad Singh. Ryan Salame, who had come and gone from the Bahamas in a flash and now seemed hardly involved with the company, was somehow the CEO of the entire international business, with twenty-seven people reporting to him. Ramnik Arora, whose official title was still Head of Product, clearly had nothing to do with product but sat on top of a small pile of people in charge of both raising and investing vast sums of money. George just put him in a little box marked "Ventures." About half the entire company reported to the first two young women Sam had hired upon his arrival in Hong Kong, Constance Wang and Jen Chan. Most of those people, George noted, were East Asian women.

Then there was Caroline Ellison. Caroline was apparently alone in charge of the twenty-two traders and developers working inside Alameda Research, about half of whom had followed Sam from Hong Kong to the Bahamas. This surprised George a bit. "She never said anything about Alameda," said George. "Neither did Sam. This was clearly wanting *not* to think about it."

In a memo dated February 6, 2022, and titled "Thoughts," Caroline had listed half a dozen ideas to improve her relationship with Sam. "Couples counselling with Lerner" was number three, in between "choose a point in the future at which to decide whether to break up" and "resolve to communicate better in the future." By the time she'd followed Sam to the Bahamas, their affair was going even more poorly than usual. On the night of April 15—ten days before they broke ground on the new corporate headquarters—they sat down to discuss their future. The next day, Caroline summarized their discussion in a memo to Sam:

- Caroline plan
  ◦ I quit Alameda and move back to the United States
- SBF plan
  ◦ break up, stay friends, try to cause as little drama
    as possible

That night, they'd argued about the wisdom of her continuing to run Sam's private hedge fund-cum-dragon's lair, as opposed to doing something else with her life. "Running Alameda doesn't feel like something I'm *that* comparatively advantaged at or well suited to do," she now wrote. ". . . I feel like I need to do a ton of things I'm not very good at . . . But yeah, I think it's plausible that running Alameda is super high EV and way higher than my next best option. I think I shouldn't consider quitting Alameda until I've spent a lot of time thinking about alternative options and their EV."

What Caroline would consider doing, and right away, was ceasing to sleep with Sam. She didn't want to move out of their bedroom in the $30 million penthouse condo purchased by Ryan that they now shared with eight other effective altruists, including Nishad and Gary. It was Sam who needed to move, furtively, into a lesser condo in the same compound. Inside the company, hardly anyone other than the few EAs Caroline had shared the secret of the relationship with had been aware that the CEOs of FTX and Alameda Research were romantically involved. "People never see what they're not looking for," said Sam. Now they didn't see that the romance had ended. Having hidden the relationship, Sam now hid that he'd broken it off, along with the fact that he was living in a different place than everyone assumed he was living. At that moment he was, in a funny way, making a truth of two lies. As it happened, it was the moment before crypto prices crashed. And also, oddly enough, the moment that I turned up to watch.

ACT III

8

THE DRAGON'S HOARD

One of the first things I noticed about Sam Bankman-Fried was how easy he was to steal from. On that early morning in late April of 2022, just about anyone could have walked right into his jungle hut and taken whomever or whatever they wanted. The guard booth fronting FTX's temporary global headquarters was unmanned. The parking lot barrier gate extended less than halfway across the entrance road and so was more an idea of an obstacle than an actual one. The door to jungle hut number 27, where Sam worked, was unlocked, and the receptionist's desk was vacant. I'd soon be asking Nishad Singh for the same premortem I'd ask of others at the top of their psychiatrist's org chart: "Imagine we're in the future and your company has collapsed: tell me how it happened." "Someone kidnaps Sam," Nishad would reply immediately, before unspooling his recurring nightmare of Sam's lax attitude toward his personal safety leading to the undoing of their empire. At that moment, it seemed reasonable that he should worry more about this than about other risks. Sam was a famous and easily trackable rich person who moved around without bodyguards while in possession of billions of dollars' worth of various cryptocurrencies, which, while not all that useful as a means of exchange, made for excellent ransom. "People with access to crypto are prime kidnap targets," said Nishad. "I cannot understand why it doesn't happen more."

The only tricky part would have been figuring out which hut Sam was in. FTX's headquarters now consisted of a dozen or so identical small single-story buildings painted tan, with dull metal roofs the color of milk chocolate. Whoever had built them had started by giving up on the idea of decoration, or charm of any sort. Nothing on the outside of any of them indicated which might house the people worth kidnapping. Of course at this hour, seven in the morning, that might not have mattered, as there were so few people. There was a fair chance that Sam was the only human being in any of the buildings, and so the hunter would only need to go from hut to hut until he found his prey. Sam would be helpless. He wasn't built to escape, or even to notice, a physical threat.

However, he wasn't there when I arrived. Nishad was, though he barely looked up when I sat down beside him at Sam's desk. A small mountain of objects that covered the desk spilled out onto the beanbag chair beside it. While Nishad typed away, I picked through the items and made an inventory:

One giant canister of Morton salt
One iPhone box with new phone still inside it
One crumpled one-dollar bill
Four fidget spinners
One deck of playing cards
One pillow and one blanket
Two large half-opened cardboard boxes filled with Miami Heat jerseys
One box cutter
One open bottle of unscented mosquito repellent in a sealed plastic bag
Four manila folders containing confidential corporate documents requiring Sam's signature

One LiftMaster automatic garage door opener

A second new iPhone box with phone inside

One ceremonial medal, presented to Sam Bankman-Fried by Francis Suarez, mayor of the city of Miami

A dozen square plastic boxes of unclear purpose inscribed with the message *FTX: Welcome to your new world of payments*

Three pairs of chopsticks

One key card to a Ritz-Carlton hotel room

One handheld Gaiatop fan

One abnormal Rubik's Cube, with all squares painted white

I was about halfway through the pile when Sam appeared. I had the briefest sensation of being discovered by a teenager while taking in the chaos they'd made in their bedroom. If he was curious how I'd gotten into his office, or why I was now picking through the contents of his desk, he didn't show it. Something new was up.

If there was any rule governing Sam's life, it was that it was never allowed to bore him. "He's like Kanye," said a Sam watcher who also spent time with Kanye West. "Wherever he goes, all this wild shit just happens." That day—the morning I turned up at his desk and took an inventory—wild shit was happening. Elon Musk was buying Twitter and Sam had been on the phone with one of Musk's advisors, Igor Kurganov. Kurganov was a Russian-born former professional poker player to whom Musk had entrusted the task, it was reported, of giving away more than $5 billion worth of his fortune. He was also a self-described effective altruist, thickening the plot. He and Sam had just spoken of the possibility that Sam might help to pay for the Twitter purchase. As it turned out, Sam had already sunk $100 million into Twitter shares and entertained a private fantasy of finding some way to buy the rest. Most of them he'd bought at $33 a share, or $21.20 a share less than Musk had just agreed to pay for the entire company.

When there was something new to buy, Sam often found it useful to talk it over with Ramnik and Nishad. Both were smart, at least in the high-IQ way that Sam understood. Both also had a curious abil-

ity to disagree with Sam without making a big deal about it, or forcing him to feel that he actually had to listen to whatever they said.
After talking to them, Sam could tell himself that he'd checked his
judgment without having done so. Now he grabbed them both and
pulled them into what passed in the jungle hut for a meeting room.
It had a single chair and a sofa, upon which Sam stretched, barefoot,
a fidget spinner on his chest. Ramnik and Nishad sat down on the
floor, cross-legged. All three wore short pants, and in the room, for a
moment, it felt like nap time for a small class of restless first graders.
But then Sam explained what he wanted to talk about: Elon Musk
really was going to buy Twitter, but he didn't really want to pay for it
himself. He was looking for allies to pick up some of the $44 billion it
was going to cost. *They want us among them. But we only have three hours
to get back to them.*

"What do you get out of this?" asked Nishad, reasonably.

"There's some random shit," said Sam, then made it clear that
the most important random shit was a new alliance with Elon Musk.
Crypto lived on Twitter, and Musk was Twitter's loudest voice. With a
single tweet, Musk could trigger a stampede of crypto traders from
Coinbase to FTX, or the reverse. He also controlled the world's biggest private fortune and, by employing Igor Kurganov, was signaling
a willingness to direct some of it to EA causes.

"How much are we thinking?" asked Ramnik.

"Maybe a billion," said Sam. An uneasy look crossed Ramnik's face
and then vanished.

"But maybe as low as two hundred and fifty million," said Sam. A
pittance. A mere extra $150 million on top of the $100 million worth
of Twitter stock they already owned, and which they could just roll
into the deal.

"Can we actually talk to Elon?' asked Nishad. "Does it actually lead
to EA stuff?"

"He's a weird dude," said Sam. He stared at the ceiling. One hand
fidgeted with his spinner, the other twirled a tube of ChapStick. The
wall behind him was one big window. Outside, a small wan palm

tree bent in the wind. Beyond, on a field of asphalt, several young engineers paced and counted their steps. "If he's primarily wanting money, there are a lot of people he could get it from," said Sam. "He could syndicate it in a week. It's not the dollar amount. It's about who has been nice to him and who hasn't."

Down on the floor, Nishad looked dubious. Ramnik, beside him, was harder to read.

"It will put us more on the map," said Sam.

"Is there anything for which being even *more* on the map is useful right now?" said Nishad.

Sam clearly thought so. Twitter fascinated him. It had turned out to be the single best way for a person like him to communicate with a mass audience. On Twitter, all the problems he had with people one-on-one evaporated. "It's moved markets five times more than anything else out there," he said. "It's a very specific brand."

"Would it be impolite to say seventy-five million?" asked Nishad.

"Twitter has two hundred thirty million daily active users," said Ramnik. "If you could get eighty million of them to pay for it— say, five bucks a month—that's four hundred million in revenues a month." Ramnik did this sometimes. He'd offer thoughts to buttress arguments Sam wanted to make, even if Ramnik himself would rather he not make them.

"This is sort of a hilarious dynamic," said Nishad, interrupting the new train of thought. "Elon treating us as a proxy investment vehicle."

They kicked the decision around only a bit longer. The entire discussion took no more than fifteen minutes. At some point Sam simply decided they'd spent time enough for every possible useful thought on the subject to be had and asked for a vote from the other two.

"No," said Nishad.

"No, or a very low amount," said Ramnik.

With that, the meeting ended. What I did not realize—but both Nishad and Ramnik by now both just took for granted—was that Sam might still hand over some large sum of money to Elon Musk. He was perfectly capable of asking for a vote and then ignoring the result. Sure enough, all by himself, Sam would soon ask Morgan Stanley, which was advising on and helping to finance Musk's Twitter purchase, if they would be willing to lend him a billion dollars to invest in Twitter and accept his shares in FTX as collateral. He would also message one of Musk's financial advisors to say he'd be willing to invest $5 billion if Musk was willing to move Twitter onto a blockchain. Twitter, like other social media platforms, was on an island without any connection to the others; if you put them on blockchains, they could all be linked up with each other. When Musk refused, Sam lost interest and decided to invest nothing at all. Six months later, he wouldn't even know if he still owned $100 million worth of Twitter, or if the shares had been sold to Elon Musk.

No one person had the full picture of the puzzle Sam had made out of money. Ramnik likely had the clearest view of it, but even his view was partial. Inside of three years, Sam would deploy roughly $5 billion on a portfolio of three hundred separate investments— which worked out to a new investment decision roughly every three days. If Sam spent only twenty minutes or so deciding whether to sink a billion dollars into Twitter, it was because twenty minutes was all he could spare: so many other investment decisions awaited. He'd invest in new crypto tokens, like Solana, and old companies, like Anthony Scaramucci's investment firm, SkyBridge. He'd acquire companies obviously relevant to FTX—a Japanese crypto exchange called Liquid, for instance—and companies that had no obvious connection to crypto, like the studio that had developed *Storybook Brawl*. The money nearly always came not from FTX but from Alameda Research, which Ramnik and everyone else thought of as Sam's private fund. Often Ramnik was intimately involved with a purchase, but nearly as often he only learned what Sam had done after the fact. Sam had invested $500 million in an artificial intelligence start-up called Anthropic, apparently without bouncing the idea off anyone else. "I said to Sam after he did it, 'We don't know a fucking thing about this company,'" said Ramnik. About the same time that he was trying to decide whether to sink more money into Twitter, Sam was handing $450 million to a former Jane Street trader named Lily Zhang, to create a second crypto quant trading fund based in the Bahamas, called Modulo Capital. So far as Ramnik could see, Sam had told no one about that until he'd done it. Back in March, Sam had promised to invest $5 *billion* with a Hollywood agent turned investment manager named Michael Kives, without consulting Ramnik or anyone else. Sam had only met Kives a few weeks before he'd made that commitment. He'd known nothing about him, not even how to pronounce his name.

When they heard that Sam was about to hurl $5 billion at a total stranger, Ramnik and others inside FTX became alarmed. With a lot of help from FTX's lawyers, Ramnik and Nishad had argued the $5 billion down to $500 million—or at least they thought that's what Sam had agreed to. Much later, Ramnik learned that Sam, as usual, simply did what he wanted to do, and pledged to invest $3 billion in various Kives-run investment funds. "I think Sam's too trusting," said Ramnik. "He's too trusting too early."

A lot of what got done inside Sam's world got done without the usual checks and balances. Others found it hard to complain too loudly. The deals seemed to involve only Sam's money: Why shouldn't Sam be able to do with it whatever he pleased? Still, there couldn't be many other cases in human history of a person his age tossing around dollars in the amounts he was tossing them without much adult supervision, or the usual constraints of corporate life. A board of directors, for instance. "It's unclear if we even have to have an actual board of directors," said Sam, "but we get suspicious glances if we don't have one, so we have something with three people on it." When he said this to me, right after his Twitter meeting, he admitted he couldn't recall the names of the other two people. "I knew who they were three months ago," he said. "It might have changed. The main job requirement is they don't mind DocuSigning at three a.m. DocuSigning is the main job." Then there was the CFO. For the past eighteen months, various venture capitalists whom Sam had permitted to invest in FTX had been telling him that he should hire a serious grown-up to act as the company's chief financial officer. "There's a functional religion around the CFO," said Sam. "I'll ask them, 'Why do I need one?' Some people cannot articulate a single thing the CFO is supposed to do. They'll say 'keep track of the money,' or 'make projections.' I'm like, *What the fuck do you think I do all day? You think I don't know how much money we have?*"

Back in Hong Kong, with The Schism still in mind, Sam had briefly entertained the idea that it might be useful to have some older people around. "We tried having some grown-ups, but they didn't do anything," he said. "This was true for everyone over the age of forty-five. All they did was worry. Here's a classic grown-up thing: you freak the fuck out about a Chinese government crackdown on crypto in Hong Kong. Their job was to be serious about problems even if the problems were not serious. And they weren't able to identify serious problems. They were terrified of regulators. Or taxes! Not that we wouldn't pay it, but we'd pay too much, and then we'd have a loss the next year, but we'd already paid our taxes." It wasn't that Sam didn't want to minimize his tax bill, or that the Chinese might not at any moment swoop in and grab him and toss him in prison. It was that the odds of the bad thing happening were low, and any time spent thinking about it was wasted. "It was a random series of completely disassociated concerns, most of which were really overblown, stated very forcefully," said Sam. "The only way to calm them down was for a new concern to come along and distract them from the other ones."

The truth was that grown-ups bored him. All they did was slow him down.

A few months later, toward the end of July 2022, I met Sam beside the tarmac of a private airfield in Northern California. I'd driven there from my home; he had come from a brief retreat with the leaders of effective altruism where they'd talked about how to spend Sam's money. As usual, he was late. When he finally arrived, he didn't so much step as tumble out of the back of a black car. Instead of a suitcase, he carried what appeared to be a small pile of old laundry.

As he drew closer, I saw that it was a blue suit and a button-down Brooks Brothers shirt. "This is my DC suit," he said, almost apologetically. "Normally I leave it in DC." Six hours in the future he was meant to have dinner with Senate minority leader Mitch McConnell, whom he'd never met. He'd been briefed that McConnell would be offended if he arrived in shorts. "McConnell really cares about what you wear," said Sam, as he walked up the steps of the private plane and plopped the suit ball onto a spare seat. "Also, you need to call him 'Leader.' Or 'Leader McConnell' or 'Mister Leader.' I rehearsed it to make sure I didn't fuck it up. Especially since it's so tempting to say 'Dear Leader.'"

I eyed the ball of clothes. Its wrinkles were not new and shallow but old and deep, reversible only with time and effort. It was hard to see how these clothes would be of any use in this situation.

"Do you have a belt?" I asked.

"I do not have a belt," he said, as he reached into a basket of vegan snacks, grabbed a sack of popcorn, and dropped into his seat.

"Shoes?"

"Uh, no shoes," he said.

It was as if he'd only received a single explicit instruction: "Bring a suit." Whoever had sent it had neglected to add, "Make sure it's wearable and that you have whatever else you need to satisfy Mitch McConnell's need for his dinner companions to appear formally dressed," and so Sam had not bothered to consider what else might be needed for a suit if it were to be successfully worn. He did this kind of thing a lot. Seven months earlier, he'd testified about crypto regulation before the House Financial Services Committee. Someone snapped a close-up of his feet under the table: the laces of his new dress shoes were still swaddled and gathered off to one side, as they come in the box. Someone must have handed him the shoes and said, without further instruction, "You should put these on."

At any rate, this one item set Sam's trips to Washington, DC, apart from all the other trips he took. Only to DC did he carry a suit: the stakes justified the sacrifice. In recent decades, the laws in the

United States had been loosened so that people and even corporations could donate effectively unlimited sums of money to political campaigns and super PACs, without the larger American public being able to see exactly what they were doing, or why. What surprised Sam, once he himself had unlimited sums of money, was how slowly rich people and corporations had adapted to their new political environment. The US government exerted massive influence on virtually everything under the sun and maybe even a few things over it. In a single four-year term, a president, working with Congress, directed roughly $15 trillion in spending. And yet in 2016, the sum total of spending by all candidates on races for the presidency and Congress came to a mere $6.5 billion. "It just seems like there isn't enough money in politics," said Sam. "People are underdoing it. The weird thing is that Warren Buffett isn't giving two billion dollars a year."

Inside United States politics, Sam was creating yet another money puzzle: even after he'd poured billions into various venture capital investments, he was willing to spend hundreds of millions more to influence public policy. Later, everything he did would be reinterpreted more cynically than it was in real time, but even in real time a lot of people had their questions about him, and a lot of the questions missed the point. His political spending was distributed sloppily into three buckets. The first, and smallest, bucket contained his narrow business interests: a few million dollars donated to politicians and interest groups willing to push for legislation that would allow Americans to trade the crypto contracts on FTX inside the United States that foreigners did on FTX outside of it. It struck him as yet another strange and senseless feature of the grown-up world that the United States, which was otherwise willing to subject its poorest and most vulnerable citizens to state lotteries and casinos and other games of chance in which the odds were stacked against them, made an exception for securities, or anything that might be construed as securities. But those were the rules of this new game, and Sam had decided, with some doubts about their tractability, to try to change them—rather than do what the other crypto exchanges were doing, which was simply to ignore them.

Oddly, the money he gave to people to make it easier for him to make even more money was the easiest money for others to see. All of it without a whole lot of trouble could be traced back to Sam, or FTX or crypto interest groups. It was the other two buckets—the money that had little to do with his own narrow financial interests—that were opaque. His attempts to change the world as he thought the world needed to be changed had little to do with his business. But to be effective, he had to hide what he was doing, lest others assume that the point of giving was to shape crypto legislation. In some not unreasonable minds, "crypto" was synonymous with "criminal." "The problem was that if it were disclosed, everyone would assume that it was crypto money," he said. Crypto money was harder to give away than it should have been, in Sam's opinion. Politicians and interest groups didn't always like the look of accepting it, even if they weren't quite sure what that look was. "There isn't anything concrete there," said Sam. "They're just uncomfortable." Their discomfort could lead to strange outcomes. "We had one group say, 'You know, we really appreciate this, but it wouldn't be good for me to take money from FTX, so I can't—besides, I have found another source of funding.' That other source of funding was Gabe, my brother."

In Sam's mind, his money wasn't crypto money. It was effective altruist money that he happened to have obtained through crypto. Along with his brother, Sam had looked at the world and decided that two EA-related causes made more sense to address with his money than any of the others. And that a lot of the money needed to be sneaky.

Their first, less sneaky initiative was pandemic prevention. On the list of existential risks to humanity, pandemics occupied a special place. Unlike, say, with an asteroid strike, the threat felt real, and politicians could be persuaded to take it seriously. Unlike, say, with climate change, hardly anyone was talking or thinking seriously about how to address the problem—even after a million Americans had just died from a new pathogen. Unlike, say, in preventing a war on humanity by artificial intelligence, there were some obvious though expensive things to do to mitigate the risk. For instance, someone really did need to take the lead in the creation of a global system of disease prediction, one that resembled the global system of weather prediction. Sam guessed that it would take $100 billion, which put it beyond his reach. "If it were ten times smaller, it's possible I could just do it myself," he said. "If FTX winds up six times bigger than we are today, we'd have to recompute that." He might not have the money right now to do it himself, but he did have the money to persuade the US government to do it. This very issue was the stated, though not perhaps the biggest, reason for his dinner with Mitch McConnell: to discuss an initiative to allocate $10 billion for pandemic response to an entity inside the Department of Health and Human Services called the Biomedical Advanced Research and Development Authority. McConnell was a Republican and in theory hostile to big government expenditures. But Sam had already decided that these politicians were far more complex devices than their tribal identities might suggest. "He's a polio survivor," said Sam. "And we think he's interested."

Badgering elected officials into taking an interest in pandemics was one part of Sam's strategy. The second part was getting some new pandemic warriors elected to Congress. Sam's political operation had figured out, or thought they had, that it made a lot more sense to spend money in primary than in general elections. Voters could be swayed in primaries as they couldn't in generals. Much of persuasion in primaries was just name recognition, which you could buy with ads. They'd also already figured out, or thought they had, that a million dollars dropped into a close congressional primary gave them a one-in-five chance of swinging it to their candidate. The problem was that they had no way to determine in advance which of the five they'd be able to influence. And so they'd adopted a strategy of finding as many congressional candidates as they could who would support spending on pandemic prevention and buying their elections in bulk, while at the same time doing their best to disguise that the money involved had anything to do with crypto.

Of course, winning one out of five congressional races meant you lost the other four. Sam's political portfolio resembled his venture capital portfolio: in pursuit of crazy rewards, it took what, after the fact, looked like insane risks. In a very short time, Sam's money had bankrolled some of the most spectacular failures in the history of political manipulation.

Carrick Flynn, for example. When Sam stumbled upon him, Carrick Flynn was a newcomer to elective politics. He was the quintessential Washington, DC, policy wonk—one of the faceless minions in blue suits who sit along the wall behind the more important people and occasionally rise and whisper something in their ears. Carrick Flynn's most important trait, in Sam's view, was his total command of and commitment to pandemic prevention. His second-most important trait was that he was an effective altruist. He could be counted on to follow the math rather than woolly-minded feelings. Conveniently, he had recently moved from DC to a newly created left-leaning congressional district outside Portland, Oregon. The seat felt so up for grabs that fifteen other candidates would eventually jump into the race. Flynn asked some fellow EAs what they thought about him running for Congress. As a political candidate he had obvious weaknesses: in addition to being a Washington insider and a bit of a carpetbagger, he was terrified of public speaking and sensitive to criticism. He described himself as "very introverted." And yet none of the EAs could see any good reason for him not to go for it—and so he'd thrown his hat into the ring. Somewhere along the EA trail he'd become known to Sam. He had a sense that Sam might support him, but he had no idea what that meant. The writer Dave Weigel captured the moment he learned, in the opening of an article in the *Washington Post*:

"We were watching a YouTube video together, a tutorial about something," said Flynn, sitting with his wife, Kathryn Mecrow-

Flynn, after a U.S. Chamber of Commerce breakfast last week, where he and other Democratic congressional candidates heard a presentation on suburban crime.

"All of a sudden, we hear a voice say CARRICK FLYNN!" remembered Mecrow-Flynn.

"And I had water in my hand," said Flynn.

Mecrow-Flynn corrected him. "Mountain Dew," she said.

"It would have been Diet Mountain Dew," Flynn said, more confidently.

Whatever he was drinking, Flynn had, at the sound of his own name in a paid political advertisement, spilled it all over himself. It was the first fusillade in the political equivalent of the D-Day invasion. Sam's political team took *ten million dollars* of Sam's money, jammed it into bazookas, and fired it into the Portland suburbs. This little primary became the most expensive in Oregon history. Then it became the third most expensive House Democratic primary in the entire country. Sam's attempt to turn Carrick Flynn into a congressman was less a political campaign than an assault on the senses of the local population. "Being in it really did feel like being in an episode of *Veep*," said Tess Seger, who ran the campaign of a rival Democrat. "The people who report on the Trail Blazers were literally complaining how many Carrick Flynn ads there were. The whole thing was kind of done unartfully."

The effects of artlessness in politics are not predictable, but what happened next made a kind of sense. People figured out where the money was coming from to buy all these Carrick Flynn ads. The other eight Democrats in the primary joined hands to denounce Carrick Flynn. "Mr. Creepy Funds," one of them called him. "This is a Bahamas billionaire trying to buy a congressional district in Oregon," said another. And it was! Sam was trying to buy a seat in Congress so that Congress might finally begin to address an existential risk to humanity. The people of Oregon not only did not appreciate the effort; a lot of them started to kind of hate Carrick Flynn. And Carrick Flynn was not designed to ignore their feelings. Attacked by other candidates during a debate, he simply walked out in the middle. His public statements began to strike even his financial backers as erratic and unwise. "He got really wounded when people said mean things about him," said Sam. "He insulted owls at one point, not realizing that there's a huge owl constituency in Oregon."[*]

In the end, which came on May 17, 2022, Carrick Flynn received 19 percent of the popular vote and finished a respectable but distant second to Andrea Salinas, who won with 37 percent of the vote. For every vote Carrick Flynn won, Sam had spent just a bit less than a thousand dollars. He actually didn't mind all that much. He'd learned a lesson: there were political candidates no amount of money could get elected. "There are limits to what money can buy," said Sam.

Anyway, to Sam, the money he'd spent on Carrick Flynn had been a drop in his second bucket. Other congressional races had worked out better. He also had one other and even more promising bucket—a vessel for political spending that was yet harder to see into than the other two. So that voters would not know where the money had come from, this bucket would be largely controlled by Mitch McConnell, or friends of Mitch McConnell. So that the disguise would be legal, Sam and McConnell would not talk about how the bucket would be used. But the bucket was very much the subtext of the dinner Sam was headed to, because in McConnell, Sam had found someone as interested as he was in another existential threat to humanity: Donald Trump. Trump's assault on the government, and on the integrity of US elections, belonged, to Sam's

---

[*] On a podcast, Flynn took the side of an alt-right group called Timber Unity in its complaints about what it saw as excessive restrictions on economic activity in the habitat of an endangered species, the northern spotted owl. "You have these people in the city who were like, 'Oh, look. There's an owl. Isn't it cool?'" said Flynn. "'We're gonna destroy all of your livelihoods in your community because we like this owl' . . . You know, it's like it's saying, like, 'Oh, I like this exhibit in the zoo more than everyone you know.'" A lot of those people in the city turned out to be the voters in his election.

way of thinking, on the same list as pandemics and artificial intelligence and climate change. Across the land, Republican primaries were littered with candidates who were willing to behave as if
the presidential election had been stolen from Trump. They faced
candidates who were forced to pay lip service to the idea. McConnell's people had already figured out which was which, and McConnell was intent on defeating the former. "He's already done the
work," said Sam. The work, he added, was to distinguish "people
who would actually try to govern versus people who would under-
mine the government."

At that moment, Sam was planning to give $15–$30 million to
McConnell to defeat the Trumpier candidates in the US Senate races.
On a separate front, he explained to me, as the plane descended
into Washington, DC, he was exploring the legality of paying Donald
Trump himself not to run for president. His team had somehow created a back channel into the Trump operation and returned with the
not terribly earth-shattering news that Donald Trump might indeed
have his price: $5 billion. Or so Sam was told by his team.

It was interesting, especially in retrospect, how well suited Sam's
mind was to understanding Donald Trump. At that moment, his
team was using their mysterious line of communication into the
Trump camp to seed Trump's mind with an idea. In Missouri, a
rabid Trumper named Eric Greitens was in what looked like a close
race with a less enthusiastic Trumper named Eric Schmitt. Schmitt
wanted to govern; Greitens wanted to tear things down. Trump had
not yet weighed in on the race, and the fear was that his endorsement
might swing the election to Greitens. Sam's team had come up with
an idea—which, Sam claimed, was just then making its way to Trump
himself. The idea was to persuade Trump to come out and say "I'm
for Eric!" without specifying which Eric he was for. After all, Trump
didn't actually care who won. All he cared about was that he would
be seen to have backed the winner. If he said he was for Eric, he'd get
the credit for whichever Eric won. "I'm for Eric!" would attract even
more attention to Trump than a more specific endorsement, and the

attention is all Trump cared about in the end. "It's very Trump," said Sam. "It'd become a meme."

As he said that, he tossed popcorn in his mouth, in a herky-jerky motion that resembled a clumsy layup. He was shooting around 60 percent, and the popcorn was flying everywhere. He'd failed to catch a dish of warm nuts as they'd hurtled past him during takeoff, and they too were still scattered all around him. As he'd ordered the political world in his mind, he'd created chaos in the space he inhabited. Finally we landed, and he ran to his dinner, leaving the mess for someone else to clean up.

We'd agreed to meet the morning after next at the town house on the back side of Capitol Hill that served as the headquarters for Guarding Against Pandemics, the organization that Sam paid for and which Gabe ran. Once again he was late. Once again he tumbled out of the back of a car, this time a regular DC taxicab. And once again he had in his hands a balled-up suit—but this time, as he emerged from the car, a single brown dress shoe fell out of the pile in his hands and into the street. As he reached to grab it, the other shoe dropped and rolled under the taxi. It was then that I noticed that the suit's color had changed: someone had taken the wrinkled suit he'd arrived carrying and replaced it with another, pressed one, reduced now to laundry. I watched as Sam entered the empty town house, opened a closet, and, without so much as a glance at the row of empty hangers, tossed the ball of clothes onto the closet floor. We then drove together to the airport and returned to the Bahamas.

Two days later Trump announced, in a post on Truth Social, his intention to name his choice in the Missouri Senate race. Next, he released a written statement: "ERIC has my Complete and Total Endorsement!"*

---

* Both Eric Greitens and Eric Schmitt instantly claimed to have Trump's endorsement, and thus Trump's influence was neutralized. Eric Schmitt wound up winning the primary and the general election, and now sits in the US Senate.

The sun was setting on the Albany resort when the effective altruists gathered to discuss how they might give their money away. Like rich people dressed up for a formal occasion, the buildings surrounding the marina looked their best when the light was lowered. In mid-day sun they were just seven crass blindingly white monstrosities barely distinguishable from one another. Only after sunset, when they became unnaturally lit, did their names make any sense. The facade of a building named Honeycomb became a stack of wax hexa-gons. The one called Cube revealed itself to be a beguilingly uneven jumble of rectangles. Orchid—the building closest to the ocean, the one with the most sweeping views—was more subtle. It looked noth-ing like an orchid in any light, but its exterior was wrapped with an aluminum sheath whose pattern was meant to call to mind the tropical flower—in the same way that the planned exterior of FTX's new headquarters was supposed to evoke Sam's Jewfro. At night its penthouse was lit purple, and the purple light made it seem glamor-ous, and elicited envy even from those accustomed to being envied. That's where the effective altruists all lived, at least until Caroline booted Sam out. Gary, Nishad, Caroline, and Sam's best friend from college, Adam Yedidia, slept in more or less identical bedrooms, all but Caroline with their romantic partners.

The interior of Orchid's penthouse contained even more stuff to be impressed by, if you were the sort of person impressed by stuff. Eleven thousand five hundred square feet of marble floors had been tricked out with enough luxury to persuade any normal rich per-son who lived inside it that whatever sacrifice he'd made to acquire such a thing surely was worth it. The problem was that the rich peo-ple inside were not normal. The effective altruists already had half ruined the splendor. One wall was now obscured by a row of com-puter monitors whose cords snaked across the marble like jungle vines. A cheap Ikea-like bookshelf groaned under the weight of the EAs' favorite board games: Galaxy Trucker, Wingspan, 7 Wonders, more than one chess set. The living room had been surrendered to a massive video game monitor. Alongside the various crystal and silver tchotchkes that had obviously come with the place, the effective altruists had deposited, without rhyme or reason, a lot of random crap they'd been too lazy to chuck: books their authors had given Sam that he'd never read, a football that Shaquille O'Neal had signed and given to Sam, fan gear sent by various professional sports leagues. In effect, they'd turned a $30 million condominium into a flophouse. From their wraparound sixth-floor balcony they had a view to die for, and yet they seldom so much as glanced at it. Just below was a semi-private beach so close that from their balcony Tom Brady could have thrown Shaq's football onto it. A year into his new life in the Bahamas, Nishad Singh had stepped onto that beach just once, and then only because some relatives were visiting. That was once more than Sam, and likely Gary too.

Caroline appeared with a glass of wine, which here counted as an act of hedonism, and the meeting began. From the moneymaking division of FTX, it was just her, Sam, Gary, and Nishad; from the money-giving side were the four employees who worked for FTX's philanthropic wing. They shared their employer's habit of turning life decisions into expected value calculations, and their inner math yielded similarly surprising results. In 2020, Avital Balwit had won a Rhodes Scholarship and turned it down, first to run Carrick Flynn's congressional campaign and then to give away FTX's money. Leopold Aschenbrenner, who had entered Columbia University at the age of fifteen and graduated four years later as class valedictorian, had just declined a spot at Yale Law School to work for this new philanthropy. Their boss, a former Oxford philosopher named Nick Beckstead, was also present, as was their spiritual guru, Will MacAskill—who was of course in some way responsible for everyone, including Sam, even being there.

Since MacAskill had first sold Sam, back in the fall of 2012, on the idea of earning to give, the EA movement had obviously changed. It had become a lot less interested in saving the lives of existing human beings than future ones. In early 2020, movement cofounder Toby Ord had published a book, *The Precipice*, which laid out where his thinking (and that of everyone in the penthouse) had been for a while now. In it he offered up rough estimates of the likelihood of various existential risks to humanity. The chance of a stellar explosion he put at one in a billion, and an asteroid strike at one in a million. The man-made risks of nuclear bombs and climate change had a one in a thousand chance of wiping out the entire species. A man-made pathogen—as opposed to a naturally arising disease—he gave a one in thirty chance. The most likely threat to humanity, Ord argued, was runaway artificial intelligence. He put the odds of AI ending life as we know it at one in ten. "If it happens, it wipes us all out," explained Sam. "Where with biological risk, even if it gets really bad, I dunno, it doesn't have the intelligence to weed out the stragglers the way AI could."

One response to these sorts of calculations is that they are a kind of gonzo science fiction. No one actually knows what the odds of any of these things are, and your willingness to make up some numbers should render you less, not more, credible on the subject. And yet . . . there clearly is *some* chance that all of these terrible things might occur. And if there is *some* chance, how can you not try to figure out what that chance might be? You are free to quibble about the specific odds. Once you're in the argument, however, you'll find it difficult to escape a certain logic: the expected value of reducing even the minuscule likelihood of an existential threat to all future human beings is far greater than the expected value of anything you might do to save the lives of the people who currently happen to be alive. "The core argument was like, look, the future is vast," said Sam. "You can try to put a number on it but obviously anything that flows through to that is going to have a vast multiplier."

One day some historian of effective altruism will marvel at how easily it transformed itself. It turned its back on living people without bloodshed or even, really, much shouting. You might think that people who had sacrificed fame and fortune to save poor children in Africa would rebel at the idea of moving on from poor children in

Africa to future children in another galaxy. They didn't, not really—which tells you something about the role of ordinary human feeling in the movement. It didn't matter. What mattered was the math. Effective altruism never got its emotional charge from the places that charged ordinary philanthropy. It was always fueled by a cool lust for the most logical way to lead a good life.

At any rate, the people sitting around Sam's living room and talking about where Sam's money was being spent weren't talking about buying bed nets for children in Africa, to prevent malaria. They were looking for clever ways to reduce existential risk. The sums they were able to give away were about to increase dramatically—or so they all imagined. After handing out $30 million in 2021, they were on pace to hand out $300 million in 2022, and then $1 billion in 2023. As Nishad had put it to me not long before, "We're finally going to stop talking about doing good and start doing it."

The list of things they had just done or were about to do was—well, soon it would be entirely irrelevant. But in retrospect it would be interesting for other reasons. They spoke for some time about proposals they had received and might fund. For instance, a Stanford economist hoped to start a new university focused exclusively on artificial intelligence and biotech and recruit as part of its student population young people from lower- and middle-income families in developing countries. An engineer at a think tank that specialized in catastrophic risk wanted to launch a communications satellite that would serve as a backup channel for emergency services if 911 ever went down. An outfit called the Apollo Academic Surveys, using FTX money, had created a mechanism to quickly determine what expert consensus was on any topic. Oddly, only economics had such a tool. The first question they put to it was how likely it was for the earth to be destroyed by an asteroid. Not that likely, as it turned out. "One less thing to worry about," said Avital.

They'd been doing this for only a year and already had been pitched nearly two thousand such projects. They'd handed out some money but in the process they'd concluded that conventional philan-thropy was kind of dumb. Just to deal with the incoming requests—most of which they had no ability to evaluate—would require a big staff and lots of expense. Much of their money would end up being used on a vast bureaucracy. And so they had just recently adopted a new approach: instead of giving money away themselves, they scoured the world for subject matter experts who might have their own, better ideas for how to give away money. Over the previous six months, one hundred people with deep knowledge of pandemic prevention and artificial intelligence had received an email from FTX that said, in effect: *Hey, you don't know us, but here's a million dol-lars, no strings attached. Your job is to give it away as effectively as you can.* The FTX Foundation, started in early 2021, would track what these people did with their million dollars, but only to determine if they should be given even more. "We try not to be very judgy once they have the money," said Sam. "But maybe we won't be reupping them." The hope was, first, that these people on the ground would know better than anyone what to do with the money and, second, that some people might actually have a genius for giving away money. "It's trying to blast through the hesitation," said Sam. "The default to inaction."

The effective altruists finished their first meeting at midnight, then returned the next night and talked until one in the morning. Nishad and Sam talked some, Caroline sipped wine and talked less, Gary said nothing at all. They were moving fast, as Sam always did. "If you throw away a quarter of the money, that's very sad," he said at one point, "but if it allows you to triple the effectiveness of the rest, that's a win."

Here was yet another game. The game was for him and Nishad and Gary and Caroline to generate hundreds of billions of dollars and use it to reduce the likelihood of the grand experiment coming to an end. Like all the games Sam loved, this game was played on a clock. He'd somehow decided that the odds were low that he, or really most people, would do anything important after about the age of forty. If he didn't sleep, or exercise, or eat properly, and always preferred action over inaction, here was why. He had to move fast. He didn't think the later years of his own life contained much expected value. To do their bit to save the species, he figured they had maybe ten or at most fifteen years.

As it would turn out, they had five weeks.

As late as the final days of October 2022, you could have ransacked the jungle huts until you were blue in the face and have had not the faintest sense that anything was amiss. Walking across the acres of asphalt toward jungle hut 27, I bumped into Ramnik and his wife, Mallika Chawla. Even as the price of bitcoin tumbled, Ramnik's mood hit new highs every day. Using Sam's money—or what he assumed was Sam's money—he was playing a new and curious role in crypto finance. Between the start of the boom in 2017 and June of 2022, crypto had re-created the institutions of traditional finance, without the rules and regulations and investor protections that exist in traditional finance. It had brokers. It also had its own banks and sort of banks that paid crypto interest on crypto deposits—though did not offer insurance on those deposits. The banks re-lent that money at higher rates of interest to crypto hedge funds—without anyone having really any idea what those hedge funds were doing with the money. It had exchanges that did not merely facilitate crypto trades but also warehoused their customers' money—without any regulator paying a whole lot of attention to how they did this. It even had the equivalent of US dollars, in the form of stablecoins. These were digital currencies on a blockchain, like bitcoin, but, unlike bitcoin, backed by actual dollars. For every dollar's worth of a stablecoin, there was meant to be a dollar held somewhere in a genuine Federal Deposit Insurance Corporation–insured bank. But again, there was no proof that these dollars were there.

The whole edifice relied on a fantastic amount of trust. By late October that trust was gone, and crypto was in a souped-up version of an old-fashioned financial crisis. In late June, the second-biggest hedge fund after Alameda Research, Three Arrows Capital, had blown up. The banks and sort of banks had suffered runs and collapsed. Unlike in a traditional finance crisis, there was no government to step in and calm everyone down. The 2008 financial crisis had only subsided after governments had agreed to bail out the banks. The 2022 crypto crisis lacked this mechanism. Instead of governments, crypto had Sam. Or, rather, it had Ramnik, who was busily evaluating which of the failed crypto businesses to save and which to let die. Sam had never been more important and so, by association, neither had Ramnik. "It's a reflection of a collapse of trust," said someone close to the business. "Now it's trust in Sam."

Trust in Sam meant trust in Ramnik, who was just then putting the finishing touches on the purchase of two failed crypto banks, Voyager Digital and BlockFi. At their peak, they'd together been valued at roughly $7 billion. Now Ramnik was acquiring them for no more than $200 million. A pittance.

Or so it seemed. Ramnik recently had asked Sam how much capital he should assume was available for possible acquisitions, and Sam had said, *Just let me know if you get to a billion.* Two years earlier, Ramnik was just a guy hoping to be able to walk to work in the morning. Now he was the right-hand man to the J. P. Morgan of crypto. In the presence of his wife, he glowed with the pleasure and the glory of it all.

"What I don't get is how he knows how to do all this," I said to his wife, as we walked into jungle hut number 27.

"I know!" she said brightly. "I ask him that all the time. *How do you know?* He just knows."

9

THE VANISHING

I was only gone for a week or so. By the time I returned, Ramnik, along with pretty much the entire corporate org chart, had fled the island. Some meaningful percentage of the company's fleet of cars had been abandoned, keys still inside them, in the Bahamas airport lot. It made for a bizarre scene: panicked employees of FTX and Alameda Research struggling to escape against an incoming tide of oblivious tourists in flip-flops and floral shirts. As they passed one another in the terminal, giant airport video screens flashed the message over their heads: *Get Free Crypto Anytime, Anywhere. Download the FTX App.* The day I landed, Friday, November 11, the signs on the airport walls were still cheerily pitching crypto—even though at four thirty that morning, Sam had DocuSigned the papers that threw FTX into bankruptcy in the United States.

It was late afternoon by the time Natalie collected me from the airport, in one of the few cars that the local creditors had not tracked down and repossessed. The night before she'd resigned from her job as head of public relations and Sam's life manager. She planned to leave the next morning without most of her possessions or a clear idea of what had happened. She knew what everyone now did: at least $8 billion belonging to crypto traders, and meant to be safe and sound inside FTX, had wound up instead inside Alameda Research. What had become of the $8 billion was not entirely clear, but it wasn't good. Natalie had wept when she'd learned that, as she put it, "there was a button on FTX. Alameda could take whatever risk it wanted to." Like most FTX employees, she'd kept her money on the exchange. Now it was all gone. Like most FTX employees, she felt as if she'd been living a dream. Already the dream was growing fuzzy and requiring effort to recall. Could it really be true that she'd been next-door neighbors with Vince Carter?

Between Sunday and Wednesday, the inner circle of effective altruists had been holed up in Sam's sleeping quarters, trying and failing to save the company. Natalie now had only a vague sense of their whereabouts or states of mind. On Wednesday, George Lerner had determined that Nishad was a suicide risk and arranged for him to be escorted out of the country and to his parents, in San Francisco. As the company collapsed, Caroline had been traveling in Asia and had remained there in an odd mood. She struck her psychiatrist, and others to whom she had spoken, as somewhere between relieved and happy. She too was now rumored to be heading back to her parents' house, in the Boston area. Gary was as silent as ever and impossible to read but apparently still around. And Sam—well, Natalie didn't know what, if anything, Sam was actually feeling, or even where he was. Tracking Sam was no longer her job.

The road from the airport to the Albany resort passed FTX's offices. Natalie was uneasy about me trying to see them. She feared they might contain the people repossessing the company cars. Still, as we approached, we slowed. The guard booth was empty. The barrier was down but blocked as little of the road as ever. There was no sign of life on the field of asphalt; the cars were gone; the jungle huts seemed entirely abandoned. Then, on the far side of the lot, a figure rounded a hut and came into focus. It was Sam, all by himself, in a bright red T-shirt and shorts. Walking circles around his former empire. Even at a distance, you could tell he could use a shower and a shave. He walked over and climbed into the car, as if he'd been expecting us. He needed a ride home, which of course raised the question of how, and why, he'd come to be here in the first place.

"You know what's weird to think about?" he said, as we left the office behind. "Saturday. Saturday everything was normal."

I did my best to reconstruct what had happened the previous few weeks, before reconsidering what had happened the previous few years. There'd been another dustup between Sam and CZ that, when it happened, had not seemed all that important. In late October, Sam had flown to the Middle East to raise money and, in the bargain, find a second home, in the Eastern Hemisphere, for FTX. On the evening of October 24, 2022, he bumped into CZ at a conference in Riyadh. It was the first time in nearly three years they'd been in the same room. They'd had a brief, awkward chat, only because it took less effort than not having it. "It was a five-minute conversation in which no real information was exchanged," said Sam. "It was like fake nice. We dispensed with our obligation to acknowledge we were both there." The next day, Sam had flown to Dubai to meet with its financial regulators. The regulators at the time hoped that FTX might make Dubai its Eastern Hemisphere headquarters. Sam later wrote up the message he'd tried to convey to them. "I love Dubai," he said.

> But we *can't* be in the same place as Binance. . . . This is for two reasons: first they are constantly devoting significant company resources to trying to hurt us; and second that they soil the reputation of wherever they are. I can't emphasize this enough: in general I hear great things from other jurisdictions/regulators etc. about Dubai and the UAE [United Arab Emirates], *except* that there's a constant refrain of: *that's the jurisdiction that accepted Binance, and so we don't trust their standards.*

It was unclear to Sam, if Dubai decided to rid itself of CZ and his exchange, whether any country in which CZ would be willing to live would accept them. In these woods, CZ was the biggest bear and Sam seemed to be going out of his way to poke him. Dubai was tiny, Houston with sheikhs. Sam's bid to turn CZ into a homeless fugitive was bound to get back to him. And yet Sam didn't leave it at that. On October 30, when he returned to the Bahamas he tweeted a joke about CZ's inability to shape US crypto regulations. "Uh, he is still allowed to go to DC, right?"

Three days later, on November 2, the crypto news site CoinDesk published an article about a curious document that appeared to have been leaked to them by someone inside Alameda Research, or perhaps someone who lent money to Alameda Research. It wasn't a formal balance sheet. There was no sign that it had been audited, or that it presented a complete picture of the contents of Alameda Research, or that it was even real. It listed $14.6 billion of assets and $8 billion of liabilities that were supposedly inside of Alameda Research as of June 30, 2022. What the CoinDesk piece wanted to highlight was that more than a third of the assets were FTT, the token FTX had issued three years earlier.

In and of itself the article struck people inside FTX as of no more than prurient interest.[*] Everyone noticed that one of its contributors was the current girlfriend of Eric Mannes, Caroline Ellison's former boyfriend at Jane Street. The previous month, the couple had visited the Bahamas and stayed with employees of Alameda Research at Albany: Had the leak somehow originated inside the company? There was also the frisson that came with catching even a glimpse of the dragon's hoard. But the piece did not alarm or even surprise anyone at FTX. FTT was, in effect, equity in FTX—it had a claim on the first third of FTX's revenues. FTX had generated a billion dollars

---

[*] Even informed outsiders were not all that surprised. Steve Ehrlich, the *Forbes* reporter who had been assigned to determine Sam's wealth, said that he said to himself when he saw the piece, Congratulations on knowing something we knew two years ago.

in revenue in 2021 and, even with crypto prices crashing, was about to do it again in 2022. Sam's biggest regret, expressed repeatedly from the moment the price of FTT had rocketed back in 2019, was that he'd created and sold it in the first place. Ever since, he'd been vacuuming it up inside of Alameda Research.

On Sunday morning, November 6, CZ posted a tweet to his 7.3 million followers.

CZ ◆ Binance ✔ @cz_binance

As part of Binance's exit from FTX equity last year, Binance received roughly $2.1 billion USD equivalent in cash (BUSD and FTT). Due to recent revelations that have came to light, we have decided to liquidate any remaining FTT on our books. 1/4

3:47 PM · Nov 6, 2022 · Twitter for iPhone

CZ still held the roughly $500 million worth of FTT that he had taken back in mid-2021 as part of his $2.275 billion buyout. (Most of the rest of his massive payout he'd taken in bitcoin and dollars, though he also took back roughly $400 million of the Binance token, BNB, that he'd used to buy his stake in the first place.) Sam hadn't thought much more about the tweet than he had about the CoinDesk article. On Saturday, November 5, he and his brother, Gabe, along with Ryan Salame, had met in Palm Beach with Florida governor Ron DeSantis. The meeting had no particular purpose. Like basically everyone else in US politics and finance, DeSantis wanted to meet Sam, and Sam was curious to know more about this person who might well one day ask him for money. "It was to figure out where he was on the scale from reasonable person to Trump," said Sam. "But I couldn't figure it out." After the meeting, he was scheduled to fly to Tampa to watch Tom Brady's Buccaneers play the Los Angeles Rams the following day. It turned out to be thrilling, with Brady leading yet another last-minute game-winning touchdown drive. Only Gabe and Ryan Salame watched it, however, as by then Sam was back in the Bahamas, to play the end of another game.

The run on FTX was in its own way spectacular. There had been $15 billion in customer deposits on the exchange. Or there was meant to be that amount, held in either fiat currency or bitcoin and ether. On a normal day, $50 million or so either came into or left the exchange. Each day between November 1 and November 5, $200 million fled. By late Sunday night, the sixth, $100 million was leaving every hour. FTX customers withdrew $2 billion that day, and then tried to withdraw another $4 billion on Monday. By Tuesday morning, $5 billion had exited, and the exchange was clearly not going to be able to come up with enough cash to pay the swelling number of customers who wanted their money back. It didn't formally shut down withdrawals, but it more or less stopped actually sending money back to the customers.

Even more interesting than the speed of the event were its inciting incidents. CZ's tweet had obviously been the first, but it wasn't the last, or maybe even the most important. Caroline had responded to CZ on Sunday morning.

Caroline
@carolinecapital

@cz_binance if you're looking to minimize the market impact on your FTT sales, Alameda will happily buy it all from you today at $22!

4:03 PM · Nov 6, 2022 · Twitter Web App

The tone—the peppy simplicity that obviously masked some other motive—sounded a lot like Sam. Caroline had actually written it. Neither she nor Sam expected CZ to accept the deal. CZ wanted to maximize the damage to FTX, and so would string out the uncertainty for as long as possible. The hope was that a concrete offer to buy at a certain price would shut him up and calm the market.

It did the opposite. A risk analysis company called Gauntlet, which studied the price movements of various crypto tokens, had maybe the best picture of what actually happened next. Within twenty seconds of Caroline's tweet came a rush to sell FTT by speculators who had borrowed money to buy it. The panic was driven by an assumption: if Alameda Research, the single biggest owner of FTT, was making a big show of being willing to buy a huge pile of it for $22, they must need for some reason to maintain the market price at $22. The most plausible explanation was that Alameda Research was using FTT as collateral to borrow dollars or bitcoin from others. "You don't tell someone a price level like $22 unless you have a lot of confidence that you need that price," the CEO of Gauntlet, Tarun Chitra, told Bloomberg News. By Monday night, the price of FTT had fallen from $22 to $7. The half a billion dollars of his own money that CZ had elected to incinerate was, in the grand scheme of things, such a trivial sum that hardly anyone paid it any more attention.

By Tuesday, the relevant math was fourth-grade level. Before the crisis, FTX was meant to be holding about $15 billion worth of customer deposits.* Five billion of that had already been paid out to customers, and so, still inside FTX, there should have been roughly $10 billion. There wasn't. The only remaining assets were whatever was left of the dragon's hoard inside of Alameda: a big pile of FTT, another big pile of Solana tokens, an assortment of crypto tokens that would be even harder to sell, $300 million worth of Bahamas real estate, and a truly massive heap of Sam's venture capital investments—including the stake in Twitter, which Sam had never

---

* I'm simplifying this, though only a tiny bit. FTX was a futures exchange, and so it lent money to its customers to make bets. At any given moment, it would not be expected to have all of its customers' money immediately on hand. But its chief selling point back in 2019 was that it had found a better way to evaluate the gambles of the customers to whom it lent money; and it had. And so it should not have been exposed to losses from its loans to customers.

bothered to sell. There was still perhaps as much as $3 billion worth of hard currency and bitcoin that they had yet to return to customers— but the vast majority of the secret stash had no immediate market. Much of what Caroline and Sam went back and forth about the first two or three days of the run on FTX was just this. Caroline, who by then was beaming in from the Hong Kong office, would appear on a video call. Sam would go down the list of the many things either he or she had bought and ask: How long will it take you to sell this? For most, the answer was too long.

On the night of November 6, Sam had called Ramnik and asked him to come to his Albany unit to talk about how they might find money. Sam had actually called him twice, in the space of twenty minutes, and Sam never called twice. The next hour left Ramnik triply confused. He thought that Sam was in Florida, watching Tom Brady play football. He thought that Sam lived not alone, on the ground floor of Gemini, but in the Orchid penthouse, with the other effective altruists. (Like almost everyone else inside FTX, he still had no idea that Sam and Caroline had been in a relationship.) Above all, Ramnik did not know why Sam so urgently needed money. Ramnik could see that money was leaving FTX, but he didn't view it as a big deal. The customers might panic and pull out all their money. But once they realized that there was nothing to panic about, they'd return, and their money would too.

Ramnik had always wanted to walk to work, and now he did. He left his place (Cube 1B) and strolled around the Albany marina, past the sleeping megayachts. They all had names that sounded like inside jokes or bad puns. *Special K. Pipe Dream. Fanta Sea.* It was curious how few people were ever around. Even in the day, there were more boats than people; at night, the entire resort felt vacant. It was a place where rich people bought homes they didn't need because that's what rich people were supposed to do.

Entering Sam's unit in Gemini, he found only effective altruists.

Nishad was in the living room, Caroline was on a video screen, and Sam was headed to his bedroom to lie down. Sam wasn't exactly incoherent so much as he was difficult to talk to. Nishad was agitated with Sam in a way that Ramnik had never seen—at one point turning on him and screaming, "Will you please fucking stop playing *Storybook Brawl*?!" Nothing any of them was saying made sense to Ramnik. Though Caroline was in charge of Alameda Research, she seemed totally clueless about where its money was. She'd come onto the screen and announce that she had found $200 million here, or $400 million there, as if she'd just made an original scientific discovery. Some guy at Deltec, their bank in the Bahamas, messaged Ramnik to say, *Oh, by the way, you have $300 million with us*. And it came as a total surprise to all of them!

Eventually Ramnik gathered that they needed to raise $7 billion, fast, to fill what they thought might be a $7 billion hole. (The exact number shifted around a lot those first few days.) To his obvious question—Why was there a hole in the first place?—Sam and Nishad and Caroline offered fuzzy answers. Gary sat quietly off to one side.

Ramnik had sat at the desk beside Gary for six months. "He'd come, sit down, start working, work twelve hours straight. Not a word on the way in, not a word on the way out," said Ramnik. Gary usually didn't arrive until early afternoon, but one day he'd turned up at eleven in the morning, and Ramnik had used the fact to try to start a conversation.

"You're in early today," said Ramnik. "It's only eleven o'clock."

"And that too in the a.m.," said Gary.

That was the only exchange they'd ever had, and Gary didn't look as if he was hoping for another. Sam, as usual, was doing most of the talking. If at that moment you had asked Ramnik what he thought Sam knew or did not know, he would have said that Sam actually didn't know what had happened. That he'd been taken by surprise. He wondered: *If these people knew there was a risk that they might not have enough money, why hadn't they even bothered to figure out how much they had? They'd done nothing.*

The next day, after lunch, an FTX lawyer named Can Sun appeared. Sam had summoned Can for the same reason he'd summoned Ramnik—to talk to investors and help him raise $7 billion. Can, too, was perplexed. "They wouldn't answer questions directly about where the money went," he said. "When I entered the room, no one acknowledged that money was being mishandled. The money was all there. We just had a liquidity issue." Sam and Can and Ramnik and others called everyone on the planet who might be able to deliver $7 billion quickly: sovereign wealth funds, private equity funds, Asian crypto exchanges. As it turned out, it wasn't easy to get people to give you $7 billion when you couldn't explain why you needed it. It was even harder to get people to give you $7 billion when you had to have it right away. Lots of people were willing to talk to Sam and Can and Ramnik, but all of them had the same question: *Where did the customer deposits go?* When that question went unanswered, everyone who had $7 billion lying around lost interest.

From the universe of people with that kind of money to spare, only one person stepped forward to say he might be willing to spare it: CZ. For obvious reasons, CZ was the last person Sam wanted to call and beg for money. Sam did not call CZ until Tuesday. "I called CZ and he's pissed," said Sam. "So I started groveling. Three hours later we had an LOI [letter of intent] signed." The agreement gave Binance the entire company, minus FTX US, in exchange for assuming its liabilities. It also gave Binance the right to inspect the books of both FTX and Alameda Research, such as they were. It positioned CZ as the first outsider on the planet to see into the dragon's lair and to know, or appear to know, exactly what had happened inside both FTX and Alameda Research.

The following evening, Wednesday, November 9, CZ said that whatever he'd seen had caused him to change his mind. Sam learned the news from a tweet:

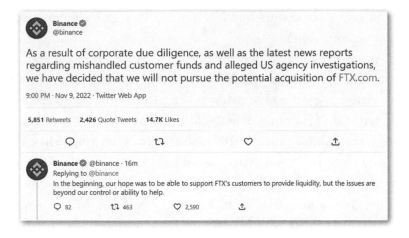

That's when everyone who hadn't already crept away bolted for the airport. They all had their reasons for their feelings of urgency. Nishad was speaking more of killing himself. Can's wife told him that if he didn't leave right away, she would file for divorce. Ramnik, who had thought himself a behind-the-scenes guy, invisible to the outside world, was receiving death threats. He was relieved to have never been told that money that should have been inside FTX was actually inside Alameda. It crossed his mind that his wife had saved him—because everyone would have known that to tell him was also to tell her. The effective altruists might have expanded their circle of trust by one, he thought, but not two.

By Wednesday evening, the trust was vanishing even inside the small circle of effective altruists. Caroline remained almost upbeat, and even tried to explain to Sam why. "I just had an increasing dread of this day that was weighing on me for a long time and now that it's actually happening it just feels great to get it over with one way or another," she'd written to him on Sunday. In the wee hours of Tuesday, Bahamas time, she followed it up with another message: "Feel weirdly good to get it over with. I've been dreading this for a long time so feels like a big weight off my shoulders." The next day, four hours before CZ tweeted his change of heart about buying FTX, she addressed her subordinates in the Hong Kong office. "I think I'll just start by saying some stuff, and feel free to ask questions?" she began, with a nervous giggle.

Caroline thought in periods but spoke in question marks and exclamation points. She made the sounds of uptalk and uncertainty while delivering a message that was brutally simple: they were bankrupt. She didn't go into a lot of detail about how it had happened but did say that Alameda had suffered losses back in June, when their biggest crypto lenders had also asked for their money back. At that time, Alameda had "borrowed" from FTX to repay its lenders. Now that they had sold—as far as she knew—FTX to CZ, Alameda would likely cease to exist. "Mostly I want to say I'm sorry?" she said. "This really sucks. It's really not fair to you guys." She understood that people might not want to stick around to help clean up whatever mess needed cleaning up, but "for people who do stick around it's possible there's some future thing." She concluded on a hopeful note, about the deal with CZ. "Repaying all of our creditors and making sure Alameda didn't go bankrupt is probably, like, good?"

"Can you say how big the hole is?" asked one of the traders in the audience, when she was done.

Caroline said she'd rather not.

"Is it closer to one billion or six billion?" he pressed.

"The, uh, latter?" said Caroline.

After her talk, Caroline approached a female employee and said brightly, *If you want to stay and help, I'd really appreciate it!*

Fuck you, the woman had said.

While Caroline happily made the case for her guilt, Nishad was unhappily searching for evidence of his innocence. At the start of the crisis, he seemed mostly concerned that the effective altruist dream had died and that he, and anyone else who had borrowed money from FTX, would soon be bankrupt, as they had no assets and still owed money to the company. At four in the morning on Monday, he texted Caroline, *i'm sad about the reflection of this on ea.* By Wednesday, November 9, his mind had turned to his legal peril. "This is wildly selfish of me but they may need to know it wasn't a ton of people orchestrating it," he messaged Sam, without specifying who "they" were or what "it" was. He followed it with another message: "Can you make it you, or you and Gary who people blame?" And then a third: "I think I need to tell Zane that I wasn't aware in orchestrating it."

That night, Nishad requested a meeting with just Gary and Sam. Once the three were alone in a room, Nishad asked, *What happens if law enforcement or regulators reach out?*

What do you mean? Sam asked.

How do we make sure we cooperate in prisoner's dilemma? How do we all make sure we say the other ones are innocent?

I don't have any reason to think any one of us had criminal intent, said Sam.

No, said Nishad. *That's not good enough. You need to talk to them. You need to tell them I had no clue.*

How could I know that? asked Sam. *You are saying that I should say that you know nothing about something I know nothing about. How is that even possible? It makes no sense.*

But I didn't know, said Nishad.

Then say that, said Sam.

It's not going to work for me, said Nishad. *Because there is code-based evidence of what I did.**

From start to finish, Gary just watched, as he'd done the entire week. He never said a word. It was as if he had made an expected value calculation of whatever he might say and decided that words still did not pay.

On Friday, Nishad was gone, which was just as well, as by then the police in the Bahamas were preparing to arrest any remaining lead-

---

* The reader is right to wonder how I know any of this. Or, as Sam might put it, What is the probability that any of this is true? The conversation comes from Sam's memory soon after. The rest of the account of the crisis was confirmed by others in Sam's sleeping quarters. I'm not sure how that affects the various probability calculations, but anything I didn't think happened I would not have included. What any of it *means* is another matter.

ers. That afternoon, roughly $450 million in crypto vanished from the wallets inside FTX. No one knew who the hacker was; everyone just assumed it was an inside job; lots of people suspected Sam and Gary. That evening, when Sam called Caroline, she didn't pick up. And never again would.

In the middle of all this, the woman responsible for the presence in the Bahamas of all the characters in the drama intervened. Christina Rolle, the Bahamas chief financial regulator, was genuinely shocked by how quickly the financial ecosystem that had grown around Sam and become populated with opportunists who had done very well off of him had collapsed—and by how those very people who had taken his money were turning on him without knowing exactly what he'd done. So long as Sam was giving away money to everyone, people loved him and nobody asked too many questions; the moment he was losing money, they turned on him—and didn't want to hear his answers to the questions they asked him. She found it troubling that the police were setting out to arrest people before anyone had any idea what they'd done. No authority had yet spoken to Sam, or to any of the other leaders of FTX and Alameda. All anyone knew was what they read on Twitter. They had no evidence to charge anyone with a crime: in the Bahamas, fraud required intent, and the intent here was unclear. Without explicit charges, anyone they arrested could be held only for so long.

The other reason she didn't want Sam and Gary arrested was that she needed their help to understand what had happened. Sam hadn't returned her calls all week. On Wednesday afternoon, she finally had a Zoom with Ryan Salame, who though still co-CEO of FTX had remained in the United States after Tom Brady's game, and Ryne Miller, the lawyer for FTX's US business. They told her that money had been moved from FTX into Alameda but that they didn't know how or why it had happened. "I found it funny that someone who was the CEO had this level of understanding that was not good," said Rolle.

It was an odd moment. All these people inside FTX suddenly

wanted to seem to know less than they did, and all these people outside FTX thought that they knew more than they actually did. On Twitter, in the blink of an eye, a rumor became a fact, the fact became a story, and the story became an explanation. Sam had made off with billions and was already on the run. Sam was in Dubai or some other place that lacked an extradition treaty with the United States. Someone posted videos of a man alleged to be Sam wandering the streets of Buenos Aires. Christina Rolle didn't think Sam was going to run, and she didn't think he was hiding billions. Her biggest worry about him was that when she asked him questions, he wouldn't give her straight answers. "I don't think he knows why people don't trust him," she said. "It's not hard to see you are being played by him, like a board game."

On Thursday she froze FTX's assets and effectively threw the company into liquidation, the Bahamas version of bankruptcy. On Friday—the day of my arrival—Sam's father, Joe, had dropped Sam at the old FTX offices to meet with the Bahamas liquidators. Three hours later, they were finished with Sam for the day. Rolle asked him to meet with her the next day at police headquarters. She wanted to question Gary, too, but the liquidators needed him to secure the exchange's assets, and so she'd put that off until the following Monday. After grilling Sam for several hours, Rolle climbed into a car with her assistant, who had observed the interaction. The assistant began to cry. "You cannot let them arrest this man," she'd pleaded. Rolle hadn't. She'd persuaded the police to take away Sam's and Gary's passports instead. And that was why, when I rolled into the FTX parking lot with Natalie, I found Sam, alone but still at large, walking in circles.

By Friday night there were only two people still waiting to exit the stage and leave it to others to find the meaning of the play. The first was Zane Tackett. I'd heard that Zane might still be around and found him the next day, Saturday, November 12. Zane had done something no one else had done: when the shooting started, he'd run toward the fight rather than away from it. The previous Sunday, he'd been at a crypto conference in Lisbon, about to leave for Abu Dhabi, where FTX was sponsoring a Formula 1 race. He was now walking back and forth across the marble floors of a unit inside Albany, shifting clothes from a dryer into a bag and drinking a bottle of rum.

From the start, Zane had been enthralled by Sam, and by the empire he might create. But he hadn't signed up to the cause blindly. Before joining FTX, he'd consulted his old friends in crypto. CZ was one of them. "It was CZ who told me about him," he now recalled. "He said, 'I think that'd be a really good option for you.' People have asked me, 'How did you come to trust Sam so much?' CZ was the start of it. But nobody had a bad thing to say about him." Zane was the gunslinger who'd been talked into making a respectable home in the town alongside what appeared to be law-abiding folk. Lots of big crypto speculators had entrusted their money to FTX because they trusted Zane.

Those people had had their doubts over the past two weeks, of course. They read Twitter too. But on Sunday, when things began to unravel, Zane had asked Sam for orders, and Sam had told him to reassure everyone. "I pinged Sam and asked, 'Should I do damage control?' 'Yup,' he said." Zane then sent Sam a message asking three questions: "One, are we insolvent, two, did we ever lend out customer funds to Alameda, and three anything I didn't ask that I need to know?" Sam didn't reply—and then went totally silent on him. He'd vanished on Zane in the same way he'd vanished on Christina Rolle.

Still, Zane figured there was no way that FTX was in real trouble. It made no sense. The price of FTT shouldn't have any effect on the value of the exchange, any more than the price of Apple stock should have on Apple's iPhone sales. Just the reverse: the exchange's revenues drove the value of FTT. "If FTT goes to zero, so what?" said Zane. The other reason it made no sense was that FTX had been so wildly profitable. "I know how much real revenue we were making: two bips [0.02 percent] on two hundred fifty billion dollars a month," said Zane. "I'm like, Dude, you were sitting on a fucking printing press: why did you need to do this?"

Right up until late Monday night, Zane had been telling his friends that everything was okay. The money that fled the exchange belonged to the people who felt nothing for it; the money that remained, at least some of it, belonged to people who shared Zane's principled belief that you stuck by your allies through thick and thin. "That fucking asshole—how could he not tell me, when I went out to defend him?" said Zane, repeating more or less what he'd said to Sam directly. "You let me go out and lie for you. Fuck you."

He was so different from the effective altruists. He didn't have Sam's interest in How to Think About Bob. If Bob was Zane's good friend, and Zane had no evidence that Bob had committed the unsolved murder, Zane would have insisted on thinking about Bob the way he had always thought about Bob. He would have gone out of his way to stand by Bob, and to make Bob feel better about what had happened. But if he'd stumbled upon Bob burying a bloody knife in his backyard he'd have shot him on the spot, without even pausing to update his probabilities. Or at least that's how I still imagine Zane.

He'd quit on Tuesday. Now he was on his way to Miami, and from there he wasn't sure where he'd go. Whatever trail he took, he wasn't going to waste time on it trying to figure out why Sam had done whatever he'd done. To Zane it didn't matter. There was one question he dwelled on: Why had neither he nor anyone else he knew seen this coming? He had the beginning of an answer. "Sam's oddness," he said. "His oddness mixed with just how smart he was allowed you to wave away a lot of the concerns. The question of why just goes away."

There remained the question of who would pass legal judgment on Sam and the others, and who would clean up their mess. The Bahamas had moved to put FTX into liquidation the day before Sam signed the papers declaring bankruptcy in the United States. Alameda Research and the small US exchange were incorporated in Delaware. FTX's bigger international crypto exchange, where the vast majority of the trading occurred, had been created in Hong Kong. Incorporated in Antigua and now headquartered in the Bahamas, the main crypto exchange forbade US citizens from using it and worked fairly hard to keep them from doing so. Any US citizens who happened to be trading on it had lied their way onto it. There was a decent argument to be made that judgment of Sam, and liquidation of FTX, should occur in the Bahamas. There was a less decent argument, made by US bankruptcy lawyers who stood to make a fortune from the case, that all the assets and the people meant to be tending them should be moved to the United States. And there was a third argument, made by Sam, that anything that happened would need to happen wherever Gary was, because Gary was the only one who could explain the code that had governed the business. "At the end of the day, the deciding factor in the jurisdictional dispute is Gary," said Sam, the night Zane left, "because he's the only one who knows how to use a computer."

Gary was the last person to leave. He pulled Sam aside in the Orchid penthouse. And he actually spoke, albeit very briefly.

I talked to my lawyer and I'm going to leave, he said.

Is there anything to say that would be relevant here? asked Sam.

The lawyer told me to leave, and I have to leave, said Gary.[*]

That was it. Gary never said when he would leave, or how he would leave—which was an issue, as the Bahamas had taken his passport. On Sunday night, without a further word to anyone, he just slipped, unnoticed, out of the Orchid penthouse. The lawyer who spirited him off arranged with US authorities to supply him with a second passport, so that they might smuggle him back to the United States before the government of the Bahamas knew what had happened. Christina Rolle never had a chance to speak with him.

---

[*] This one I witnessed from a distance. It felt like a kind of miracle.

10

MANFRED

Once everyone who felt the need to run had fled, the Albany resort reminded me of New Orleans a week after Hurricane Katrina. No people, but lots of stuff, and a surface quiet that masked the deeper chaos. You could wander into any one of a dozen luxury condos and find not just shelter but food and clothing, too. The most glorious five-bedroom units in Honeycomb or Cube were yours for the taking, and stocked with mountains of Chinese snacks, dress for any occasion, and enough alcohol to sink a pirate ship. Sam's parents had flown to the Bahamas and would remain in the Orchid penthouse with their son till the end, as would his psychiatrist. A single FTX technologist named Dan Chapsky had stayed on, but he was an odd case. He'd held the title Chief Data Scientist, but Sam barely knew who he was, or what he did, or why he had stayed— and neither did he. On bankruptcy Friday, he had emerged from his own luxury condo with the haunted look of a man after an air raid and sought out George Lerner.

"Why am I here?" he'd asked.

George had looked him in the eye for a long moment and said, "You need to leave."

For whatever reason, Dan hadn't left. He'd soon be employed by both the US and the Bahamas bankruptcy teams and, right after that, be caught up in the war between them for control of the company's remaining assets. Both needed someone to help them figure out the contents of FTX's database. Dan was the only one left who knew how to use a computer.

At the peak, Albany had housed as many as seventy employees and guests of FTX and Alameda Research. By Monday, November 14, the only other sign of FTX life inside the walls of the Albany resort came from a house directly behind Sam's place in Orchid. The Conch Shack, it was called. The Conch Shack was Ryan Salame's finest purchase: a drop-dead gorgeous six-bedroom house that, unusually for Albany, was in proportion to its surroundings. Ryan had paid $15 million for it and assumed that Sam would live in it. Sam had taken one look at it, seen that some of its bedrooms were bigger than the others, and decided he'd instead take the Orchid penthouse, where he and the other effective altruists could live in virtually identical conditions.

The Conch Shack had been handed to Constance Wang, the longest-tenured FTX employee in the Bahamas outside of Sam's inner circle of effective altruists. Hired on April 1, 2019, she'd been FTX's first Chinese and eighth overall employee. At the moment of the collapse of the exchange she still had the title chief operating officer, and added to it was CEO of FTX Digital Markets. Even after all her colleagues had taken flight, Constance remained at the Conch Shack with her two cats. The cats were a sticking point. Lucky and Money, they were called. It would take Constance a couple of weeks to obtain the permit to fly them back to China, and even then the airlines would only allow her to return home with a single cat. If she'd been forced to choose, she'd have picked Lucky, but the thought of leaving Money behind was unbearable, and Constance was relieved not to have to think it. Her good friend Quinn Li had stuck around to help. Along with Natalie Tien and Zane Tackett, Quinn was one of the forty-eight people below Constance on George's org chart. "She stayed because of me," said Constance. "I need her help to bring my cats home."

It wouldn't have been the first time I'd seen people risk it all for a pet. That had happened during Hurricane Katrina too. But Lucky and Money were obviously not the only reason that Constance had stuck around, as she'd remain long after she'd obtained their travel documents. Sam still held out hope that he might resuscitate the exchange. That hope rested on a Chinese-born crypto billionaire named Justin Sun, who'd come to Sam with a plan. Sun, founder of Tron, a blockchain, wanted to hand out his own private cryptocurrency, Tronix, to FTX creditors, in exchange for their claim on the remaining assets. Seeing that he needed someone who spoke Mandarin, Sam had begged Constance to stay. "I want to make sure Sam doesn't kill himself," said Constance, who didn't think much of Justin Sun's plan. "Though sometimes I feel that is not my responsibility."

More than anything, though, Constance wanted to understand what had just happened. That was the most important reason the chief operating officer of FTX had stayed in the Bahamas and risked detention or arrest: she couldn't stand not knowing how FTX had operated. "I like to figure things out," she said. "If I can't figure things out, it really bothers me."

On that Monday morning after the collapse, I found the two young Chinese women in the Conch Shack kitchen. Constance had already gotten her hands on a small stack of what amounted to classified documents from FTX and Alameda Research. Quinn had just returned from a failed attempt to retrieve fresh vegetables from the houses and apartments around the island previously occupied by FTX employees. (The places were already locked and guarded.) Both were dealing with parents back in China freaking out that their children were refusing to come home until they'd finished their investigation. The entire situation had been inflamed by the media; even in China, all anyone was talking about was Sam and FTX. "FTX got so famous," said Constance. "This is literally what FTX was trying to achieve. We achieved it by going bankrupt!"

Both women had used various tricks to get their parents to leave them be. Quinn argued to her mother that Sam's parents were now in the Bahamas with no one to console them. "I said to my mom,

'They are two old people, and they have no one with them,'" said Quinn. "My mom says, 'I'm old people too!'" Constance was able to silence her mother only by telling her that if she kept calling and hollering at her and did not allow her the space to find closure in this chapter of her life, her sadness might spin out of control into emotions she'd be unable to survive. Amazed by the success of Constance's strategy, Quinn had tried it on her own mother. "I said to my mom, 'I'm really sad. Do you want to make me more sad? If you say one more thing, I'm going to kill myself.' And it didn't work! She said, 'I have given you enough pity! You are working all the time and you still have no boyfriend!'"

Constance took the lead in their investigation, using Quinn mainly as a sounding board. As she was the more perplexed, she was also the more motivated. She'd met Sam before he'd started FTX, when he was still just another crypto trader no one in Asia had ever heard of. Back in late 2018, she'd been working in Huobi's Singapore office when the exchange had either frozen or misplaced some of Alameda Research's money. "They don't speak Chinese, and customer support does not speak English," said Constance. "They found me, and they found their magic fix to their problem."

After Sam decided to open his own crypto exchange, he'd hired Constance away from Huobi. She became the person he took with him to any meetings in which Mandarin might be spoken. "He was literally nobody, and nobody was taking him seriously," said Constance. In those first meetings, Sam's leg would bounce up and down so violently that the table where they sat would bounce too, and Constance would feel the need to reach over and put her hand on his knee, to still him. He'd just look at her and nod, but his leg would relax. Often he'd leave her feeling uneasy about how much he'd disclosed, and to perfect strangers. "There are some times I told him in the early days, *You don't have to be so honest. In crypto everyone bluffs.* Sam is always, *Let me show you my last card.*"

Back then, crypto was still a small world. "You go to a few conferences, you host an event, and you know everyone, basically," said Constance. So that people might get to know Sam, she'd taken him to a dance party ("Sam has one move, bouncing straight up and down") and kept him there until three in the morning. They had a meeting scheduled at nine. Constance awakened at six, hungover, and texted Sam to postpone. He replied immediately. "He never sleeps," she said. "I asked him once how he can be happy, and he said, 'Happiness does not matter.'"

Four years later, in the kitchen of the Conch Shack, she paged through the private documents she'd unearthed (how I never learned) that described some of what Sam had done with his surplus waking hours. The first was an internal spreadsheet of FTX's spending on endorsements. On George's org chart, Constance oversaw all of FTX marketing. Until then, she'd never seen FTX's biggest marketing expenditures. The numbers boggled her mind. Three-year deals each with the Coachella music festival, Steph Curry, and Mercedes's Formula 1 team for, respectively, $25 million, $31.5 million, and $79 million. The five-year deal with Major League Baseball for $162.5 million. A seven-year deal with the video game developer Riot Games for $105 million. ("Just because Sam likes *League of Legends*," said Constance.) On it went, for a very long time, until it reached the smaller deals, which actually didn't look so small: $15.7 million to *Shark Tank*'s Kevin O'Leary, for example, for "twenty service hours, twenty social posts, one virtual lunch and fifty autographs."

Virtual lunch! Constance of course knew that Sam had been loose with money. She'd just assumed that he had so much it didn't matter what he handed Kevin O'Leary. "I tried to question it," she said. "But I thought they were using the profit from Alameda. Or that Sam's investments were making a ton of money."

The next document in her stack was a rough balance sheet of Alameda Research that differed in important ways from the rough balance sheet that had inspired the CoinDesk article now being credited with bringing down the entire business. It appeared to Constance that it had been hastily concocted either by Sam or Caroline, or maybe by both. Constance had first come across it the previous Tuesday, after FTX had ceased sending money back to its customers. "When I saw it, I told my team not to respond to external parties because I did

not want them to lose their good name and reputation," she said.
The list of assets included the details of hundreds of private investments Sam had made over the previous two years, apparently totaling
$4,717,030,200. The liabilities now had a line item more important
than everything else combined: *$10,152,068,800 of customer deposits.*
More than $10 billion that was meant to be custodied by FTX some-
how had ended up inside Sam's private trading fund. The document
listed only $3 billion in liquid assets—that is, US dollars or crypto that
could be sold immediately for dollars. "I was like, *Holy shit,*" she said.
"The question is: *Why?*" It was the same question Zane had asked. "We
had so profitable a business," said Constance. "Our profit margin was
forty to fifty percent. We made four hundred million dollars last year."

These first two documents in Constance's private haul helped her
to see how the money had been spent. The others revealed who, ultimately, had picked up the tab. She now turned the page to a list
of FTX's top fifty creditors: the fifty biggest accounts whose owners
had been unable to remove their money from the crypto exchange,
ranked by the size of their losses. At the moment of its collapse, FTX
had had more than ten million account holders, to whom it owed
$8.7 billion. Nearly half of those losses, or $4 billion, were concen-
trated in these fifty accounts. The biggest losers not employed by
either FTX or Alameda were high-frequency trading firms. Near
the top was Jump Trading ($206,160,600.00), and at the bottom
was Virtu Financial Singapore ($10,095,336.83). The real names of
about half the list were concealed. The entity listed as Tai Mo Shan
Limited—and out more than $75 million—was actually another
affiliate of Jump Trading. Many of the disguised accounts belonged
to FTX employees. Constance herself had lost around $25 million.
She still had $80,000 in an ordinary bank account she'd kept from
her previous life, but otherwise she'd lost everything.

As she had also overseen the sales team, she knew most of the
names on the list, especially the high-frequency traders. She knew
that every one of them had been intensely suspicious about the relationship between FTX and Alameda Research. "Everyone cared
about it," said Constance. "It was literally the first thing I was asked

every day. Is Alameda Research front-running us? Does Alameda Research get to see other people's trades? Does Alameda get less latency?" In other words: Did Alameda enjoy the same unfair trading edge on FTX that the high-frequency traders enjoyed on Nasdaq and the New York Stock Exchange? Oddly enough, it had not. Instead, FTX had simply loaned Alameda all of the high-frequency traders' deposits . . . for free!

FTX had also done other things to jeopardize the high-frequency traders' money, along with everyone else's. It had exempted Alameda from the risk rules that governed all the other traders. The trades made by every other trader on FTX were liquidated the moment their losses exceeded the collateral they had posted. That's why FTX felt so much safer than the other crypto exchanges. No single trader was allowed to lose so much money that it put the exchange, and everyone who traded on it, at risk. For Alameda Research, however, an exception had been made. Sam's private trading firm was allowed to lose, in effect, infinity dollars before its trades were liquidated. "*No one* ever asked about liquidation," said Constance. "And *no one* ever asked, 'Is our money actually inside Alameda?'" Sam was right: People don't see what they aren't looking for.[*]

Till this point, Constance had been calm and detached. It was as if she were inspecting the medical charts of a total stranger to determine the cause of death. When she arrived at the final document, her tone changed. She'd uncovered a complete list of FTX's shareholders, along with the number of shares owned by each. At the end of each year, as part of her bonus, she, like other FTX employees, had been allowed to buy a certain number of shares in FTX. Everyone agreed that these shares were the finest possible investment. Right up to the very end, the world's most famous venture capitalists had been clamoring to buy them, at a higher price than employees

---

[*] Sam said much the same thing to me. "No one ever asked about the risk engine," he said. "I don't know what I would have done if asked. I would have done one of two things. Either I would have answered a different question, or I would have made a word salad."

were asked to pay. "Sam decides how many each employee is allowed to buy," said Constance. "Most everyone maxed out." She'd maxed out herself, but she'd never really known what that meant. When she'd come upon this document, her eyes had naturally searched for the number alongside her own name: 0.04 percent. Not 4 percent; not four-tenths of 1 percent: four *one hundredths* of 1 percent. She'd of course known how many shares she'd been given, or had been allowed to buy cheap, as part of her annual bonuses. She'd never thought to calculate exactly how much of the company she owned, or how much anyone else owned. She of course knew that Sam owned 60 percent and that Gary and Nishad, the next biggest shareholders, had between them another 23 percent, because those numbers had been published. *Forbes* had needed them to rank not just Sam but also Gary and Nishad on its list of billionaires.

About all other FTX employees, including herself, Constance was in the dark. Now she compared her number to the numbers of some of the other people at the top of George's org chart. Ramnik owned many times more shares than she did, as did Brett Harrison, the former CEO of tiny FTX US, who had only joined in May of 2021 (and resigned sixteen months later). As did . . . basically everyone at her level. She thought back to conversations she'd had over the past three years with potential investors. Several had told her that they had seen FTX's cap table—the list of shareholders with meaningful stakes—and had been surprised that her name was not on it. She hadn't thought much about it. "I always trusted Sam to treat me fairly," she said.

That's when Constance's feeling about Sam changed: when she saw how she'd actually been treated. Until then she'd been simply sad. On their last day in jungle hut 27 the previous Thursday, she and Quinn had fallen into each other's arms and wept. They'd lost everything, but felt bereft, not bitter. Not until Constance saw how little Sam had given her compared to others did she see red. Enraged, she marched up to the Orchid penthouse and confronted him. " 'It's not possible,' he said. 'I thought you had at least a million shares.' " She had less than a quarter of that. "Sam said to me, 'I never intended for that to happen to you,' and I said to him, 'It does not matter what you intended!' "

That revelation would set the tone for the next month. Constance would stick around and make a show of helping Sam with his absurd plan to resuscitate FTX. She'd meet with him nearly every day and tend to his linguistic needs and even cook him dinner. What she was really doing was trying to understand exactly what he'd done. Eventually the US Department of Justice would find her, and she'd agree to serve as a witness in the case they'd bring against Sam. But before that, she intended to ask Sam a few questions. Get him to explain himself. See if she could catch him out. Coax him into a confession. At the very least, she might find the holes and the contradictions in his story.

The story Sam told Constance ran as follows. There had been two different ways that money that should have been in cold storage inside FTX instead wound up in Alameda's hot little hands. The first was through Alameda's normal trading activity. Like every other trader, Alameda had been allowed to borrow from the FTX exchange by posting collateral. As collateral, Alameda had used, among other things, FTT—the token that was, in effect, equity in FTX. The price of FTT had collapsed with FTX. The collateral was now worthless, and some of the loans remained unpaid. In Sam's story, there was a reason that Alameda had been exempted from the rules that governed every other trader on FTX, and had liquidated their trades when the losses exceeded the value of their collateral. Back in 2019, when FTX was created, Alameda was by far its biggest trader. At the start, Alameda was on the other side of most trades that occurred on FTX. It helped the market on the exchange to work better if Alameda could occasionally run losses—for example, if they needed to step in and acquire another trader's losing positions after FTX liquidated them.

In Sam's telling, FTX had switched off Alameda's risk limits to make itself more appealing. The losses caused by this unsettling policy were in any case trivial. Ordinary trading loans made by FTX to Alameda constituted a small fraction of the losses to customers; on their own, they wouldn't have posed a problem. The bulk of the customers' money inside of Alameda that should have been inside FTX—$8.8 billion of it, to be exact—resided in an account that Alameda had labeled fiat@.

The fiat@ account had been set up in 2019 to receive the dollars and other fiat currencies sent by FTX's new customers. Alameda Research had created the account only after FTX had been unable to get its own bank accounts. Back in 2019, no real bank in the United States had been willing to offer its services to a new international crypto exchange. The crypto entities that they did bank, like Alameda Research, usually disguised their association with crypto. The biggest US crypto exchange, Coinbase, had by some miracle persuaded Silicon Valley Bank to give it an account—and thus a mechanism for Coinbase to receive US dollars from, and send US dollars to, its crypto trading customers. A US bank account had thereby given Coinbase a big advantage, but how exactly they'd obtained the account was a story for another day; the story for this day is how FTX failed to find its own US bank for sending and receiving dollars. From its founding in the spring of 2019 until July 2021, when it finally persuaded a bank in San Diego called Silvergate Capital* to open an account in its name, FTX had no straightforward way to accept dollar deposits.

In Sam's telling, the dollars sent in by customers that had accumulated inside of Alameda Research had simply never been moved. Until July 2021, there was no other place to put them, as FTX had no US dollar bank accounts. They'd been listed on a dashboard of FTX's customer deposits but remained inside Alameda's bank accounts. Sam also claimed that, right up until at least June 2022, this fact, which others now found so shocking, hadn't attracted his attention. He wasn't managing Alameda Research; Caroline was. Toward the end of 2021, when the flow of new dollars into the fiat@ account trickled to nothing—as customers could now deposit their dollars directly onto FTX, through a US bank—Alameda Research had a net asset value of $100 billion. That number was of course wildly

* The institutions that stepped up to bank crypto wound up paying a huge price. Of the four that collapsed in the spring 2023 run on regional US banks, three were the earliest bankers of crypto firms: Silicon Valley Bank, Silvergate Capital, and Signature Bank. The fourth, First Republic Bank, was not important in the crypto financial ecosystem but did have an account with $200,000 in it in the name of Sam Bankman-Fried.

unreliable, as it was simply the market value of lots of cryptocurrencies for which the market might vanish, if Alameda tried to sell into it. But even if you valued the contents of Alameda more rigorously, as Sam sort of did in his head sometimes, you could still easily get to $30 billion. The $8.8 billion that should not have been inside Alameda Research was not exactly a rounding error. But it was, possibly, not enough to worry about. As Sam put it: "I didn't ask, like, 'How many dollars do we have?' It felt to us that Alameda had infinity dollars."

That feeling would have changed by late spring of 2022. Between the start of April and the middle of June, the price of a bitcoin fell from just over $45,000 to under $19,000. Entering that summer, the relative importance to Alameda of the $8.8 billion had skyrocketed. But Sam wasn't managing the risk inside Alameda Research, according to him. Caroline was. Perhaps because he and Caroline were barely speaking by that point, she hadn't bothered to raise, directly with him, her worries about the risks she'd been running.

Right up until October 2022, in Sam's telling, he'd had only two brushes with this huge unexplained pool of other people's money that had accumulated inside Alameda, and that Alameda was increasingly dependent upon. The first was truly bizarre: in mid-June, Caroline had become alarmed to discover that the fiat@ account had swelled from $8.8 billion to $16 billion. She shared her worries not with Sam but with Nishad, who in turn informed Sam and Gary—whereupon Gary discovered that it was just a bug in the software. The real number in the fiat@ account hadn't changed: it was still $8.8 billion.

Three months later, in September, Caroline pulled Nishad aside and told him that she was growing more and more worried about Alameda's market exposure. Nishad had taken Sam out onto the balcony of the Orchid penthouse and relayed the message—but without explicitly mentioning the fiat@ account. At that point, in Sam's telling, Sam thought that Alameda might be in trouble. He decided to dig into its accounts on his own and understand the problem. By October, he had a clearer picture. It was only then that he could see that Alameda had been operating as if the $8.8 billion in customer funds belonged to it. And by then it was too late to do anything about it.

Constance heard Sam out. She listened to his story. But she refused to believe it. She suspected that he was omitting some big, important fact—say, a sudden trading loss inside Alameda Research that had caused him to actively grab customers' money and move it into Alameda. "It is crazy," she said. "He made me try to believe it was an accounting error." She didn't know how or why he had consciously decided to take customers' money and use it as his own, but she felt sure he had. "I always feel disappointed that Sam did not explicitly say he moved the funds," she said. She decided to find out what had happened on her own, the way she had obtained the company's internal documents. She poked and prodded at Sam when his guard was down. She lurked over Dan Chapsky's shoulder as he searched FTX's computer code for evidence that Sam was not telling her the whole story. A month into it, she hadn't found anything.

Just once did she feel she might have tricked Sam into a confession. She'd been talking to him about how to present his story to the public. "I said to Sam, 'You have to explain why you moved the funds.' And he never denied that."

Yet he'd never actually said that he had moved the funds. His story, implausible as it sounded, remained irritatingly difficult to disprove. Constance's own experience working for FTX didn't help. It would not have surprised her at the time, for instance, to learn that, to maintain markets on the exchange, they'd needed to exempt Alameda's traders from FTX's risk rules. She'd seen how critical Alameda's willingness to trade anything with anyone at any time had been to the successful launch of FTX. She didn't even think it fishy that a crypto exchange had its own internal trading team. "Most of the exchanges did this,"[*] she said. "All the Chinese ones. It's only a matter of how big the trading team is and what they are doing." She couldn't even disprove Sam's wild story about the fiat@ account. Up

---

[*] The lawsuit filed against Binance by the SEC alleged, among other things, that the world's biggest crypto exchange used an internal trading team to manipulate its volume and removed billions of dollars' worth of customers' money and sent it to a trading firm, owned by CZ, called Merit Peak Limited.

until late 2021, when she had moved her own dollars from her personal bank account onto FTX, she'd needed to wire it not directly to FTX but to various accounts owned by Alameda Research. Some of the dollars inside fiat@ had been hers.

For the better part of the month, I watched Constance return from her encounters with Sam. "I try to poke, and each time I poke, he says a little more, and more," she said. Nothing he said, however, left her feeling that her situation had been explained. One night in early December, she stood with Quinn in her kitchen and considered what, if anything, she had learned about Sam Bankman-Fried over the past month. There'd been only one serious revelation, she'd decided. Over and over, she'd confronted Sam with the suffering he had inflicted upon the very people who had been most loyal to him. A very short list of characters, topped by CZ and a few Western male former FTX executives, had exited FTX better off than they'd been when they'd arrived. Most FTX employees had lost their life savings. Some had lost their spouses, their homes, their friends, and their good names. There were Taiwanese employees of FTX still in Hong Kong who couldn't afford plane tickets home. "I asked Sam: 'When you were doing this, have you ever thought how much this event will be hurting people, and does that count as part of your initial expected value calculation?'"

Even here, however, she found herself talking past Sam: in his telling, he hadn't realized how much risk he'd subjected others to, without their permission. Constance nevertheless sensed that he didn't really register the damage he'd caused to other people in the way that, say, she might have. "He has absolutely zero empathy," she said. "That's what I learned that I didn't know. He can't *feel* anything."

The morning after she said that, I returned to the Conch Shack kitchen and found a handwritten note. "*Why can't Sam love?*," it read. "*By Quinn.*"

I had a different question. It preoccupied me from the moment of the collapse: Where had the money gone? It was not obvious what had happened to it. And it would be hard to understand why the

effective altruists had done whatever they'd done with their customers' money without knowing how much of it they had lost and how
they had lost it. In the days after the collapse, I created what might
have been the world's crudest financial statement. It treated FTX
and Alameda Research as a single entity: Sam's World. One column
listed all the money that had entered Sam's World since its inception,
in April 2019; a second column listed all the money that had exited
Sam's World. Both ignored the year and a half of Alameda's existence
before the creation of FTX, as the numbers involved were relatively
small. All the numbers were obviously very rough estimates. Some
came from Sam, but all were confirmed by former insiders who had
no reason to lie to me. At any rate, when I was done, my extremely
naive money-in, money-out statement looked like this:

MONEY IN:

Net customer deposits: *$15 billion*

Investments from venture capitalists: *$2.3 billion*

Alameda trading profits: *$2.5 billion*

FTX exchange revenues: *$2 billion*

Net outstanding loans from crypto lenders (mainly Genesis and
    BlockFi): *$1.5 billion*

Original sale of FTT: *$35 million*

Total: $23,335,000,000

MONEY OUT:

Returned to customers during the November run: *$5 billion*

Amount paid out to CZ: *$1.4 billion* (Just the hard cash part of the
    payment. I'm ignoring the $500 million worth of FTT Sam
    also paid him, as Sam minted those for free. I'm also ignor-
    ing the $80 million worth of BNB tokens that CZ had used to
    pay for his original stake, worth $400 million at the time Sam
    returned them as part of his buyout of CZ's interest.)

Sam's private investments: *$4.4 billion* (The whole portfolio was

$4.7 billion, but at least one investment, valued at $300 million, Sam had paid for with shares in FTX. He likely did the same with others, and so this number is likely bigger than it actually was.)

Loans to Sam: *$1 billion* (Used for political and EA donations. After his lawyers explained to him that taking out loans was smarter than paying himself a stock dividend, as he'd need to pay tax on the dividends.)

Loans to Nishad for same: *$543 million*

Endorsement deals: *$500 million* (This is likely generous too, as in some cases—Tom Brady was one of them—FTX paid its endorsers with FTX stock and not dollars.)

Buying and burning their exchange token, FTT: *$600 million*

Corporate expenses (salaries, lunch, Bahamas real estate): *$1 billion*

Total: $14,443,000,000

Obviously, this wasn't the way Ernst & Young would have drawn it up—though these lists I made for myself didn't look much different than Sam and Caroline's various attempts to summarize their affairs. In the previous three and a half years, nearly $9 billion more had entered Sam's World than had exited it. When FTX stopped returning funds to customers, on Tuesday, November 8, it still had $3 billion on hand. That dropped the missing sum to $6 billion. (The roughly $450 million stolen in the hack three days later is irrelevant to this calculation.)

There were some likely explanations for the missing money. The more you thought about them, however, the less persuasive they became. For example, Alameda traders might have gambled away $6 billion. But if they had, why did they all believe themselves to be so profitable, right to the end? I'd spoken to a bunch of them. Several were former Jane Streeters. They weren't stupid. They'd all been chirpy and upbeat and even a bit boastful about how much more money Alameda made per trader than Jane Street. Alameda may have lost a lot of money trading, but how those losses occurred was not easy to see. The most hand-wavy story just then being bandied about was that the collapse in crypto prices somehow sucked all the money out of Sam's World. And it was true that Sam's massive holdings of Solana and FTT—and other tokens of even more dubious value—had crashed. They'd gone from being theoretically worth $100 billion at the end of 2021 to being worth practically zero in November 2022. But Sam had paid next to nothing for these tokens; they had always been more like found money than an investment he'd forked over actual dollars to acquire. He'd minted FTT himself, for free. For his entire haul of Solana tokens, he'd paid no more than $100 million. His fleece cloud fortune had evaporated, but that didn't explain where all those hard dollars had gone.

I found him alone that evening of November 14 in the Orchid penthouse—the home to the polycule, as his club of effective altruists was now being called in the *New York Post*. The outside world was just then entertaining the most lurid fantasies about Sam's inner circle. Inevitably, word had got out that the effective altruists took a principled stand against monogamy. After that, a rumor spread that they spent half their time in the Orchid penthouse finding new ways to have sex with each other. Mostly what they had done with each other was play board games. In the heat of bughouse chess matches, they'd explored every possible combination and position; otherwise, not so much. But the confusion was understandable. They'd granted themselves hunting licenses without ever really wanting to learn how to handle a gun. Who does that?

In the weeks after the collapse, the Orchid penthouse never lost the feeling of a smash-and-grab crime scene. Each bedroom remained as it had been at the moment of its occupant's departure. In them were preserved not just possessions but states of mind. Caroline's room was still the giddy mess she'd left it when she'd gone on vacation with a new boyfriend: the outfits she'd decided not to pack were still on her bed. Nishad's bedroom was perfectly clean. He had needed persuading to leave the Bahamas, and had taken the time to leave his space feeling like a hotel room waiting to be checked into.

Gary's bedroom, into which Sam had moved, told its own, more complicated story. Three packed bags remained in a corner: Gary had somehow decided to pack, then left his bags behind. Yet he hadn't packed everything: his dirty clothes were still scattered all over his room. On his desk remained a half-eaten package of oil-fried noodles. His toothbrush was still on the bathroom counter. He appeared to have prepared to leave, changed his mind, stayed for a few days and lived as if he planned to stick around, then changed his mind again— whereupon he cleared out as fast as he could. "It's what people do when they're afraid," said Sam, as I picked through the abandoned possessions. "It tells you something about how and why people left. Like what if they just took an extra hour and packed? He stayed for *days*. Why not stay for days and one more hour? It's not like he said, 'I've got one hundred six hours to be here,' and then he got to one hundred six and had to run." He paused, then added. "I'm guessing his lawyers told him that he'd be facing criminal charges if he stayed."

The list of questions I showed up with whenever I met with Sam always felt like one of those trick drinking glasses that refills itself after you've taken a gulp. His answers always led to even more questions. *What happened to those six billion dollars?* should have been at the top of my current list. Constance's documents had raised a lot of other, obviously less important questions, however, and one of them I just had to get off my chest.

"You paid Kevin O'Leary for virtual lunch?" I asked. "Seriously?"

"It wasn't that much," said Sam, stretching out on Gary's bed, which, now that he no longer could afford the Albany maid service, remained unmade. The Albany resort was making noises about shutting off the water and the power, too. "It was like two million a year."

"Five million a year, for three years," I said. For some tweets and autographs. From a *Shark Tank* person. And not even the most famous *Shark Tank* person. Maybe not even the second-most famous *Shark Tank* person.

"So," said Sam. "There's one type of product that's like shampoo. The way shampoo works is, you want shampoo, you buy shampoo. You don't tweet about shampoo. Financial products are different. Why do you trade on Robinhood? Because your friends trade on Robinhood. It's a conscious decision."

He'd entered the mode that maybe came most naturally to him. I thought of it as Sam's *patiently-explaining-things-to-an-idiot* mode. He'd have made a great high school physics teacher.

"You agreed to pay fifteen million dollars to Kevin O'Leary," I said.

"How do you get people on FTX?" he continued, ignoring me. "Investing is a social network. It makes no sense, but it is. And Kevin O'Leary is a social influencer. And when you look at who has influence in this social network, there aren't that many people."

With that, he began to list the people who might count as social influencers in finance. Kevin O'Leary hadn't even been at the top of that list. Sam had tried and failed to hire *Mad Money*'s Jim Cramer.

"It's Kevin O'Leary!" I was almost shouting.

"Who listens to him?" said Sam. He'd actually thought about Kevin O'Leary, the way he'd thought about all the other endorsements. "The answer isn't no one. One million people follow him. And they follow him for his financial advice. It's shocking. But it's true. Anything you can do to grow out this exponential network helps. I can't claim Kevin O'Leary is who matters. But I don't know who matters. How many people who are expected to give financial advice have one million followers on Twitter? There's not some huge number of them. There's thirty. Twenty will say no to us for various reasons. He said yes. That's reason number one."

"What's reason number two?" I asked.

"Reason number two is he came to us."

Eventually we arrived at the question whose answer might offer clues to other puzzles: Where did the money go? It wasn't the last time I'd ask it. Like Constance, I'd poke and prod and always come away with the sense that I'd learned less than I needed to know. But on that evening, Sam filled in one piece of this particular puzzle: FTX had lost a lot of money to hackers. To avoid encouraging other hackers, they'd kept their losses quiet. The biggest hacks occurred in March and April 2021. A lone trader had opened an account on FTX and cornered the market in two thinly traded tokens, BitMax and MobileCoin. His purchases drove up the prices of the two tokens wildly: the price of MobileCoin went from $2.50 to $54 in just a few weeks. This trader, who appeared to be operating from Turkey, had done what he had done not out of some special love for MobileCoin. He'd found a flaw in FTX's risk management software. FTX allowed traders to borrow bitcoin and other easily sellable crypto against the value of their MobileCoin and BitMax holdings. The trader had inflated the value of MobileCoin and BitMax so that he might borrow actually valuable crypto against them from FTX. Once he had it he vanished, leaving FTX with a collapsing pile of tokens and a loss of $600 million worth of crypto.

The size of those hacks was an exception, Sam said. All losses due to theft combined had come to just a bit more than $1 billion. In all cases, Gary had quietly fixed the problem and they'd all moved on and allowed the thieves to keep their loot. "People playing the game," was Sam's description of them. (He really was easy to steal from.)

The hacks reduced to $5 billion the number of unexplained missing dollars. Sam was no help in reducing the number further. Either he didn't know where the money had gone or he didn't want to say. He dismissed the most obvious explanation: Alameda had suffered some big trading loss in the great crypto crash of 2022. The collapse of FTX felt a bit like the case of the missing Ripple, but on a far grander scale. This time the question of where the money was would take longer to answer, and the person most qualified to figure it out was soon gone.

It was a Monday evening, December 12, and Constance and Quinn had just finished watching a funny YouTube video about stinky tofu. They were making their short nightly trek to Orchid to help with dinner when they spotted, just ahead, the men in uniforms. It looked like an episode of *CSI*, and they caught up to the guys on the sidewalk outside Sam's building to ask why they were there. The men wouldn't say. Instead, they said, *You're welcome to go up and find out for yourselves.* Which isn't something that men in uniforms normally invite you to do. So they did.

Moments earlier, a small crowd—Albany officials, *CSI*-looking people, one very large Bahamian police officer—had stepped off the elevator and into the penthouse. There was a long hallway from the elevator to the living room. Coming down it, the big policeman asked, "Is Mister Sam Bankman-Fried here?" He was reading from a paper in his hand—apparently a warrant. When George stood up from his chair in the living room, the policeman approached him and asked, "Are you Sam Bankman-Fried?"

At first no one could find Sam. As it turned out, he was tapping into his phone in Gary's bathroom. Less than an hour earlier, his lawyers had called to say that the US government was giving him an hour to decide whether to return to the United States or face arrest in the Bahamas. He'd been rushing to send in his written testimony to the House Financial Services Committee, which was about to hold an inquiry into the collapse of FTX. Sam had hoped to cut a deal that would allow him to appear in person without being detained by US authorities, but that clearly was not going to happen. Before he'd hit Send, he'd landed in an argument with his mother about what he planned to say. The opening of his testimony included the sentence "I fucked up." *You cannot say "fuck" to a US congressional committee,* argued Barbara. That point now seemed moot,[*] as the Bahamian police officer had him in handcuffs before he could finish what he was doing. Barbara stopped arguing with Sam about what he could say to Congress, and started arguing with him about what he should wear to jail. She wanted him to put on long pants. Sam insisted on remaining in his cargo shorts.

As the police explained the charges and produced the warrant,

---

[*] It wasn't. The document fell into the hands of reporters, who forwarded it on to the committee. Members of the committee saw Sam's document. They agreed with his mother.

Constance and Quinn entered and tried to make themselves useful. To the mess Gary had left behind, Sam had added his own sedimentary layer of laundry. They searched through it for clothes Sam might want to take with him to jail. *He needs socks*, thought Quinn, as the police officer led Sam from the room. *Because he likes to change his socks a lot. You can't take him away yet, because I have not finished picking up his socks.* George was now in the room too, looking for things Sam might need. He came across a keepsake box. It surprised him. He hadn't known that Sam had the sentiment in him. He opened it. It had very little inside. A few medals from high school math competitions. A copy of *Forbes* magazine, with Sam's face on the cover. And a box of business cards, from his time at Jane Street Capital.

It was Manfred that caught Constance's eye. Manfred was Sam's stuffed animal. He'd had it since birth and refused any substitutes, and so Manfred was about to turn thirty-one years old. She'd first seen Manfred in Hong Kong—Sam had brought it with him from Berkeley. Even then, Manfred was so old and worn it was hard to determine his species. Might have been a dog, could have been a bear. Manfred had made the journey from Hong Kong to the Bahamas and, Constance assumed, might soon be going to jail. Sam liked having Manfred around that much. Constance and Quinn had gone back and forth on the meaning of Sam's childhood friend. Sam didn't care about real animals. It had been an expected value calculation, rather than emotion, that had led him to go vegan. Quinn thought that Sam kept Manfred so close because "he doesn't need to share Manfred with anyone." Constance saw Manfred in a different light. "I think it is very, very important for him to have an emotional attachment," she said.

11

TRUTH SERUM

When the lawyer from Sullivan & Cromwell sent him the message asking him to sit tight because something big might be coming his way, John Ray had no idea what that big thing might be. All he knew was that whatever got to him would be a corpse. He knew nothing about crypto or its culture. He wouldn't have even wanted to be able to explain bitcoin. He certainly didn't know anything about FTX, and when the Sullivan & Cromwell lawyer referred to "SBF," he didn't know who or what the guy was talking about. "I thought it might mean 'small box Ford,'" said Ray. After a phone call on the night of Tuesday, November 8, the Sullivan & Cromwell lawyer had left him hanging. Finally, late Wednesday morning, Ray received a text: *It's insane. I'll try to get back to you later.* Then crickets until 12:33 a.m. on Friday, November 11. At that improbable hour, the Sullivan & Cromwell guy sent John Ray a text: *they are still considering whether you are the right candidate for the job.* Two hours later he texted again: *SBF has gone underground.* A part of John Ray thought that he was getting too old for this game.

The game still needed John Ray, however. The wild and wonderful world of US corporate bankruptcy was increasingly dominated by big law firms, but there were still a few of these lone actors, like Ray, who played the role of wildcatters. The law firms brought in the wildcatter to take over as CEO of the failed firm, and the wildcatter in turn hired the law firms. As a legal matter, at 4:30 in the morning on Friday, November 11, 2022, Sam Bankman-Fried DocuSigned FTX into bankruptcy and named John Ray as FTX's new CEO. As a practical matter, Sullivan & Cromwell lined up John Ray to replace Sam as the CEO of FTX, and then John Ray hired Sullivan & Cromwell as the lawyers for the massive bankruptcy.[*]

Sullivan & Cromwell was present on the scene only because the firm had done a bunch of work for Sam back when everyone loved him. They'd actually served as FTX's lawyers when the exchange had gone before US regulators to answer questions like: Are there any conflicts of interest between FTX and Alameda Research? Sam had never heard of John Ray, and he hadn't wanted to sign the bankruptcy papers. Or rather, there had been a period of about two hours on the morning of November 11 when he'd been willing to sign them. Up to that moment, he'd listened to the lawyers from Sullivan & Cromwell, and to his own father, with the combination of disinterest and polite skepticism that he reserved for grown-ups who were just telling him to do whatever grown-ups normally did. They were all saying that if he didn't sign the documents, he was going to be thrown into bankruptcy by various barbaric countries: he and FTX would be in safer hands in the United States than in other jurisdictions. Sam wasn't sure this was so.

While Sam stewed, John Ray read up on him and this company he'd created. "It's like, What is this thing?" said Ray. "Now it's just

---

[*] In the first seven months alone, the professional fees would top $200 million, with Sullivan & Cromwell the top fee earner, and they'd only just gotten started. A study made by one creditor projected that by the time they were done, the various advisors to the bankruptcy would have taken out a billion dollars.

a failure, but it was once some kind of business. *What did you guys do? What's the situation? Why's this falling into bankruptcy so quickly?*" He briefly considered the possibility that the failure was innocent: *maybe they got hacked.* "Then you start looking at the kid," said Ray, the kid being Sam. "I looked at his picture and thought, *There's something wrong going on with him.*" Ray prided himself on his snap judgments. He could look at a person and in ten minutes know who they were, and never need to reconsider his opinion. The men he evaluated he tended to place in one of three bins in his mind: "good guy," "naive guy," and "crook." Sam very obviously was not a good guy. And he sure didn't seem naive.

Sam had been led to believe that whoever succeeded him as CEO would at the very least use him as a resource, to help find the missing money. That was never going to happen. In the early days of his career in bankruptcy, back in the 1990s, John Ray had learned a lesson the hard way. One of the crooks he'd replaced engaged him in conversation and then lied about what had been said. In the first few days after he signed the company over to Ray, Sam reached out to him, over and over, with these pitiful emails. *Hey John, I'd really love to talk.* Ray took one look at them and thought, *No way, José.*

His unwillingness to interact in any way with Sam of course made it more difficult to figure out what Sam had done, or why he'd done it. "It's literally like you're pulling out a box of puzzle pieces and some of the pieces are missing and you can't talk to the guy who created the puzzle," said Ray. He'd spoken only long enough with the other members of Sam's inner circle to see them for what they were. Nishad Singh struck him as a naive guy. "He's narrow," said Ray. "It's tech, tech, tech. There's never a problem he can't solve. He's not going to steal money. He's not going to do anything wrong. But he has no idea what's going on around him. You ask him for a steak and he puts his head up the bull's ass." The bankruptcy team had located Caroline Ellison by phone on the Saturday after Ray became FTX's new CEO. She at least had been able to explain where some of the wallets storing the crypto were stashed. Other than that, she wasn't much use. "She's cold as ice," said Ray. "You had to buy words by the vowel. An obvious complete fucking weirdo."

As Caroline spoke, Ray had tried to figure out where she was. She claimed to be in Boston. Ray knew that wasn't true. He made chitchat that sounded more innocent than it was. *Was it a long flight from Hong Kong? How's the weather where you are?* The FBI was looking for Caroline, and he intended to help them find her.[*] He had a clear, narrowly defined job: to find as much money as he could and return that money to the creditors. Almost as soon as he became the new CEO of FTX, he took on a second, far more loosely defined one: helping US prosecutors make their case against Sam Bankman-Fried. "There's people that are born criminals, and there're people that become criminals," said Ray. "I think he became a criminal. The how and why he became a criminal I don't know. I think maybe it takes an understanding of this kid and his parents."

Then all was chaos. Sam signed the papers and announced eight minutes later that he'd changed his mind, only to have Sullivan & Cromwell inform him that there was no updating after you'd declared bankruptcy. That cleared the way for Ray to be briefed on FTX. He now learned that FTX owned thirty different crypto exchanges—not just in the Bahamas and the US but also in Turkey and Japan and, well, you name it. Wherever people traded crypto in size, FTX had incorporated an exchange and sought a government license. Each exchange had money on it and customers who in theory could log in and withdraw their deposits. So far as Ray could see, which was not very far, no money was moving. "There was no sheet of paper with bank account information on it," he said. Inside scores

---

[*] They'd find her in a raid of her parents' vacation house in New Hampshire. She'd moved from Nassau to Nashua.

of small banks and far-flung crypto exchanges, FTX or Alameda or one of the more than one hundred other corporate entities they controlled held many dollars and other fiat currencies. There were also, on some Amazon server, passcodes that gave you access to virtual wallets with crypto inside. "The wallets were in the cloud," said Ray. "You lose the passcodes, you lose the money."

If the money was hard to find, it was in part because there was no person inside of FTX—at least no person Ray was willing to speak with—in charge of knowing where it all was. "There was no structure," said Ray. "No list of employees.* No org chart." Six days into his new job, Ray filed a report with the US Bankruptcy Court for the District of Delaware. "Never in my career have I seen such a complete failure of corporate controls and such a complete absence of trustworthy financial information as occurred here," he wrote.

Instead of grilling the people who had created the mess, Ray hired teams of hard-nosed sleuths—many of whom he'd worked with before. "Serious adults," as he called them. The Nardello firm was a lot of former FBI guys. (Corporate motto: *We find out.*) Chainalysis, the crypto sleuthing firm, was new to him. Ray told his people to "do a Zoom interview with every single FTX employee. And if they don't contact you to arrange a time, they're fired." Maybe eighty employees got themselves fired that way. Just about everyone else would be fired after their Zoom call. Even if you came out of the woods with your hands in the air you got shot. "He was acting like every single person who was not in the United States was part of a crime, but he didn't know what the crime was," as one FTX employee put it. On a group Zoom call to talk about the mysterious roughly $450 million hack that had happened the day of the collapse, Sam himself popped up. *Hey, Sam here!* Ray said, imitating Sam's chipper tone, itself an imitation. "We were trying to figure out what the fuck is going on and who

---

* There was one of these, too, but it was as elusive as George's org chart. Natalie had given it to me but with a whisper that might accompany the transfer of a classified document.

hacked us," said Ray. "He knows nothing about the hack. He keeps saying, 'You have to ask Gary.' He pops up later and says, 'I need my passwords to get into the system.' I'm like, *Fuck no.*"

Within a few weeks, Ray had fired pretty much everyone with deep knowledge of whatever had happened inside FTX and Alameda Research. He could think of but one exception. "I think they're still paying the psychiatrist," said Ray.

That was in early 2023. By late April, John Ray's head was on a swivel. "This is live-action," he said. "There's always something every hour." One day, some random crypto exchange got in touch and said, *By the way, we have $170 million in an account of yours: do you want it back?* Another day, some random FTX employee called them out of the blue to say that he'd borrowed two million bucks from the company and wanted to repay the loan—of which, so far as Ray could see, there was no record. Of course, once you heard about one loan, you had to wonder how many others like it you'd never hear about. The search for money inside Sam's World reminded Ray of the Easter egg hunt he'd just run for his grandchildren. "At the end they have a count," he said. "Five are missing. They go out and look for them. They come back with six." The extra egg was a yellowing relic undiscovered the previous year. His teenaged grandchild had said to him: *This is just like your new job!* And it was true! John Ray was on a bizarre Easter egg hunt with no prior egg count. With no idea how many eggs he was looking for, he'd never know when to end his search.

Several months into the hunt, Ray's sleuths had discovered that "someone had robbed the exchange of four hundred fifty million." They'd stumbled upon not the simple hack of November 2022 but the complicated BitMax and MobileCoin hacks of $600 million in the spring of 2021. (The dollar value changed with fluctuations in the price of the stolen crypto.) They'd tracked the hacker not to Turkey but Mauritius. "We have a picture of him going in and out of his house," said Ray. He was pretty sure he was going to get most of that money back. "We believe there are a lot more of these," said Ray. Eventually, I figured, he'd find the $1 billion or so lost in hacks that Sam would have just told him about, if he'd been willing to talk to Sam.*

It was true, as Sam said, that people don't see what they're not looking for. It was also true that they have a talent for seeing whatever it is they expect to see. John Ray expected to see evidence of a crime. To our meetings he always brought new and seemingly damning pieces. One time, he'd found Alameda Research's US tax forms from 2021, for instance. Alameda had reported a loss of more than $3 billion. If it was what it seemed to be, it would help to explain the hole in my private balance sheet; but it was actually just a piece of a bigger and more complicated puzzle. That year, Alameda Research had sold short FTT at the same time an entity it controlled bought the same quantity of FTT. The price of FTT had gone up, a lot. Alameda Research suffered a multibillion-dollar trading loss; the second entity had taken in a precisely corresponding multibillion-dollar gain. The accounting rules for Alameda Research allowed it to report unrealized market losses as tax losses; the accounting rules for the other entity did not require that it do the obverse with its gains. Alameda's tax lawyers, a group that included Sam's father, had argued for taking the tax loss, as it could be offset against current gains. It was, as one of the lawyers put it, "a fake loss."

Back in June 2022, Nishad Singh had filled my ears with the many devious ways people sought to extort money from FTX. Several employees had joined the firm, been found wanting at their jobs, and been fired—then had sought out one of several law firms that

---

* Former FTX employees were more skeptical of Ray's sleuths. Sam's World controlled a great many virtual wallets, and you sort of had to know what you were looking for to find them. "They have no idea what are in these wallets," said one former employee. "Even after five years, they will not know." As an example, he mentioned a collection of 101 Bored Ape Yacht Club non-fungible tokens, or NFTs, that Sam had bought at auction for $24.4 million back in September 2021. They had not been on Ray's list of recovered assets. The former Hong Kong staff thought there was a lot like that.

famously specialized in shaking down crypto firms.* Nishad had been outraged not merely that the various accusations the fired employees had made were pure inventions but that everyone involved knew that FTX would rather pay out several million dollars than endure the cost of a false accusation. "The American employees are the problem," he said. "The Chinese employees don't do this." FTX had finally cooked up a strategy they called Operation Warm Blanket. Operation Warm Blanket identified the law firms that engaged in the shakedowns and retained them to do legal work, so that they couldn't sue FTX. At the time, it seemed smart; less so two years later, with John Ray waving documents and arguing that Sam had paid hush money to settle whistleblower complaints.

To John Ray it felt like an Easter egg hunt. To me it felt more like an amateur archaeologist had stumbled upon a previously unknown civilization. Unable to learn anything about its customs or its language, he just started digging. The artifacts unearthed by the excavation lent themselves to an interpretation that would have puzzled the aboriginals who had created and used them. But the pleasure Ray took in whatever he unearthed was so infectious that I often didn't have the heart to say, "I'm not quite sure that you've found exactly what you think you have found," or "I actually know what that is, and it isn't what you think." At some point his team discovered that a Hong Kong subsidiary of Alameda Research called Cottonwood Grove had bought vast sums of FTT, for example. To the innocent archaeologist, it was evidence of Sam's World artificially propping up the value of FTT. Ray didn't know that FTX had been obligated to spend roughly a third of its revenues buying back

---

* One of the lawyers responsible for at least one of the resulting raids on FTX, Kyle Roche, would be fired by his firm after making a video explaining how he shook down crypto companies that had actually done nothing wrong. He'd claim that he had been drugged and tricked into saying what he had. Another story for another day.

and burning its token, and that Cottonwood Grove was the entity that did it.

From my perch on the side of the dig, I would occasionally shout down to the guy running it my guess about the most recent find, but he'd just look up at me, pityingly. I was clearly a naive guy. During one of our meetings, Ray asked, "Did you ever hear of this guy Zane Hacket?" He'd gotten the name wrong but he'd discovered that Zane had pulled many thousands of dollars' worth of crypto off the exchange in the weeks before the collapse. And he had! In the weeks before the collapse, Zane had bought some stuff. But Zane had also deposited a million and a half dollars' worth of crypto onto the exchange the Sunday of the collapse. He had the receipts to prove it: when FTX vanished, much of Zane's wealth vanished with it. Zane's problem wasn't that he was a crook but that he was too trusting. The same was true of almost all of FTX's employees, many of whom had lost everything. Their lost civilization had been built not on cynicism but on trust.

That was hard for the archaeologist with no prior knowledge of it to see. Ray's first impression of Sam and his inner circle was the starting point for a narrative that could be imposed on almost any of the remaining fragments of Sam's World. The hundreds of private investments made by Alameda Research, for instance. When we first met, in early 2023, Ray went on about how fishy these all were. He had a theory about why Sam had thrown money around the way he had: Sam was buying himself some friends. "For the first time in his life, everyone ignores the fact that he's a fucking weirdo," said Ray. As an example, he cited the dollars Sam had invested in artificial intelligence companies. "He gave five hundred million bucks to this thing called Anthropic," said Ray. "It's just a bunch of people with an idea. Nothing." A few weeks later, Google and Stark Capital and a few other companies invested $450 million in Anthropic. The terms revalued the stake Sam had bought for $500 million to $800 million. I knew at least one investor who thought that if that stake was broken up into smaller pieces and slowly sold off, it might easily fetch a billion.

Once Ray's people had finished doing the math, they concluded that FTX still owed its customers $8.6 billion. There were at least three ways the money might be found to repay them. The first was the Easter egg hunt, the search for company funds that might still be stashed in banks and crypto exchanges. A second was to sell whatever was left over inside the dragon's lair—not just the stake in Anthropic but the hundreds of other private investments and the vast pile of lesser-known cryptocurrencies. The third was to claw back money from the people Sam paid to be his friends—his investments in other people's funds, his political donations, even his philanthropic gifts.

To wring the money out of the people Sam had hurled it at, John Ray needed to prove two things. The first was that FTX hadn't received equivalent value for its money. You couldn't claw back money from a plumber who'd been paid some normal sum to unclog an FTX drain. But you could claw back money from the researcher to whom FTX had handed a grant to invent drains that never clogged. Simply not getting value for money was not enough for Ray to get it back, however. He also had to prove that at the moment Sam gave money away, it wasn't his money to give. And the only way it wasn't Sam's money was if FTX, in the moment he gave away the money, was insolvent, or nearly so. Ray's various attempts to claw back money raised an interesting question, which his team had yet to answer in an intelligible way: At what point was there less money in all of Sam's World than was supposed to be inside of FTX? Exactly when did FTX go broke?

Instead of answering the question, Ray launched a blitzkrieg of lawsuits against various people to whom Sam had handed money. These were really fun to read. They were still legal texts, but they all had subtexts. Plus, Ray wrote to attract media attention. "You have to tell a story," explained Ray. "Nobody wants to read X dollars wired to

Y, blah, blah, blah. You need the imagination of a child to write this stuff." In the first eight and a half months, he filed nine of these claw-back lawsuits. Ray mainly targeted insiders—Sam, Sam's parents, Caroline, Nishad, and so forth—or people to whom Sam had forked over huge sums to invest on his behalf.* His most revealing target, at least to me, was FTX's lawyer Dan Friedberg.

In Sam's World, Dan Friedberg—who was in his early fifties—had been the only important grown-up. At the behest of Sam's father, he'd left a multimillion-dollar-a-year job at the law firm Fenwick & West to chase after Sam wherever he went. He was FTX's general counsel. He was also the babysitter. To a baby who terrifies his parents and is calling the shots. He'd followed Sam to Hong Kong and then moved again to the Bahamas, where he spent a lot of time looking

---

* In a suit filed against Michael Kives for return of the $700 million Sam had invested in his K5 group of funds, Ray led with a dinner party Kives hosted on February 11, 2022, attended by Sam. "True to Kives's reputation as a high-profile 'super-networker,'" he wrote, "the attendees at the dinner party included a for-mer Presidential candidate, top actors and musicians, reality TV stars and multi-ple billionaires." He then quoted from a memo he'd found, written by Sam, which described Kives as "one-stop shop[ping] for relationships that we should utilize" and a provider of "infinite connections." I'd actually gone to that dinner party with Sam. Neither of us, nor any of Sam's colleagues, had any idea who Kives was. The dinner party invitation had come more or less out of the blue, along with a hint about the guest list. Sam was going to be in Los Angeles anyway and decided (as always) last-minute to see if it was real. He worried a bit how to pronounce the name of his host. (He guessed it was KY-ves; it turned out to be KEE-vus.) His employees worried that the invitation was a ruse to get Sam to a house in Beverly Hills so that he might be kidnapped. Adam Jacobs followed in a car with a small team and was ready to rush the house and save Sam if he cried for help. In this spirit, and of course wearing cargo shorts, Sam rolled into the home of a total stranger, only to be ushered to the back lawn, where maybe sixty other guests had already gathered. Among them: Hil-lary Clinton, Leonardo DiCaprio, Chris Rock, Katy Perry, Kate Hudson, Orlando Bloom, Jeff Bezos, Doug Emhoff, and at least four Kardashians. For a moment it seemed like a play drawn up by Fox News to dramatize one of their arguments in the culture war—but then we spotted Dallas Cowboys owner Jerry Jones, a solid Republican, and Los Angeles Rams owner "Silent Stan" Kroenke, who had donated a million bucks to help pay for Trump's inauguration. Sam pulled out his phone and texted Jacobs: *I think it's real.*

out of place in Bermuda shorts. Friedberg was who Sam usually had in mind when he complained about the pointless stuff that grown-ups asked him to worry about. Even in good times, it was obvious that Friedberg had had only so much influence on him, or on the opera-tion, though Friedberg's name of course appeared on many official documents. He'd helped to set up the bank accounts that received the deposits from FTX's customers. He'd helped to execute Opera-tion Warm Blanket. But in the week of FTX's collapse, he'd been the first employee to abandon ship, and had gone immediately to the US financial regulators and the FBI. Even then, he didn't know exactly what had happened between FTX and Alameda—just that whatever it was was bad. And he was completely, totally crushed. He'd sort of gotten swept up by the enthusiasm of the effective altruists. "I wanted there to be a Sam," as he put it.

Friedberg's most serious offense, I suspected, had been commit-ted after the collapse. After he'd joined FTX, he'd moved about a million dollars' worth of crypto from his account on Coinbase onto FTX US. He'd tried, and failed, to attach himself to a suit brought by other creditors to prevent Sullivan & Cromwell from controlling the bankruptcy, and thus all the evidence of what had happened. No one had asked Dan Friedberg to reach out to the bankruptcy judge; all by himself he'd just filed a declaration with the Delaware bankruptcy court. The literary energy of the thing exceeded even John Ray's. It explained that, back in late 2020, Friedberg had hired a Sullivan & Cromwell partner named Ryne Miller to become the general coun-sel for FTX US. He wrote that Miller had told him back then that he hoped to return to Sullivan & Cromwell—and so he needed to direct as much FTX legal work as he could toward his future employer. FTX had subsequently paid Sullivan & Cromwell between $10 mil-lion and $20 million in fees. In one instance, Friedberg alleged, Sul-livan & Cromwell had billed FTX $6.5 million for work that should have cost a small fraction of that amount.

At any rate, in the week of the collapse, when it became clear that FTX was bankrupt, the lawyers argued about what to do. Along with all the other lawyers, Friedberg had resigned. Miller alone had stayed on and pushed for Sam to sign the bankruptcy documents and for Sullivan & Cromwell to run the bankruptcy proceedings. It was also Miller, wrote Friedberg, who pushed for FTX US to be included in the bankruptcy—even though FTX US was a wholly separate entity and appeared to be solvent.* Miller had done this for two reasons, Friedberg alleged. The first was to strengthen the case for the lucrative bankruptcy to unfold in the United States, as opposed to, say, the Bahamas. The other was that FTX US controlled a pool of $200 million that could be used to pay Sullivan & Cromwell. At the end of his declaration, Friedberg wrote, "I am not the only former FTX employee who has serious concerns about S&C. Both former and current employees are scared to raise these issues because S&C might take adverse action against them."

Inside the US bankruptcy system, there existed a frustrating and often frustrated character called the trustee. Employed by the US Department of Justice, the trustee was meant to serve as a check on the insiders who profited from the bankruptcy. (And who controlled the evidence for any criminal cases.) But the only power the trustee had been given by law was the power to bitch and moan to the bankruptcy judge, himself usually a former bankruptcy lawyer. The US Trustee assigned to the FTX case, Andrew Vara, had written a strongly worded letter to the judge, John T. Dorsey, arguing that Sullivan & Cromwell shouldn't be allowed to run the bankruptcy, and that an independent examiner should be brought in to police it. Dorsey had denied the request. He did the same with Dan Friedberg's. At the hearing to decide whether Sullivan & Cromwell could run the bankruptcy, witnesses were allowed to appear in person or

---

* John Ray told me that it was not but did not supply evidence. An employee of FTX US who worked on a small team that studied the question in early November 2022 told me, "When we ran the calculation on the US balance sheet, it was a solvent entity."

by Zoom. Friedberg had Zoomed in, uninvited, and offered to testify under oath. Dorsey refused to allow it.

Outside the US courtroom, Friedberg had one of the better views of what had occurred inside Sam's World and maybe the finest view of the role Sullivan & Cromwell had played in it. Inside the courtroom, Dan Friedberg's experience was deemed irrelevant. And that, it seemed, was the end of it. US bankruptcy judges have sensational powers to determine which evidence to admit in a case.

But then in late June, John Ray made Dan Friedberg relevant again, by suing him in bankruptcy court. Ray had his own response to the dispute between Ryne Miller and Dan Friedberg. He thought Miller "a naive guy." He thought Friedberg "a born criminal."

Dan Friedberg hadn't been charged with a crime. He was cooperating with the Department of Justice in their investigation. Ray didn't have the power to charge Friedberg with a crime. In his lawsuit, which sought to claw back all the money FTX had paid Dan Friedberg, Ray listed the bad things he thought Friedberg had done. He also listed the monies that he wanted Friedberg to return. Most of the money was in a single line item. "In July 2020, "wrote Ray, "the FTX Group caused Friedberg to be granted 102,321,128 Serum tokens, a digital currency launched by the Solana Foundation in 2020. . . . At the time of Plaintiff's bankruptcy filing the value of Serum was estimated at $.33 per token, and therefore Friedberg's Serum holdings were worth $33,765,972.20."

Before I read that line, I had only ever heard Ray refer to Serum (and Solana and FTT) as "Sam Coins" or "shitcoins." His view of crypto was a bit like his view of people. There was "the good shit" and "the bad shit." (Though no naive shit.) I'd never tried to argue with him, in part because I thought he was sort of right. Still, there were distinctions worth making that he hadn't bothered to make. FTT received an actual cash flow—the robust revenues from FTX— and so was more like corporate equity. Solana, because it could process tens of thousands more transactions per second than Bitcoin, was perhaps better designed than Bitcoin to fulfill Satoshi's original vision and become a means of exchange. In any case, because a sufficient number of people had come to believe that story, there was a real market for Solana tokens, and the pile that Sam had accumulated still had value.

Serum was, by comparison, a dubious proposition. Serum was more like a currency in the private board game Sam never stopped playing inside his own mind.

Serum was Sam's bet on blockchains replacing, say, the New York Stock Exchange or, for that matter, FTX. Blockchains were just communally maintained records of who owned what and when they'd owned it. They could keep track of any transaction. It was at least theoretically possible that they could keep track of all financial transactions. The Serum tokens that Friedberg had been paid gave their owner trading discounts on, voting rights over, and a slice of the tiny fee charged for any financial transaction that occurred on the Solana blockchain. Which sounded great. The problem was that there were relatively few financial transactions on the Solana blockchain. Sam had simply cooked up the idea with Solana's founders, minted ten billion of these Serum tokens, kept most of them for himself—but handed some to his employees, as pay.

The Serum tokens Sam paid to employees like Friedberg appeared to be fetching $.33 at the time of his bankruptcy. Their true value was not as clear. The FTX employees' Serum tokens were "locked"; the employees were forbidden from selling them until they became unlocked. The person who did the unlocking was Sam. Initially, the tokens were meant to be unlocked over the course of seven years, starting at the end of the first year. Employees could sell one-seventh of their Serum at the end of that first year, and another seventh at the end of each of the following years, until they'd sold it all.

Soon after Serum's creation, its price had skyrocketed. Sam clearly had not anticipated this. He now had all these employees who felt ridiculously rich. (At least in theory, the value of Dan Friedberg's Serum stash peaked, in September 2021, at over $1 billion.) In Sam's view, everyone at once became a lot less motivated to work fourteen-hour days. And so he did a very Sam thing: he changed the terms of the employees' Serum. In the fine print of the employee Serum contract, he'd reserved for himself the right to extend Serum's jail time, and he used it to lock up all employees' Serum for seven years. Sam's employees had always known that he preferred games in which the rules could change in the middle. They now understood that if he had changed the rules once, he might do it again. They became less enthusiastic about their Serum. "It was very unclear if you had it or if you didn't have it," said Ramnik, who had watched in irritation as Sam locked up a bunch of tokens that he'd bought with his own money on the open market before he joined FTX. "I guess you would know in seven years."

The market even for ordinary Serum tokens wasn't great. There was no chance that Dan Friedberg could have sold 102 million Serum tokens at the stated market price. Serum that you effectively would not possess for seven years and maybe not even then—who would have the courage to guess what that was worth? Zero, perhaps? That's what *Forbes* magazine had concluded, even as Serum's price was peaking, when they valued Sam's holdings. They'd treated his locked Serum tokens as if they didn't exist.

And yet now, somehow, in John Ray's book, the locked Serum was good shit. Primo crypto of the finest vintage imbibed by all gentlemen of good taste. And who knows?—maybe one day it will be. But if Serum was a token to be taken seriously, Sam Bankman-Fried and the world he created needed to be viewed in a different light. At Serum's peak price, the stated market value of Sam's stash of it was $67 billion. On November 7, 2022, Sam's pile of mostly locked Serum was still "worth" billions of dollars. If even locked Serum had that kind of value, FTX was solvent right up to the moment it collapsed. And John Ray would have no grounds for clawing back money from any of the many lucky people on whom Sam Bankman-Fried had showered it.

Six months into the Easter egg hunt, there was a decent argument to be made that FTX was solvent right up to the moment it collapsed, even if Sam's Serum was worthless. The hunt had gone better than anyone without a very deep working knowledge of Sam's motives and methods could have expected. At the end of June 2023, John Ray filed a report on his various collections. "To date, the Debtors have recovered approximately $7 billion in liquid assets," he wrote, "and they anticipate additional recoveries." Seven point three billion, to be exact. That haul didn't include the Serum, or any large clawbacks, or the money stolen by the guy in Mauritius, or the stake in Anthropic, or most of the other private investments. An investor who was hoping to bid for the remaining portfolio told me that, if it was sold intelligently, it should go for at least $2 billion. That would raise the amount collected to $9.3 billion—even before anyone asked CZ for the $2.275 billion he'd taken out of FTX. Ray was inching toward an answer to the question I'd been asking from the day of the collapse: Where did all that money go? The answer was: nowhere. It was still there.

Caroline had been the first to plead guilty and take whatever deal the prosecutors had implicitly offered. Gary and Nishad soon followed. All sorts of people who had no idea exactly what had happened inside Sam's World now thought they knew all they needed to know. A surprising number of them thought the crime should have been obvious all along. It hadn't been. Hedge fund managers who had shorted the stocks of US banks that banked crypto routinely spread nasty rumors about the banks' crypto customers, like FTX, in an attempt to damage the banks. If any of these people had known the truth about FTX, they most certainly would have said it. They didn't. Even those who had expressed suspicion about Sam or FTX had failed to say the one simple thing you would say if you knew the secret they were hiding: *the customers' deposits that are supposed to be inside FTX are actually inside Alameda Research.*

The authorities in the Bahamas had jailed Sam and after a lot of the usual Sam-induced complications extradited him to the United States. In an indictment brought by the US attorney's office for the Southern District of New York, the US Department of Justice charged Sam with various crimes and then allowed him to post $250 million bond as bail. Sam hadn't posted $250 million. Sam's parents had posted their home and assumed the risk that he would jump bail—in which case they would, in theory, owe $250 million to the US government. They didn't have $250 million. The prosecutors didn't mind; they seemed to care mainly that the press report that Sam Bankman-Fried was still in possession of at least $250 million. Once that happened, lots of people who should have known better but who'd fallen into the habit of speaking without thinking took to Twitter to say that Sam's ability to fork over $250 million made up their minds about his guilt. But most people hadn't waited even that long. "Your son is a dirty, filthy rotten typical criminal hooky-nosed selfish greedy jew," someone calling himself J. Revick had emailed Joe Bankman, the day FTX filed for bankruptcy. All the Bankman-Frieds received lots of messages like it. Joe had written back: "Isn't Revick a Jewish name?"

Mobs now gathered and sentiment now hardened more quickly than ever. From a distance, it was soon easy to make up one's mind about what had happened inside Sam's World, even before Sam had his day in court. From a distance, it became almost taboo to raise any doubts about the nature of Sam's crime.[*] Up close, it was hard not to have such doubts. The closer a person was to him, and to the business, the more questions they had about it. Zane Tackett, for instance, could not understand why, toward the end of 2021, Sam hadn't simply replaced the customers' deposits inside of Alameda Research with loans from the crypto banks. Back then, Alameda could have borrowed $25–$30 billion without much trouble. Why not take that money and move the $8.8 billion of customer money back into FTX, so that if Alameda blew up it would take the crypto banks, rather than FTX, with it? Ramnik had a different question.

---

[*] And basically no one did, with one fabulous exception: Kevin O'Leary. Say what you will about his influence, he's got some nerve.

He and Sam had invested billions of dollars of Alameda's money—
and yet he'd never seen Sam pay attention to the risks Alameda was
running. Sam's attention always seemed to be somewhere else. The
question Ramnik wanted to ask Sam was, "Why the fuck did you
spend the last year playing *Storybook Brawl*?"

I had my own questions, of course. The first one had to do with
financial incentives. None of the characters in this financial drama
had behaved as financial characters are expected to behave. Gary
had owned a piece of Alameda Research, but his stake in FTX was
far more valuable. Nishad owned a big chunk of FTX and none of
Alameda Research. Ditto Caroline, who ran Alameda Research but
owned shares only in FTX. None of these people had any interest in
moving money out of FTX into Alameda Research in a way that put
FTX in jeopardy. Just the reverse: it might as well have been their
money that was being moved. And yet at least up until late spring
of 2022, when crypto prices began to plunge, and possibly much
later than that, none of them expressed disapproval of the risk being
taken with their fortunes. Why not?

And of course there was the question that would sit in the middle
of Sam's trial, if indeed there was a trial. Ninety percent of those
accused of crimes by the US government in 2022 had accepted a deal
and pleaded guilty. Less than half of 1 percent had been acquitted.
Going to trial against the government felt a bit like playing an away
game against an opponent that started with vast material and psychological advantages. Sam was hell-bent on going to trial—insisted
that he was innocent of fraudulent intent. To persuade others of his
innocence, however, he'd need to explain why his three closest colleagues were now willing to plead guilty. Why would anyone say they
had committed a crime when they had not? Why did they seem themselves *to believe* they had committed a crime?

Sam now had a lot of time to think, and he spent a lot of it thinking about this. Human nature had always been something of a puzzle
to him, but puzzles could be solved. He sat down to write a memo,
very like those he'd written in response to Caroline's. He was days

away from a gag order being imposed by the judge presiding over his case, Lewis A. Kaplan, in response to a request from federal prosecutors. But for the moment, he was still allowed to share his thoughts. "People seem to have a really hard time having *thoughts* that go out on a societal limb," he wrote, "*even if they never have to say anything about them.*" He followed this curious premise in the usual business memo–like manner:

1. It's almost always easy to criticize, even if you're talking about something popular; nothing is perfect and you never really get punished for pointing out the bad parts of otherwise good things.
2. And it's easy to praise something that society praises
3. But it seems like the thing that *really* scares people—more so even than the threat of jail—is acknowledging internally, to themselves, that *they* are an example of the person who society disparages.

To which he added, "It's sometimes easier for people to publicly be the villain, than to privately have thoughts that others *would* judge harshly were they to be public . . . in other words: sometimes courage of thought is even harder than courage of action." When the social pressure reached a certain point, it was easier for people to cave to it than to preserve their true identities.

As he wrote those words, he sat alone in a room in his childhood home. He'd come full circle. He was back to where he started, only he now wore an ankle monitor and was guarded by a German shepherd. Unable to afford security, his parents had instead bought this extremely large dog, named Sandor. Sandor had been flown in from Germany, where he had been trained to kill on command. The commands were in German, however, and while Sam's parents had learned them, Sam had not.

The dog was there to protect Sam, and yet Sam couldn't generate the faintest interest in the dog. Joe had bought and read a book called *Inside of a Dog*; Sam still thought books were sort of dumb and better reduced to blog posts, and anyway he didn't care what was inside of Sandor. And so when Sam was in a room with the dog, it always felt as if some accident was waiting to happen. Some terrible misunderstanding very like the misunderstandings Sam had with other people. The odds of any accident were obviously hard to estimate. Lower than an asteroid strike, but surely greater than some artificial intelligence slipping its leash and wiping humans from the face of the earth. But it would have been very Sam Bankman-Fried to have been eaten by his own guard dog.

CODA

At the end of the week of the collapse and after everyone had fled, George Lerner had gone into the office. Walking around, he finally came to jungle hut 27 and Sam's desk. That's when he saw the toppled king. Someone had taken the piece from an office chessboard and placed it sideways on Sam's keyboard. George had removed it but otherwise he'd left the place untouched.

Six months later, it remained in nearly the same state. The Bahamas liquidators had taken it over and used it for an office until they'd run out of money, but it was as if their workers had been instructed to preserve the place as you might a sacred burial ground. The framed Steph Curry jersey still hung on the wall. The tchotchkes and coffee mugs and even the eyeglasses of the former occupants remained on the desks exactly where they had been when the volcano erupted. The shelves were still packed with unhealthy vegan snacks, and FTX beer was still stacked inside the refrigerators. "Brewed by pirates for pirates," read the sides of the cans.

To many of the former inhabitants it was all starting to feel as if it had been a dream. Their experience had been so different from experiences they'd had before in their lives that it was growing harder to believe any of it had really happened. Collectively, they were shaking themselves awake and getting back to whoever they had been before they'd fallen asleep. You could see this happening in real time. Even before she left the magical island, Constance Wang had begun the process of syncing up her future with her life before the dream. "Do I need a purpose?" she'd asked me. "Sam made me feel like I have a purpose. Now I don't know if I need a purpose. Or what my purpose should be."

I'd come back after they'd all gone, to look for something. After searching the jungle huts I was prepared to agree with others that it, too, had been no more than a figment of the imagination. But there was one last place to check, an old storage unit that no one had bothered to go through. The facility was just off the road that Sam drove every day between the Albany resort and the jungle huts. To the naked eye, it wasn't a place you'd store anything of value, just lines carved in the jungle by tired-looking buildings with corrugated metal fronts. But it was there that I found it. It was just inside one of the ten unmarked FTX sheds. The wooden crate had been addressed to Ryan Salame. It must have been far too heavy to move farther into the unit, so they'd just dumped it right at the front. The tungsten cube.

ACKNOWLEDGMENTS

Elizabeth Riley and Jacob Weisberg read and commented upon parts of this book. Will Bennett and Christina Ferguson researched crypto and other questions and helped me to understand my subject better than I ever could have on my own. Pamela Bain and Valdez Russell kept me looking forward to yet another trip to the Bahamas. Nick Yee taught me about games, and David Chee schooled me in *Storybook Brawl*. Janet Byrne is still somehow considered my copyeditor, but with each book her influence extends further into places that normal copyeditors never reach. And I owe more than I can express here to my editors, Tom Penn and, of course, Starling Lawrence.